Jimmy Outlaw:
Tiny Mite Tiger

Jimmy Outlaw:
Tiny Mite Tiger

Edited and Annotated by Perry Outlaw

Autobiography transcribed from audio and video recordings and conversations

ISBN: 978-1-954693-98-2

V-9

Published by

www.IntellectPublishimg.com

Season Schedule

Dedication

I dedicate this book to my wife, Harriet, who knows nothing about baseball, but nonetheless, is supportive of a baseball family…

Just like my Mother

Pregame Announcements: Dee Outlaw

He was a big man in a small town… but he was also a small man in a big town. Check out his name. Jimmy "Runt" Outlaw. The name of a champion. He grew up in Jackson, Alabama, which is a small town. But he was short in stature in Detroit, Michigan.

Uncle Jimmy earned his name because of his size, a small 5'7" tall and that may be stretching it a little. He was a world champion with the Detroit Tigers in 1945. I held his World Series ring. He even let me try it on. He probably let all his nephews try it on.

This book tells the saga of moving from Jackson to Auburn and on to Detroit with a few stops along the way. He was a winner as a baseball player. He was a winner and a hero in our family.

In his first game in the big leagues with the Cincinnati Reds he got three hits off of Hall of Fame hurler Dizzy Dean. Another Hall of Fame pitcher, Bob Feller, had a major league record with seven one-hitters. You guessed it….Jimmy had one of those hits.

I had the pleasure of putting together a brochure about his career to enhance his chances to get in the Alabama Sports Hall of Fame. Sure enough, he was elected along with the likes of Pat Dye, Ray Perkins and Wimp Sanderson.

It was a crowded podium the night he was enshrined. It was a crowded table in the audience, also. It appeared that all the Outlaw family was there, along with half of Jackson.

He was a hero to the people of Jackson. He even coached little league. How many World Champions coached Little League back in their hometown?

In 1983 he was named "Citizen of the Year" for the City of Jackson for his active work in the Methodist Church, the Civitan Club, the Boy Scouts and the Jackson Little League.

He played ten years in the big leagues with a steady .268 batting average. That would earn him millions today.

Uncle Runt would be modest about all this attention, but he was a World Champion and a Hall of Famer. He is also forever enshrined in the Outlaw Hall of Fame.

And that, to me, may be the biggest honor of all.

Introduction of Starting Lineup
Perry Outlaw, Editor

He was the best dad anyone could want. I know how blessed I am to have had him and my mother guide, inspire, and encourage me. Growing up as the son of a famous baseball player and a member of the 1945 Detroit Tigers World Series Championship team was just the norm for me. I didn't know anything different. He was Dad to me – and baseball was second to his family. Now, in my older years, I see what an amazing man he was. I always respected and admired him, but now I look back and realize the character he had was unusual, indeed.

We were blessed to have him until he was in his nineties and also blessed that his memory was perfect until near the end of his life. He loved to talk to people and was always the life of any gathering. In reference to his professional ball career, he was humble, always saying that he was so lucky to have been able to play ball. He realized what an accomplishment the World Champion Team had earned in 1945 and relished every moment he was asked about it. But he never bragged or put himself in the center of the story. It seems he always ended every comment with a chuckle.

My mother had compiled the news clippings and other memorabilia in a scrapbook during the years 1934-1950. He reproduced that scrapbook for his grandchildren and the original is still in perfect condition – the primary source of my information other than his taped interviews and conversations I had with him. In his home in Jackson, Alabama, he had displayed some of items most important him: bronze shoes and glove, bat he used in the series, bat signed by 1945 Detroit team members, trophy, and original photos.

We stayed very close to each other throughout his life, as did all of the Outlaw family members – and they still do. He willingly answered questions, made classroom visits, joined in professional ball appearances, and was interviewed on multiple occasions. Many of those interviews were recorded or transcribed and are in our family collection. My cousins Bert Outlaw and Dee Outlaw are just two of the people who helped maintain the firsthand information he shared.

My wife, Harriet, helped to assemble all of his interviews, scrapbooks, video tapes, primary source information, and other publications to compile this anthology of his life. The book is written in first person because the information is from Jimmy Outlaw, himself. If the reader feels there are discrepancies between factual information and this printed volume, we can only say that we are transcribing his memories. Readers can ask him about those details one day.

In the text, we have cited sources we were able to contact and have conducted due diligence in obtaining permission to use all of them. Many of the sources are no longer alive, no longer exist, nor are in business. We are talking almost 100 years ago – hard to realize that.

Special thanks and appreciation go to Cheryl Krebs and Dee Outlaw for proofreading and to Paul and Jen Outlaw and Penny Taylor for photo formatting. Our editor, John Woods, is a magician! Many, many others have contributed to our memories of my Dad.

I hope you sit back and enjoy the life of the *Tiny Mite Tiger* as recollected by the man himself, Jimmy Outlaw.

Jimmy Outlaw:
Tiny Mite Tiger

Inning One
Early Life
1913-1930

I guess I was there. They tell me I was born there. That was in Orme, Tennessee. You will have to look it up on a map to find it. It is near South Pittsburgh. We had a devil of a time trying to get there back a few years ago when we went to visit where I was born. The railroad station says it was Orme, anyway. My older brother Cornell was born there, too, but my oldest sister Gladys had already been born at Coble on Wolf Creek, down where the mill was.

Perry, Paul, and Jimmy Outlaw, Orme Tennessee train depot, 1988

My father, James Franklin Outlaw, was born in 1877 in Corbandale in Montgomery County, Tennessee, near Clarkesville. He worked on his father's tobacco farm near Corbandale on the Cumberland River. The old Outlaw family home was on the Cumberland River, but the children did not all stay there for long. My father left home at a very early age.

Four generations of Outlaws lived in this house: George, Grandfather of William Penn; Alexander, Uncle of William Penn; Alexander C., first cousin of William Penn; and Alexander K.; first cousin once removed from Wiliam Penn. The famiy lost the house in 1932.

Lumber camp in Tennessee. James Franklin Outlaw is on far right holding the two-man saw.

Papa left home about age 16, like his oldest brother Alex did. Alex had settled in Stuart County, the next one over to the west, but Papa went into the lumber trade, following lumber camps. Papa never finished school. He had a great life with only a fourth-grade education. He learned a lot and achieved a lot on his own. He mostly manned a two man saw, and he played it as well. He played a guitar, too. When the two brothers, Alex and Jim, went to a family reunion in Tennessee in the 1940s, it was the first time Papa had seen his brother in decades.

Bertie Jane Grimes was the prettiest girl Papa had ever seen. He was still moving around with lumber camps. The story goes that he was coming down the road while his camp was working at Indian Creek, near Hohenwald, and he saw this young platinum blond girl. He asked her for drink of water; scared her half to death. She took off running back to the house. They got married in 1907 – a family story told over and over. Bertie's parents were hard-shelled Baptist and were very strict. Actually, none of the Grimes children remained in the Baptist church after they were grown. They had enough of that rigid life to last a lifetime.

Bertie Jane Grimes, mother of Jimmy Outlaw

The preacher who married them was named Reverend King, who folks say was attracted to Bertie Jane as well. He always said, "She could have been a King but chose to be an Outlaw."

Some folks said the preacher would not let them get married in the Salem Church at Indian Creek near Hohenwald, so Rev. King came outside and married them while they were sitting in the buggy. Other folks told me that Bertie Jane had told them she was too embarrassed to go into the church. Mother became member of the Church of Christ while they were still living with the lumber camp in Coble. She never changed her church membership, but she always went to the Methodist Church with Papa after they moved to Jackson.

Salem Church at Indian Creek near Hohenwald, TN

They wasted no time starting their family. Gladys was born in 1908 and soon Bert Cornell followed. Papa got working for a man named Gooch – maybe in Coble. Seemed to kind of go where he went. Probably part of the same crew. Typical workcamps were made up of thrown-together shelters. When the camp moved to Orme, Papa and family went with him and I was born there.

Jimmy, Gladys, Mildred, and Cornell Outlaw, 1918

Then their camp moved to Akron, Alabama. Then from Akron to Jackson, and on to Coffeeville. My sister, Mildred, was born in Coffeeville. When they moved back to Jackson, they were on a barge being pushed by a small lumber mill steamboat on the Tombigbee River. There was Mama in the middle of the barge, scared to death we would all be drowned for sure. She was like a mother hen keeping us all right next to her. She probably could not swim. Papa could swim, and he taught me how when I was older by just throwing me in the water.

Stave mill in Jackson, Alabama circa 1918

We lived at the lumber mill worker community on the Tombigbee River near the stave mill. Staves are the curved slats used to make wooden barrels and kegs. At some time before that, Papa got out of cutting timber and bought into a stave mill on the Tombigbee River near the railroad track in Jackson. The train trestle was between our house and the mill, and during WWI, I could see the soldiers on the bridge guarding it from sabotage.

When Cornell and I were sent to take water to my father, he would put us to work stacking staves more times than we could count. Even back then we loved baseball. We would use one of the staves as a bat and rocks as balls. Later Mama made me a ball by wrapping twine and cloth around a round rock and she also made me a hat. When it got wet, though, the cardboard bill would flop down in my face.

When we lived on the river my playmates were Filligoo, Lallihoo, and Peter Wood. Their father worked for the mill. Besides baseball, one of our favorite entertainments was running a tire down the road by hitting it with a stick. Uphill was hard but keeping up with it going downhill was harder. Taught me to run fast. Papa got on to Cornell and me one time for being down on the riverbank and told us that he wanted us to run back to the house. The smart boy, Cornell, ran on home. I decided I wasn't going to run; I was going to walk. Papa walked along beside me and swatted me a lick on the butt with every step. But I never did run.

William Penn and James Franklin Outlaw on porch of house in lumber mill workers' camp near the Tombigbee River in Jackson, Alabama.

Admiral Raphael Semmes Bridge across the Tombigbee River connecting Washington and Clarke Counties, Alabama

When they were building the Raphael Semmes bridge across the Tombigbee River near where the ferry was, I got a job carrying water to the workers up on tall scaffolding and tried to keep it a secret from Mama and Papa. But he found out and let me keep doing it and didn't tell Mama.

We moved from the river into town, and at first lived in a house near the school. Then we moved into the "big" house on College Avenue. That is the one we all think of as our family home. The garden was in the back. Everybody lived off their gardens for the most part. One spring there was a late freeze. Papa went through the house gathering up all the girls' bras to use to cover the tender tomato plants.

412 College Avenue, Jackson, Alabama, family home.

Mama had a cow which she milked every day, twice a day. We kept that cow until well after my brother Dan was born, even after my son Perry was born. One day Dan was milking, and he called Perry over and squirted him with milk straight from the udder. From then on Perry called him 'Bad Dan.' The nickname stuck and he laughed every time he heard that.

Papa was sometimes an impatient man. Once, after we moved into town, he bought us all a pair of shoes and some of them didn't fit, so he knocked the toes out with a poker, gave them back, and said, "Now they do." I remember him resoling our shoes by tacking leather onto the bottoms.

There were seven of us children living in that house. One brother had died as an infant. Edith had been born while we lived in the river house, and Mack and Dan

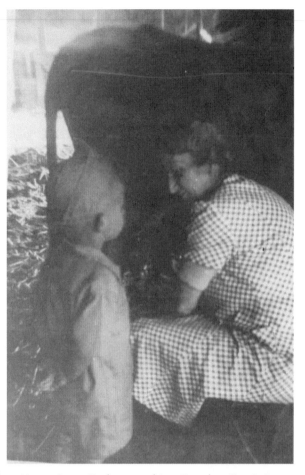

Young Perry Outlaw watching Grandma Bertie Jane Outlaw milk the family cow, 1943

were born after we moved to town. We made our own fun back then. We would get paper boxes and slide down the pine straw in the gullies. Cornell and I experimented with hot air balloons. We took a paper bag and rigged up a way to put the candle in it to make it rise. The last we saw one of them, it was glowing and going toward the gully.

Papa got a car that had a thermometer that stood up on the hood, maybe a Reo. We got in it one day and started it, and it took off through the garage. It broke the thermometer off the front hood, and we had to tell him when he got home. He was not too pleased.

My grandfather, William Penn Outlaw, a War Between the States veteran, came to live with us in Jackson. One day, he took me and Cornell out fishing on the Tombigbee in a boat. Mama was really upset about that. My sister Edith said that Grandpa taught her how to read when she sat in his lap while he was reading the paper.

For some reason he was called "Prink." Once, while on a train in Tennessee he looked at a girl across the aisle and asked her, "Don't I know you?" She answered, "You should. I am your daughter." Grandpa got sick while living in Jackson. Papa had to take him by train to Mobile. He died there and they brought his body back to Jackson where he was buried.

William Penn Outlaw, Grandfather of Jimmy Outlaw

My best friends were Robin McCorquodale and Lilburn Odom. Lilburn's dad drove the train on the narrow gage railway out to the camp where he loaded the logs and took them to the sawmill. Lilburn and I went off to play pro ball at the same time. I stayed best friends with Robin my whole life. I never played high school baseball because for two years in a row, just before the season, I broke my arm. I graduated in 1930 from the State Secondary Agricultural College (Jackson High School.)

State Secondary Agricultural College was commonly called Jackson High School.

We used to turn the outhouse over when someone was in it. Terrible, terrible! My sixth-grade teacher would also become my son's sixth grade teacher. This was the school where Gladys was elected *Queen of the Sanitary Toilet*. Never sure why.

Outlaw family (LtoR) Back: James Paulus Outlaw (m Grace Windham). Curtis Dan Outlaw(m Dot Boone), Mildred Outlaw Farish (m Bob Farish), Gladys Wanda Outlaw, Edith Outlaw, Mack Outlaw (m Dora Alice York) , Bert Cornell Outlaw(m Madge Bradford.) Seated: James Franklin and Bertie Jane Grimes Outlaw

All of us children ended up living near our parents. Of course, there were years that some were away in college or serving in the military or had jobs elsewhere. Even when I was playing ball, we were in Jackson and Alexander City during off-season most years. Dan worked away from Jackson awhile, but later moved back with his wife and children. My father had strokes and died when he was 82 years old, and my mother lived to be over 100. We all got together in the old house most Sunday afternoons and every Christmas. After my ball career, we lived in Alexander City awhile, but I moved my family to Jackson when Perry was in the sixth grade. Jackson is my hometown.

Inning Two
High School and College
1930 - 1932

First Baptist Church, Jackson, Alabama, old Sanctuary, location of high school graduation ceremonies, 1930

I was 17 when I graduated from high school in 1930. It was the spring right after that Black Friday when the whole country started in the Depression. We didn't feel too much right away being in a small country town, but the stave mill was starting to lose some business. So, I worked there until I could save enough to go to college. My parents really wanted their children to go on with their educations.

We listened to college football and baseball games on the radio. In fact, we would also all go to the Jackson Theatre to hear the games. The radio was not loud enough for all of us to hear, so they showed the progress of the football game on a big board drawn off like a football field in front of the screen. They would move the markers shaped like a football after each play so we could see the game on the board. They would write up there which end of the field each team had. I liked Auburn because they had such a good team, and it was also the cheapest to go to, being a land grant school. I knew I could not play football but thought maybe I could make the baseball team.

COACH McFADDEN

Coach Bill McFadden, Auburn Freshman Athletics, 1932.

I was playing some town baseball then, too, and was traveling to a few other places for games. I played summer league ball for Jackson for a couple of years with Sammy Barnes as manager. Sam was a former pro player and manager. He was with Detroit a short time in 1921. We were a part of the Tri-County League. We didn't get paid, but we were usually fed and got gas to drive to the games on Thursday and Sunday afternoons. Back then most towns pretty much shut down on Thursday afternoons. There was not an admission charge, but they would pass the hat around for donations. Sam recommended me to Coach Bill McFadden, the Freshman coach at Auburn.

So, in the summer of 1932 I had saved enough to add to what Papa could provide and headed to Auburn, Alabama, in the fall. My sister Gladys had graduated from Montevallo Teacher College and was already teaching. She sent me some money, too. The college was then named API, Alabama Polytechnic Institute. At first, it was East Alabama Male College, but women were going there when I went. It was already a big school and the buildings sure seemed to be massive to this small-town boy.

· Samford Hall ·

Sturdivant Hall, Alabama Polytechnic University, Auburn, 1932

Glomerata, API Yearbook, 1932

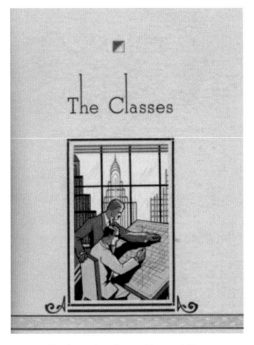

Engineering Cover Page, API
Glomerata, 1932

I am so glad I could afford a copy of the 1933 Yearbook, the **Glomerata**. The cover has a drawing of the Empire State Building that had been completed in 1931. Oh, what a time to go to college. I loved the architecture of the thirties and thought I would like to be a part of that, so I looked into Engineering.

I was interested in Civil Engineering since my childhood days watching the Semmes Bridge being built over the Tombigbee River, and that seemed like something I would like to do. I enrolled and signed up for the classes they told me to. I was afraid I would not be able to keep up with the other students who were from bigger cities and schools, but Jackson High School had given me a very good background and I did just fine. I took a class in surveying and my partner and I had a project to survey an area. We were supposed to end up right back where we started, but we were about six inches off. The teacher made us do it again and we got it right that time.

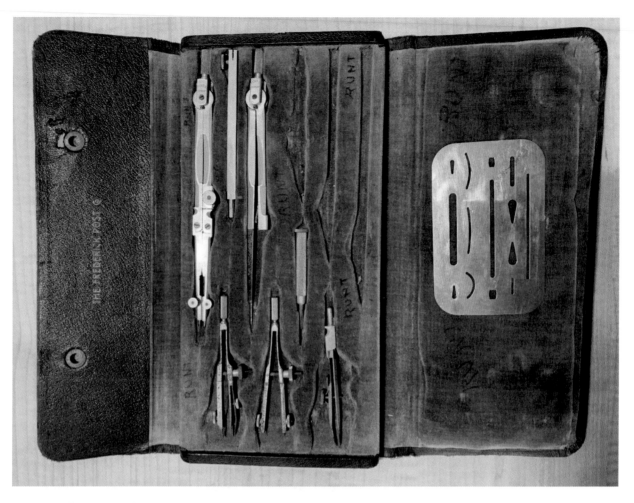

I had a little trouble with Chemistry, but you have to remember that Jackson did not even have a science lab. Of course, that was before the Periodic Table had been invented, too, so we didn't have as much to learn as today. I could never learn all that stuff now.

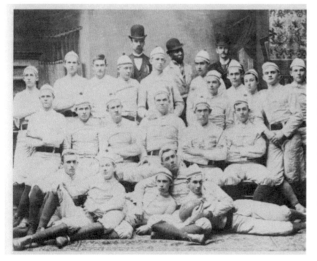

Auburn's first football team, 1892. Coach George Petrie.

My Current Events professor was George Petrie. I really enjoyed his class. He knew what he was talking about. He was in charge of the Graduate School and he was old even then, but he had a great reputation. He had been Auburn's first football coach and later had written the *Auburn Creed*.

Editor's Note: The story of George Petrie's life is literally the story of Auburn athletics for the fifty years he served the college. In 1892 he formed a team which played four games that he personally arranged. He had used his own funds and secured a loan to provide the team uniforms and equipment. He selected burnt orange and navy blue for the team's colors.

It was officially Alabama Polytechnic Institute but was always commonly known as Auburn. The college also played its first intercollegiate baseball game that year. (Courtesy of **Auburn Man, the life and times of George Petrie** *by Mike Jernigan, 2007, The Donnell Group, Montgomery Al ISBN 978-0-9985904-0-0.)*

GEORGE PETRIE
A.M., Ph.D., LL.D.

Sigma Phi Sigma, API, 1932

Nearly everyone was in a fraternity and there were at least 22 on campus. Some had big houses. I pledged Sigma Phi Sigma and was a rat for the first half of the year before I was initiated. All freshmen were called rats actually, not just fraternity pledge boys. I don't think the Auburn chapter of the fraternity even exists anymore. I remember one of our fraternity guys was known for his sleep walking. We loved to follow him to see where he went. He would get up, get dressed, and walk across campus. Usually he went into the library that was always open, and just sit there awhile. Then he would walk back to his room, get undressed and go back to bed. The next day he couldn't remember any of it.

All men were required to be in ROTC. I was in an Artillery Corps. We had classes two days a week and drilled one day a week. We had training with the cannon that was a French 75 from WWI like the one that is in front of the Fire Station in Jackson now. [*It was later moved to the Veterans Memorial in front of City Hall on Commerce Street.*] I knew I didn't want to have to carry a rifle around all the time and clean it every day, so the cannon seemed a little easier to me. We were issued a uniform that we had to turn back in but could keep our insignia. I have my crossed cannons lapel pin and my hat pin.

MILITARY SCIENCE AND TACTICS

Major G. H. Franke, F.A., D.O.L.

ARTILLERY

Captain Edward S. Ott, F.A., D.O.L.	First Lieutenant T. S. Gunby, F.A., D.O.L.
Captain W. A. Metts, Jr., F.A., D.O.L.	First Lieutenant H. L. Watts, Jr., F.A., D.O.
First Lieutenant J. V. Phelps, F.A., D.O.L.	First Lieutenant W. C. Huggins, F.A., D.O.L.

ENGINEERS

Captain Roy W. Grower, C.E., D.O.L.
First Lieutenant F. O. Bowman, C.E., D.O.L.

"The Field Artillery"

Our duty when battle is raging,
Is to keep to the rear and concealed
Till the time comes to help out the doughboys.
Now isn't that nice for the Field?

It is rumored and whispered at Auburn,
By many the statement is made,
That the Field—now wouldn't this jar you?
Always show up the best at parade.

If you feel you must get in the army,
But had still rather keep out of harm,
You've the doughboys on duty to guard you,
So join the auxiliary arm.

"The Engineers"

There are only three classes of kaydets,
He that graduates first, takes all bets—
In a class by himself—Other Engineers next.
And last come all other cadets.

The pride and the boast of the Army,
They'll shout it right into your ears
"Oh! this is the way that we do it,
So listen to us Engineers."

If you think that you're anxious to join us,
I'll give you a tip, so get wise.
If you're not smart enough, just keep up yo
bluff.
If you know you are smart—advertise.

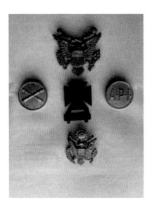

You know me, my real interest was sports, so I got to know some of those athletes really well. I ran into or played with or against a lot of them later on in my career. When I first got to Auburn, I started going to every football game I could. I went to Atlanta to see us play against Georgia Tech. I rode with a friend who had a car, but I had to ride in the rumble seat all the way there and back. One thing really different back then was that everyone dressed up to go to the games.

On our campus, the stadium was called Drake Field. It was awful. The grass was never good – and the stands were temporary wooden ones that would only hold about 700 people. We usually just stood around. And those uniforms were nothing like they are today. We only played a few games on the home field as Auburn was hard to get to and because our stands were so small. They finally built a real stadium after I left. They named it Hare Stadium after my Chemistry teacher, Dr. Cliff Hare. He had played on the first team in 1892. He knew his Chemistry, too.

DR. CLIFF HARE

Talking about that stadium: when they added on to it, they named it Jordan-Hare Stadium and I knew Shug Jordan while I was at Auburn, too. He was my baseball coach. He and Coach McFadden worked with all the freshman athletes, so they coached the freshman football team and helped with the varsity football. Auburn varsity football had a winning team that year mainly because of the coaches. Coach "Chet" Wynne and Coach Kiley led the team to tie Tennessee for the Southern Championship Crown. They had won every game until the last game of the season. The opponent was South Carolina, but the Auburn boys all got sick before the game. They had a 20-0 lead at halftime, but the sickness caught up with them and

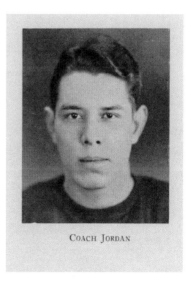

COACH JORDAN

they were so weak that South Carolina scored 20 points, ending in a tie. That cost them a trip to the Rose Bowl.

Jimmy Hitchcock, Auburn *Glomerata,* 1933

Another famous man who was there at that time was Jimmy Hitchcock. He was a senior during my freshman year. I had already heard of him from his reputation as the "Phantom of Union Springs" when he played high school ball there. He got all sorts of honors. His last year at Auburn he was named All-American Halfback and also selected for the All-American baseball team. He played major league baseball during the Depression. *[Jimmy Hitchcock played major league ball from 1933-40, served in the Navy in WWII, and then played ball in 1946.]* He died so young, only 48. But I remember when he was inducted into the 1969 Alabama Sports Hall of Fame after he died.

Billy Hitchcock

Jimmy's younger brother, Billy, was the one I had more contact with later on. He played for Auburn while I was in the majors. He played when Auburn went to its first bowl game. [*The Bicardi Bowl, Havana, Cuba; Auburn v Villanova, 7-7 tie, 1937.*] They also played Michigan State in the Rhumba Bowl and won 6-0. He then went on to play major league while I was playing. He was with the Tigers the year before I was, but then he was one of those who went off to war. I think he served in the Army Air Force in the Pacific. We kept up with our boys who were off to war. And they sure kept up with us. We were all brothers who loved the game and loved America. I tried to enlist, but the Army wouldn't take me because I had flat feet and the Navy said I was too colorblind. Anyway, I saw Billy quite a lot after he came home. He was with Detroit for a short stint in 1946 before he was traded to Washington. He played, then managed, and coached with several teams. Billie was third base coach for the Tigers in 1960 after I had retired from ball and he was president of the Southern League from 1971-1980.

Editor's Note: *Auburn named the newly renovated baseball field after him in 2003. He died April 9, 2006, at age 89 - THE SAME DAY THAT RUNT DIED*

PRIM
T. Wt. 191 Senior

WOOD
G. Wt. 166 Senior

HOLMES
T. Wt. 245 Junior

Hannis Prim (on left), Auburn Glomerata, 1933. Tackle, Wt. 191, Senior

Hannis "Red" Prim was from Salitpa, Alabama, and went to Jackson High School a little ahead of me. He was a senior at Auburn in '31-'32 and played on the football team. Hard to believe, but ROTC had a Polo Team and Red played polo on their first team in the Spring of 1932. Later, he was head coach at Clarke County High School (Grove Hill) before WWII. After the war, he was at Hartford High before he came back to Grove Hill. He coached there, then later was principal. He was principal and coach when my son Perry was hired to teach and coach there. The stadium, Prim Field, is named for him and he was inducted into the Alabama High School Athletic Association Hall of Fame.

It really is a small world. Red had a brother named Ray who was playing for the Cubs against Detroit in the 1945 World Series. He was about seven years older than I was and everybody called him "Pop." He was a pretty good pitcher and started one of the series games. He played in a couple of others, and we had kept up with each other until he died just a few years ago [1995.] I think he stayed in the Majors just one year after the '45 series. He went to play minor league with the Angels then. Right now, he is still the last Cub to lead the league in ERA. [*as of 2014*]

Ray Prim (Pop)

I got this article mailed to me written by Sammy Barnes from P.O. Box 492, Louisville, MS 39339.

*Editor's Note: The article was published by Zipp Newman in the **Birmingham** News on Sunday, September 14, 1975. The article refers to Sammy Barnes as the "Louisville Mississippian who gave the Old Duster eye-witness account of the Ty Cobb and Umpire Billy Evans fight."*

Dear Jimmy:

Enclosed is the story – as is rewritten by Zipp Newman of the Birmingham News – in this past Sunday's paper.

I am disappointed that in his re-write he left out so much. He had also promised not to use my name. At 76, I don't want or need any publicity.

I enclose also a Xerox copy of the story as I sent it to him in the original typing. I am not a sportswriter but I'm damned if my story isn't better than his. However, newsprint paper is so high now that newspapers are economizing, too.

Anyway, two deserving fellows got some recognition that they should have gotten 30 years ago.

I'm sorry he didn't do a better job because he is certainly capable of improving on what I sent him.

Regards,

Sammy

The Typed Article written by Sammy Barnes:

SAMMY BARNES

"The old cliché that the world is a small place after all has been said by many persons many times.

"Proof of this age-old statement is borne out by the fact that in 1945, nestled in the rolling red clay country and hills of southwest Alabama there was a town of about 2500 inhabitants. Across the state situated on the plains of east Alabama there was a University with an enrollment in 1945 of around 5000. Both the town and the institution had something going for them though because they shared the distinction of having two hometown athletes who were alumni of the same university, one on each of the World Series clubs. A confrontation of the home grown combatant and fellow alumni was imminent.

"The town is Jackson, now grown to be a prosperous little city of approximately 7000 people. The institution is Auburn University with a current enrollment of around 15,000 students.

"Try as we have, we are unable to come up with any other town of the size that Jackson was 30 years ago that can also lay claim to having a regular player on each club of the World Series. It also marked the first time that Auburn University had an alumnus on each of the competing clubs in the World Series.

"The two major league clubs of 1945 vying for the most highly prized honor in baseball – the World Championship – were the Chicago Cubs of the National League and the Detroit Tigers of the American League.

"The two players were Jimmy Outlaw, the regular 3rd baseman for the 1945 Tigers, and Ray Prim, one of the regular starting hurlers for the Chicago Cubs. Detroit's manager was Steve O'Neill while Charlie Grimm was at the helm for the Chicago club.

"On October 6 of that year, Ray Prim who had won 13 games for the Cubs during the regular season, was given the nod by Manager Grimm to hurl the 4th game of the fall classic. Jimmy Outlaw was at his accustomed position at 3rd base for Detroit.

"The radio broadcasters as well as sports writers at the national level of the day and age completely overlooked so many coincidences in the early careers of these fellow townsmen and future major leaguers that the writer of this column believes they are worthy of being called to the attention of baseball fans in Alabama and elsewhere.

1) Both Jimmy Outlaw and Ray Prim lived in Jackson, Alabama, their homes being about four blocks from each other.

2) Both finished high school in Jackson; Prim in 1928, and Outlaw in 1930.

3) Both played on the Jackson High School baseball team. [*This is not correct. Jimmy did not play high school ball due to a broken arm each year.*]

4) Both were coached in high school by the same coach, Eddie J. Pace, a Birmingham Southern alumnus.

5) Both Prim and Outlaw played on the hired summertime semi-pro club of Jackson in the Tri-County League; Prim in 1926 and Outlaw in 1933. [*The Tri-County League was made up of towns in Clarke and Washington Counties in Alabama and Wayne County in Mississippi.*]

6) Both boys played for the same manager in the Tri-County League, a native of Jackson with experience in the Majors and AAA Minors. Both players developed rapidly in this level of competition, the class of ball being much faster than high school, and both boys rose in determination and ability to meet the keener competition they were facing.

7) Both Prim and Outlaw enrolled at Auburn and played for Auburn University: Prim in 1929 and 1930; and Outlaw in 1932. (Prim's coach as a freshman at Auburn was R.C. "Red" Brown, the old "Red-Head" of Mountain Brook in Birmingham.)

8) Both boys chose to go into pro baseball rather than go on for a scholastic degree at Auburn University.

9) Each of the two boys played briefly with other big league clubs, Prim with Pittsburgh, Outlaw with Cincinnati, before finally making the grade with Chicago and Detroit, respectively. (While with the Cincinnati Reds, Outlaw combed the illustrious and late departed Dizzy Dean for three hits in one game.)

10) Since retiring from pro ball both Outlaw and Prim have suffered tragic losses in their immediate families.

"Jimmy Outlaw played every inning of each of the seven games in the '45 Series. He was held hitless in only two of the seven games, batted in three runs, and played errorless ball in the field, making a total of 15 assists and four put-outs in the seven games.

"In the 6th inning of the 6th game Outlaw figured in a play which was a bad break for the Cubs. Claude Passeau, who had held Detroit to one hit, a single by Rudy York in the 3ʳᵈ game of the series, was pitching and in the 6ᵗʰ inning, Outlaw's hard smash to the mound ripped the nail off the middle finger of Passeau's pitching hand, forcing him to leave the game at the close of the inning. Evidently, Jimmy Outlaw had not changed his style of hitting from back in his days of playing for his hometown of Jackson, he was always a line drive hitter.

"Jimmy Outlaw still lives in Jackson and is the wholesale distributor for the largest dairy products business in the area. He has one son, Perry, who is pursuing a career of teaching and coaching in high school circles. Unfortunately, Jimmy lost his wife of 37 years, the former Grace Windham of Jackson, in the fall of 1974 when she died of a heart condition. He states he has adjusted reasonably well except at the close of his workday when the loneliness gets pretty depressing. However, friends say Jimmy Outlaw is a man of deep religious faith and they are unanimous in the belief that he will continue to adjust with the passage of time.

"Ray Prim and his wife Ethel live in Whittier, California, where Ray has a used automobile business in which he has done very well indeed. When asked what he considered his best pitch he occasioned some surprise when he stated that it was his fast ball. He was not overly fast, but he learned to turn his wrist inward when he threw, and he says the ball would really move for him. Even as a youthful southpaw growing up in Jackson, he always had unusually good control. In organized ball he only averaged about 25 bases on balls per season.

"In 1965 Ray and Ethel lost their son of a brain tumor, leaving them with a lovely daughter-in-law and four grandchildren. Like all grandparents, they enjoy their grandchildren very much, and are devoted to their daughter-in-law.

"Someday Ray will visit his old hometown of Jackson, Alabama, and he and Jimmy Outlaw will again face each other – not in sports combat, but in genuine friendship spanning a period of over 45 years."

it

I earned a letter for playing baseball my freshman year and gave the sweater to my sister Mildred. I think she just wore out. But she didn't go to Auburn. She went to Montevallo for her teaching certificate, then to Livingston State Teacher College for her degree, and was a math teacher for her whole life. Even though I could only go for one year, I have always been an Auburn fan and those were some of the greatest days of my life.

Inning Three
From Town Ball to Pro
1933-1936

Tri-County League, Alabama – Tryouts, Bartlesville, Oklahoma - Beckley, West Virginia Black Knights-Jeannette, Pennsylvania Reds - Ft. Worth, Texas Panthers (Cats) – Decatur, Illinois Commodores -Nashville, Tennessee Volunteers - these were the teams I played with during this time.

1933

TRI-COUNTY LEAGUE

When I returned home from Auburn in 1933, I had several jobs, mostly helping out at the stave mill. But Auburn had given me a taste of serious baseball and I played again on the Jackson semi-pro team with Coach Sam Barnes. Sam played for Detroit in 1921 for one year. I got to know guys playing on other teams in the area. We traveled around a good bit in old cars and the backs of pickup trucks. In the Tri-County League we played against the Alabama towns of Millry, Helwestern, Thomasville, Chatom, and also Waynesboro, Mississippi.

Jimmy in early uniform he brought
from home

1935 Ball and Glove

We mostly made our own uniforms. Well, my mother made mine. Sometimes we had custom made uniforms, but the balls and travel were the main expenses, which we mostly paid for ourselves. If we had a company sponsor, the company would pay for the uniforms and equipment. We each had our own bat, but we shared a lot, too. The gloves were not nearly as big as they are now. Not much padding at all! Usually, the home team would give us a little money to help with gas and food.

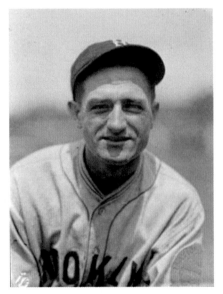
Milt Stock

Sometimes there were guys watching us that we did not know were scouts. Milt Stock was a scout for the Cincinnati Reds and after one game came up to me and two of my teammates and asked if we would like to try out for the National League the next spring. I must have had a pretty good game that day.

He also signed Lilburne Odom of Jackson and Casey Kimbrell of Thomasville the same time. I had been at Auburn when Kimbrell was on the football and track teams there. He was two years ahead of me in college, but we were the same age. He went to Auburn right out of high school.

Casey Kimbrell, upper left. Track at Auburn, 1933

1934

OKLAHOMA TRYOUTS

BECKLEY, WEST VIRGINIA

JEANETTE, PENNSYLVANIA

TRYOUTS IN OKLAHOMA

Tryouts in Bartlesville, Oklahoma

I started my pro ball career in 1934. We caught the train north of Grove Hill at Thomaston. We picked up some other ball players on the way. There must have been 300 men there in Bartlesville, Oklahoma, when we got to the ballpark. They gave us a room which I shared with three other guys. We slept all over the floor mostly. Remember this is the Depression.

We were at the city ballpark, Bartlesville Athletic Municipal Field, which had just opened in 1932. [*It has since been renamed the Bill Doenges Memorial Stadium.*] There must have been guys there from all over the country. Every day there were games played and each morning there was a list posted of the players who were sent home. The three of us from home all made the final cut. In the photo, I am in the second row with the white hat cocked all crooked. We were wearing the uniforms we brought from home.

From there we went to Cincinnati for a little while until we were transferred to farm clubs. That year there were four lower bracket teams affiliated with Cincinnati: Bartlesville (Oklahoma), Beckley (West Virginia), Jeannette (Pennsylvania) and Wilmington (North Carolina.) Their AA team was Toronto and their A team was Topeka. This was much more loosely organized than it is today. A minor league team may have changed affiliations from year to year, but all of the ones I was with were part of the Cincinnati network until 1939.

BECKLEY, WEST VIRGINIA BLACK KNIGHTS

JEANNETTE, PENNSYLVANIA REDS

Milt Stock, who had signed me, was associated with Class C Beckley, West Virginia, and he took me with him back to West Virginia. The Beckley team, the Black Knights, was in the Middle Atlantic League. I played a few games, then they sent me down to Class D in Jeannette, Pennsylvania, where I played games in the middle of the season. The manager was Ray Ryan and they were part of the Penn State Association. My batting improved to .340, so I was pulled back up to Beckley. I did much better the second go around in West Virginia and finished the season there.

I remember the field at Beckley. There was not a blade of grass anywhere. It was all sand. It was hard to distinguish the ground balls from the playing field, especially under the lights at night. Actually, Beckley did have lights five years before MLB. Lots of people came to the games after their work day, so the team was a success. There was a short left field fence. Part of the foul line down the right field line was the fence. It curved around after the seating and I hit one home run, probably because they had a short outfield line there.

The team was later the Bengals of the Mountain State League and was associated with Detroit in 1937. They won the league championship in 1937 and 1938.

In the fifty-five games I played for the Jeannette Reds, I was at bat 209 times and hit 9 homeruns. Back at Beckley, I ended up playing a total of 50 games with a batting average of .255 but had 4 homeruns. Beckley was where the longest homerun ever hit was done. A railway was just outside the fence of the park. A ball hit over the fence went right into the open door of a boxcar and just kept right on going – who knows how far that ball went.

1935

FORT WORTH PANTHERS – "CATS"

Left photo: LaGrave Field, home of Ft. Worth Panthers.

Right: John Heving

The Fort Worth Panthers had a new stadium, Panther Park, only a few years old and that was where I ended up for 1935 Spring Training. A local newspaper writer named Pop Boone was sports editor for the Fort Worth Press and we had a lot of laughs together. He was a funny man and liked to talk. His weekly column was called *Pop's Palaver*. The Cats were not affiliated with any major league team at that time, and he was pushing for the Cats to keep me there. He talked to Skipper John Heving about me and wrote all about that conversation in his column.

Knothole Gang section of the Panthers of Fort Worth

I had the best hitting streak of my career that spring. It looked like they were throwing basketballs to me. Pop claimed I must have had an .800 average. Johnnie Heving had just left major leagues and was the manager of the Fort Worth Cats. Pop kept at him to keep me, and that looked like a good prospect. Heving said my batting was the talk of the squad, but my fielding needed work.

Pop felt my hitting overcame my weakness in the field, and that I would come along, "What impressed me was the power he had for such a small fellow. Some of the fans accused me of being over enthusiastic when I said Outlaw could hit the ball as hard as Pete Turgeon usta hit 'em for Wichita."

1935

DECATUR ILLINOIS COMMODORES

As things worked out, I spent the next year with Decatur Commodores in Illinois. We were a part of the Triple I League: Illinois, Indiana, and Iowa. That year they were a Class B team, and when I was there, they were an independent team without official affiliations with any major league team. Most years they were associated with the St. Louis Cardinals.

Jimmy, 1935, Decatur,

44

Fans Field, Decatur, Illlinois, 1935, Home of the Commodores (Commies)

Our home field was called Fans Field and the managers were John Butler and Cliff Knox. We were called the Commies, but it was for Commodores, not Communists! They stopped calling them that later on.

"Two Commies at race to lead the club in batting for 1935: With only five points separating them, Jimmy Outlaw, (right) and Jerry Tiemann, clever first sacker, are having a merry fight for the 1935 batting championship of the Commie Club. Both have added many a base hit to the box scores this season and should have quite a battle before the winner is declared, assuming that Knox or some other athlete doesn't slip in to capture the honors. Outlaw is hitting .369 and Tiemann .354"

We played 113 games and won 59 of them. I had 157 hits. The stats say I had 6 homeruns. I was playing third base and outfield. The first baseman Jerry Tiemann was a great hitter, too. We were neck and neck all season. I ended up with a .351; a little better than Jerry.

"Knoxmen out to avenge that Bloomington defeat yesterday twin bill today"

This photo ran in a story about a double header against Springfield. I hit two homeruns over the left field fence to help us win the second one. They quoted me as saying, "Just swing where he throws it, and that is all there is to it." I guess I must have said it.

DECATUR FANS FIELD   2022

NASHVILLE TENNESSEE VOLUNTEERS

Nashville Volunteers Team Photo, 1939, Jimmy Outlaw standing sixth from left on back row

My good year with Decatur led to my being moved up to a Class A team, the Nashville Volunteers. They played at Sulphur Dell, the field right downtown near the Capitol. They were a farm team for the New York Giants in 1934-1935, but changed to the Reds the year I went there. They were a member of the Southern League.

SPRING TRAINING

In Spring Training, Coach Jimmy Hamilton talked to me about my mental and emotional side of baseball that would make me a major leaguer. It changed me. *[Nashville News article, March 25, 1937, relates an event that happened after the Vols Spring Training in 1936 in Tampa.]*

At spring training, Jimmy Hamilton was about the only one who thought I had the makings for the majors that year so he "stuck the stocky little Jackson, Alabama, boy at third base and made them hit grounders for hours to him. He not only became a smooth fielder but showed his stamina by wearing out three hitters every day."

We had played the Giants in a pair of games in Pensacola. I played pretty good but evidently I didn't say a word the whole game - if you can believe that. I rode back to De Funiak Springs with Jimmy and a couple of other players. We stopped to eat at a sandwich shop at 2:00 in the morning, and Jimmy had a heart-to-heart talk with me. He said he was going to put me at third base for the Vols and, "You'll stay there because I believe you can be a star. As soon as you realize within yourself that you are a big leaguer, you'll be there." I think I kept my head down the whole time he was talking. And I only said, "Yessir." He told me I had all the natural ability in the world but wasn't acting like I cared. "You are not fair to yourself by getting out there and acting like a dummy. You can field balls and have a great arm, but you never say anything. You will never be a standout that way. We don't want a ballplayer like that. You should have a good ten years in the majors if you get some life and fire about you and show some hustle." He

Jimmy Outlaw, Nashville Volunteers, 1937

sold me on the idea that scouts would not notice me if I was a lifeless ball player, so the next afternoon I didn't shut up. I even kidded Scharein for being so quiet. The paper said I bubbled over with confidence. Jimmy held to his word and I played with the Vols all year.

Sulphur Dell, home field of the Nashville Volunteers

Sulphur Dell was kind of mashed in, at least in one of the outfields. The ground in the infield was flat but as the field went toward the fence, the ground rose up to create a pretty steep incline. All the outfielders played on top of that mound because they could run down the hill a lot easier than up the hill. The old stadium had been replaced in 1927 so it was pretty nice. In the old one, the batter had to face the afternoon sun, but in the new one, he faced northeast. The shape of the field was something to see. It had a short fence in right field, just 262 feet. The terrace went all the way around the field but was the highest in right field. The top of the terrace was 22.5 feet above the infield. Right fielders were nicknamed mountain goats because they had to go uphill center and right. There was a 10-foot-wide shelf about one-third of the way up the incline that was worn so much there was no grass there.

It was near the dump and the stockyards. The fellas always said that Babe Ruth refused to play there because of the smell. The water fountains pumped up the sulphur water from the springs that were there. That didn't help either. It was one of the oldest parks, been there since 1850 or so. The Vols started there in 1901.

Aunt Maude, my daddy's sister, [*Maude Estelle Outlaw Brown*] who lived in Sylvia, not too far away, would come to Nashville to see me play. She would sit behind home plate eating peanuts and dipping snuff. Whenever I would make a good play, she would yell, "EEEEEE Little Ol' Choice," referring to me. When my teammates asked me who that lady was, I just said, "I don't know."

Sulphur Dell

"One veteran and three youngsters compose what Nashvillians regard as the best all-around infield to represent the Vols in many seasons, a unit that will play an important part in the playoff series with the Birmingham opening at Sulphur Dell Tuesday night. From left to right Outlaw, 3b, Scharein, ss, Rodda, 2b and Wasdell, 1b. Redda has been with the Vols longer than any player."

When we played a double header in Chattanooga, I rapped out six hits and played good outfield, too. At that time Freddie Russell wrote in a blurb that I had a thirteen consecutive game hitting streak. I did go hitless on the second day of the season against Ken Chitwood and Hobart Scott at Knoxville, but later in August I had four hits including a homer and drove in two. I usually had a good game there at Caswell Field. August stats say that out of eight games we had played there so far, I had 15 hits, scored ten runs in 38 times at bat. (.392) At the end of the season I had played in 155 games and was at bat 643 times, 212 hits; 7 of them were homeruns. I ended up with a .330.

We were second place to Atlanta Crackers when we went into the playoffs and we came in second. But Atlanta was next to last. On the Atlanta team was Paul Richards, the League's All-Star Catcher. We ended up playing on the same team later on with Detroit.

Nashville had more men placed on the All-Star roster than any other Southern League team. We had Speece, Peacock, Taitt, Dwyer, and me. That was five members from our team of the 17 players selected for All Star Team.

Nashville was a town that really supported the ball club. They always turned out in big numbers and at least 200 even went all the way to Atlanta for the league playoffs. After the loss, this poem was published:

Sack Cloth and Ashes

By H.W. Fleer

Our team has lost the pennant, boys
'Tis hard and sad, but true.
Get out the crepe, can all the joys,
In mourning for our crew.

We all had such a lovely dream,
A few short months ago,
Of how we had the better team
Than all the rest could show.

We could not see, with just half-luck,
How we could lose at all,
But we've since found, tho' full of pluck,
Sometimes the mighty fall.

We held our team in high regard,
That might be understood,
With every man a drawing card,
On paper, they looked good.

We must not fail to mention here,
That each man had the goods,
But steadily and without fear,
They drove us to the woods.

We've two good men behind the plate
As steady as a clock,
Both of them are catchers great,
O'Malley and Peacock.

We've George Sharein as our shortstop,
He is a fielding kid.
A batter fine, and at his spot,
When anything is did.

Old Bill Rodda, tho' slightly aged,
Is always on his toes,
Many a sparkling play he's staged,
By great and accurate throws.

We come to third, that corner hot,
A new recruit is there.
Outlaw's the boy, who fills the spot,
With smoothness and eclair.

Three outfielders make up the slate,
Ty Cobb was never greater.
Triplett, Dwyer, and "Home Run" Taitt,
Not one a second rater.

Eiland, Speece, Hilcher and Starr
Make up the pitching crew,
That keeps first place not so far,
But they alone won't do.

Some few others we also tried,
Their names I'll have to pass,
For "Take them out," the fans all cried.
"Back to the 'ole tall grass."

With this array we cannot win
The cherished Southern flag,
Just wipe our brow, and with a grin,
Pack up the old bat bag.

So get the sack cloth, ashes too.
Brace up and wipe our tears,
But hats off to our crew,
The Nashville Volunteers.

The one thing I most remember about the Southern League is that it was hot. Of all the places I ever played, Little Rock was the hottest. Being small anyway, I sure couldn't afford to lose much weight by water loss. I lost water weight during each game, so after every game, I would stop and buy a gallon of ice cream. Then I would get back to the hotel as quickly as I could and go out on the fire escape and eat the whole thing before it melted.

Winder Stadium, Little Rock, Arkansas, formerly Travelers Field

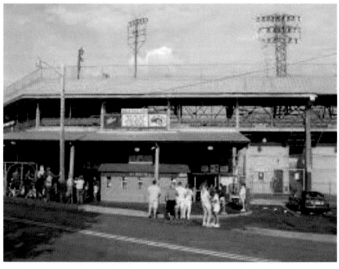

Arkansas Travelers Stadium, Little Rock

Inning Four
Majors and Back to Minors
Cincinnati Reds and Syracuse Chiefs
1937-1938

ear the end of the season with Nashville, prospects seemed pretty good for several of the players. Lance Richbourg had done an excellent job managing. Larry McPhail, sports executive, was general manager and chief executive of the Cincinnati Reds from 1933 for a couple of years. Projections were that some of us would move on up. Sure enough, his prophecy came true

In the fall of 1936, Jimmy signed with the Cincinnati Reds

Larry McPhail

Lance Ritchbourg's 1936 edition of the Vols finished higher in the Southern League race than any Nashville team since 1929. Reading left to right, front row: Whitney Hilcher, Byron Speece, Joe Dwyer, Bill Rodda and Jimmy Outlaw. Middle row: Jim Wasdell, Sidney Weiss, Manager Ritchbourg, Junie Barnes, Coaker Triplett and Johnny Peacock. Back row: Ray Starr Cowboy Thornton, Al Pladgett, Sharkey Eiland, George Scharein, and Poco Taitt. Catcher Rae Blaemire was not on hand.

Joe Dwyer is in the middle of the front row in the picture and I am on the far right of the front row. In an editorial in the Nashville Newspaper, McPhail said he was "Looking at John Vander Meer, and Joe Dwyer is also being looked at by the Reds. You can be sure that Outlaw will be pulled up. Prepare for an exodus from the Dell to the majors next year." Johnny was playing in Durham part of the season to get a lot of playing time in. He needed to work on his control.

On September 4, 1936, the president of the Nashville Baseball Club announced that he had offered me, outfielder Joe Dwyer, and pitcher Johnny Vander Meer to Cincinnati Reds for $60,000 or several players. The Reds had a working agreement with the Vols, but President Murray said if the Reds turned down the offer, he would peddle us to the Giants or the Red Sox, who were interested in Dwyer and me.

Charlie Dressen

Tom Sheehan was the scout who bought me from the Vols for the Reds. He had seen me play one of my best games against Chattanooga. And another thing happened about that time. A second division National League club offered Warren Giles, general manager of the Reds, $20,000 for me. When Charlie Dressen, manager of the Reds, heard about the offer, he butted in and said that if I was worth $20,000 to them, I was worth $40,000 to the Reds.

Spring Training with Reds

1937

Editor's Note: 1937- Cincinnati Reds, contract from April 20, 1937 to Oct. 3, 1937, but played for the Reds about half the season. Then sent to the AAA affiliate at Syracuse on option for the second half. National League: 49 games; PA – 170; AB – 165; R 18;; H 45; RBI 11; OBP .273

So, I went to Spring Training in Tampa with the Reds. The coaches really worked me at third base going to my right. I really needed to improve that if I wanted a chance for third that Lew Riggs played. Of course, he had the experience that I lacked, and no one was sure how I would do facing a real competitor on the big field. Charlie Dressen was quoted saying he liked my "fire and pepper" that I showed on the third sack. I guess I took that talk from Jimmy Hamilton seriously because I had a reputation as a "chattering hustler."

"Showing plenty of zip, as he dashes after a wide one headed to the beach."

In April, reporters kept saying I was making a name for myself:

- "...he rose to a chance with the Cincinnati club last year after hitting .330 and being something of a base-stealing bandit with Nashville of the Southern Association."
- Sports Sparks from Lou Smith: "another Pepper Martin according to scouts who had seen him play for Nashville in the Southern League last summer."

SCHEDULE OF
1937
EXHIBITION GAMES

Thursday	March 18–New York (A. L.) at St. Petersburg
Friday	March 19–New York (A. L.) at Tampa.
Saturday	March 20–Detroit (A. L.) at Tampa
Sunday	March 21–Brooklyn (N. L.) at Clearwater
Monday	March 22–Brooklyn (N. L.) at Tampa
Tuesday	March 23–Boston (A. L.) at Sarasota
Wednesday	March 24–Boston (N. L.) at St. Petersburg
Thursday	March 25–Newark (I. L.) at Sebring
Saturday	March 27–Philadelphia (N. L.) at Tampa
Sunday	March 28–Brooklyn (N. L.) at Tampa
Tuesday	March 30–Brooklyn (N. L.) at Clearwater
Wednesday	March 31–Boston (N. L.) at Tampa
Thursday	April 1–Detroit (A. L.) at Lakeland
Friday	April 2–St. Louis (N. L.) at Tampa
Saturday	April 3–Washington (A. L.) at Tampa
Sunday	April 4–Boston (A. L.) at Tampa
Monday	April 5–Philadelphia (N. L.) at Winter Haven
Tuesday	April 6–Rochester at Leesburg
Wednesday	April 7–St. Louis (N. L.) at Daytona Beach
Thursday	April 8–Jacksonville at Jacksonville
Friday	April 9–Savannah at Savannah, Ga.
Saturday	April 10–Binghamton at Spartanburg, S. C.
Sunday	April 11–Asheville at Asheville, N. C.
Monday	April 12–Boston (A. L.) at Winston-Salem, N. C.
Tuesday	April 13–Boston (A. L.) at Durham, N. C.
Wednesday	April 14–Boston (A. L.) at Rocky Mount, N. C.
Thursday	April 15–Detroit (A. L.) at Danville, Va.
Friday	April 16–Detroit (A. L.) at Charleston, W. Va.
Saturday	April 17–Detroit (A. L.) at Dayton, Ohio
Sunday	April 18–Detroit (A. L.) at Cincinnati, Ohio

FACTS ABOUT THE
1937 REDS

Twenty-six years, nine months, is the average age of the Cincinnati Reds. This is raised to this point because the outfield's average age is slightly higher than 29 years and 6 months. The average height is 5 feet 11⅞ inches and the average weight is 181 pounds.

Eddie Miller is the youngest player on the squad, born November 26, 1916. The oldest player is Hazen Cuyler, born August 30, 1899. Steve LeGault is the tallest player, 6 feet 6 inches, and Alex Kampouris and James Outlaw are the shortest men, 5 feet 8 inches. Don Brennan is the heaviest, 212 pounds, and Leonard Kahny is the lightest man on the squad, 155 pounds.

California leads the States in representation on the Reds' roster. Ten of the thirty-six players are from there.

HOTEL HEADQUARTERS DURING LEAGUE SEASON

Philadelphia	Benjamin Franklin
New York – Brooklyn	Governor Clinton
Boston	Touraine
Pittsburgh	Schenley
St. Louis	Coronado
Chicago	Belmont

Spring training booklet, schedule of exhibition games ,and facts about the 1938 Reds

Charlie Dressen, Cincinnati manager, was thinking he would put me at Toronto as a reserve infielder, but then in spring training in Tampa, he told a reporter he thought I might be a better player than Lew Riggs.

PEPPER MARTIN

Spring Training included exhibition games. There were several kinds of contests before each of the games. Before the game against St. Louis, there were races held. Pepper Martin was playing for the Cardinals then and we were pitted against each other in a footrace. I was ahead of him and he grabbed me by the belt and held me back. I guess he won. Much later, when I was managing the Miami Beach Flamingoes, Pepper was managing Miami in the same league. So I was connected with him at the beginning and also at the end of my professional career.

Here in this picture I am with Lew Riggs and Campbell, "just foolin' around." I think a photographer even posed us that way! I got along fine with Riggs, but we were competing for third base job. On March 25, 1937, Charlie Dressen passed the word to Lance Ritchbourg, the Vols manager, that he would open the 1937 season with me on third.

"Bicycle built for two had to manage three: Riggs, Campbell, and Outlaw"

At Spring Training, I made friends with Ival Goodman, who had been with the Reds two seasons already. "Goody" asked me if I had a place to stay yet, and I answered that I didn't. So, he said, "I have room at my place. You can stay with me." I lived with him until I went to Syracuse about halfway through the season. He was a regular right fielder for the Reds and actually hit 30 homeruns in 1938, a team record for then. He was there in 1939 and I played against him while I was with Boston that year. That is the year that the Reds went to the World Series. They didn't win it then, but the next year they were World Champs. He stayed with the Reds through 1942, and then went to Chicago. We stayed in touch our whole lives until he died in 1984.

Ival Goodman autogtaphed baseball card

Johnny Vander Meer

Johnny Vander Meer was another Vol that was pulled up. He was a great left-handed pitcher. Strangest pitch I've ever seen. It was sort of a side-arm pitch, not underhand but close to it. He did not have enough control to stay there; was sent to Syracuse to work on his control, and the Reds recalled him in September. The next year, in 1938, he pitched a no hitter for the Reds against the Boston Bees and then in his next appearance, he pitched another one against the Brooklyn Dodgers. That was at the first night game ever held at Ebbets Field. He still holds the record as the only pitcher who has ever pitched two consecutive no-hitters.

Jimmy Outlaw chatting with Red Barber at Crosley Field "press box"

Johnny Vander Meer and I are talking to Red Barber in this picture. Red became quite famous, but he always knew me when we ran into each other later on. He was the sportscaster for Cincinnati for about four years. He had started with the Reds a couple of years before this, when Crosley bought the team in 1934. Larry McPhail was the president of the Reds who hired him and when McPhail went to the Dodgers in 1939, so did Red. His voice was one in a million and people loved his down-home Mississippi expressions. When a long ball was hit, he would say, "Back...back...back" until it was caught or over the fence! If the game was one-sided, he would say it was "tied up in a croaker sack." If a team was on a winning streak, he said they were "tearin'up the pea patch." I always got on to him for saying my name wrong. Every time he would say, "Outlar." He said he tried and tried to say Outlaw, but just couldn't.

"The one bright spot in the Redleg defeat yesterday at Crosley Field was the playing of the youngster, Jimmy Outlaw, at third base. At bat he got three hits. Here he is batting a double in the third."

Proof sheet for promo shots of Jimmy Outlaw, Cincinnati Reds

In my first game at Crosley Field, Reds lost to the St. Louis Cardinals, but I handled pitcher Dizzy Dean. To this day I find it hard to believe I got three good hits off of him out of five times at bat in my first game in the majors.

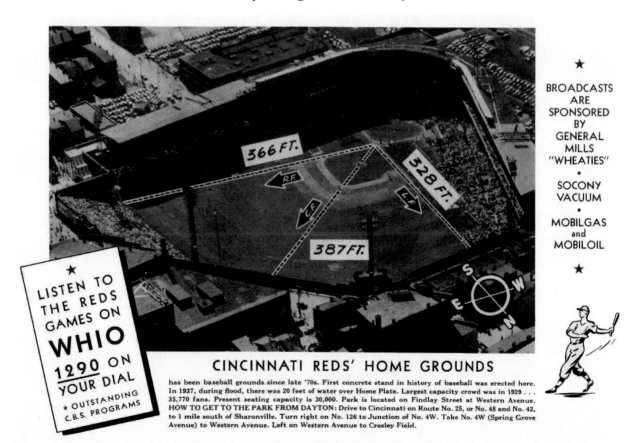

BROADCASTS
ARE
SPONSORED
BY
GENERAL
MILLS
"WHEATIES"
•
SOCONY
VACUUM
•
MOBILGAS
and
MOBILOIL

LISTEN TO THE REDS GAMES ON **WHIO** 1290 ON YOUR DIAL

★ OUTSTANDING C.B.S. PROGRAMS

CINCINNATI REDS' HOME GROUNDS

has been baseball grounds since late '70s. First concrete stand in history of baseball was erected here. In 1937, during flood, there was 20 feet of water over Home Plate. Largest capacity crowd was in 1929 . . . 35,770 fans. Present seating capacity is 30,000. Park is located on Findlay Street at Western Avenue. HOW TO GET TO THE PARK FROM DAYTON: Drive to Cincinnati on Route No. 25, or No. 48 and No. 42, to 1 mile south of Sharonville. Turn right on No. 126 to Junction of No. 4W. Take No. 4W (Spring Grove Avenue) to Western Avenue. Left on Western Avenue to Crosley Field.

Editor's Note: The Cincinnati ballfield was Crosley, known as the first major league park to have lights. It was the Reds' home location from 1884 until 1970 when they moved to Riverside Stadium. The first field was League Field. Seating was added and it was named Palace of the Fans. All the old stadium was demolished, and Redland Field was built with concrete and steel on the same spot. The name was changed to Crosley in 1934 when president Larry McPhail insisted the name be changed to honor the new owner, Powell Crosley, who is credited with rescuing the team. Crosley oversaw hundreds of improvements to the park. Several minor league parks already had lights, and Crosley pushed for approval to install the lights to save the team by allowing more fans to attend games. The first game under lights was against Phillies on Friday, May 24, 1935, with the switch flipped by President F. D. Roosevelt while he was in Washington in the White House.

Crosley field from the air after 1937 flood.

Crosley was in Queensgate on the Mill Creek, surrounded on all sides by factories, mainly a linen mill. In 1937, Mill Creek flooded, and the field was under 20 feet of water. Pitcher Lee Grissom and John MacDonald got in a rowboat and rowed over the fence in left field right out to the pitcher's mound. I don't know how they knew where it was.

Crosley Field

That field had a 15 degree rise in the outfield, not as high as Nashville, but it was there. There was a warning track, too. It was all the way around the field but was mostly in Left Field. Sometimes, they would use that for seating and put a rope in front of it. In 1935 Babe Ruth fell flat on his face on that terrace. It was an odd shaped field.

At the left center stairway there was a sign on the low fence that said, "Batted ball remaining back of barrier – 2 base hit. Bouncing out, in play." I went back later on after I was out of ball and they had built a new scoreboard right there so was no need for that ground rule, but there was another one posted: "Batted ball hitting wall on fly to right of white line – home run." It was right above the 387' sign in right-center field.

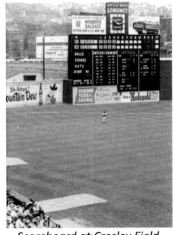

The scoreboard installation proved to be an impediment to homeruns as it was in the play area, and many hits that would have been homeruns in other parks bounced back and were doubles. Just at the very top there was a Longine's clock. To the right of the clock was a sign that read "Free suit from Local Tailor to any Reds player to hit the sign." I often wondered if a free suit or a home run would be better. Balls hit over the fence were the origins of two ball legends. One was hit into a passing truck and traveled for 30 miles. Another was hit by Jimmy Wynn right over the Center Field and onto Highway 75.

Scoreboard at Crosley Field

Right over the left field wall on York Street, there was a huge factory, the Superior Towel and Linen service. One of the advertising murals on the walls was from Seibler Suits awarding a suit to any batter hitting their sign with a ball. Wally Post won eleven suits just that way. Runner up was Willie Mays with seven.

Polo Grounds in Harlem

Polo Grounds, New York, home of the Giants

While with Cincinnati, at a game at the Polo Grounds in New York with the Giants, the German passenger airship Hindenburg flew over the field on its way to land at Lakehurst, New Jersey. It was one of the largest airships made [*812 feet long, 135 feet in diameter containing 7,063,000 cubic feet of lighter than air hydrogen gas, a very flammable gas.]* At the approach of the airship over the stadium, the game was stopped while all eyes looked up at this giant airship. We learned later that while she was preparing to be moored at Lakehurst, the hydrogen container caught on fire and the ship crashed to the ground in flames. Of the 97 people on board, 36 were killed and many others were wounded. The date was May 6, 1937. We listened to repeats of the eyewitness news report of the crash, quite an upsetting broadcast.

Move to Syracuse, 1937

After I played in 49 games with Cincinnati, I still couldn't budge Lew Riggs off regular third base and my batting average was .273, so the managers sent me to their AAA team, Syracuse Chiefs in New York. That was really okay with me.

1937 Syracuse

Syracuse, New York, MacArthur Field

The Syracuse team was managed by Mike Kelly that season and our home park was MacArthur Stadium. We ended up in the playoffs for the International League against Newark Bears. We ended the season with a record of 78 wins and 74 losses for third place in the league.

I played a strong third base for the Chiefs and batted a .307 in the 65 games I played. I credit Milt Stock for helping me at third base when I first played at Beckley. He showed me how to field slow-hit balls, and how to get down on ground balls. You know, he had played third in his major league playing days. I was recalled to the Reds at the close of the Chiefs' season September 1937.

Grace Windham, soon to be Mrs. Jimmy Outlaw

But in the meantime, something wonderful happened. Grace Windham, my high school sweetheart, agreed to marry me. We had planned to be married at the end of the season regardless of where I was playing. As it turned out, I had just returned to Cincinnati, so she came up and we got married across the Ohio River from Cincinnati in Covington, Kentucky, on October 6, 1937, in the home of Reverend R.C. Goldsmith.

Cincinnati Reds

1938

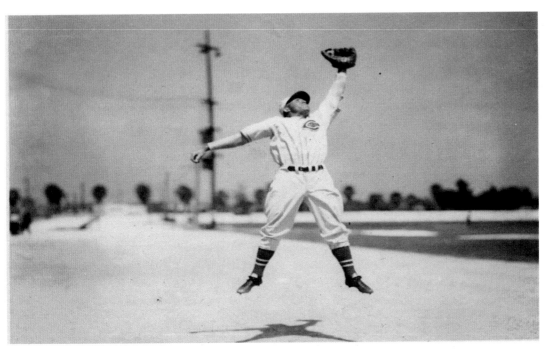

1938 spring training, Cincinnati Red catching a high fly ball

The 1938 Spring Training found Riggs set firmer at the Reds' hot corner. They let me start the year with Reds but I only got to play four games. Syracuse showed an interest in bringing me back to New York. My contract with Cincinnati actually only lasted from April 19 to May 7.

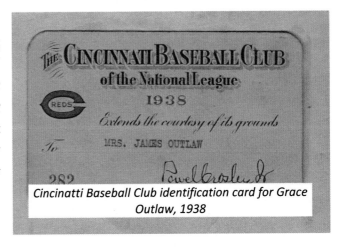

Cincinatti Baseball Club identification card for Grace Outlaw, 1938

Sportscasters were glad to see me come back, saying I had helped the Tribe end in third place the last year. President Jack Corbett announced he had purchased me as an infielder. I liked action and wanted to play and did get to play regularly from the first day I showed up and put on the uniform, Number 18. (*Meet the Chiefs No. 18 Jimmy Outlaw* by Jack Durkin.)

Dick Porter took over as manager when Bottomly was asked to leave gracefully. He moved me to centerfield, and I did much better there than at third that year. I snagged a hit by Babe Herman of Jersey City in the fifth of a game on June 30. His hit was called the longest one ever hit at the stadium. A drive right to the 455-center field fence, but I made it to the fence and caught it. In any other stadium it would have been an out-of-the park homerun. I also remember a running catch of a line drive in right center from Mayo Smith with the Toronto Maple Leafs. It had all the earmarks of a triple, but I pulled it down. Smith glared daggers and machine guns at me. We both played for Buffalo a couple of years later.

We called Dick Porter "Twisty" because of his batting shenanigans. When he got into the batter's box, he would twist his bottom like nobody's business. One time in a pregame show another player came out to the field wearing a pair of ladies' bloomers over his uniform. He picked up a bat, went to the plate, and while getting in position, he really made fun of Twisty. The crowds loved antics like that. Dick was known to court the fans. That year, the Chiefs held a contest to see which player was the fans' favorite.

Dick Porter with Tim the Terrier prize for most popular player voted by the fans, Syracuse.

72

The fans voted me in as the most popular. Funny story about the prize they gave me at the beginning of the playoffs against Buffalo Bisons. The prize came from a local pet store. It was a wire-haired terrier. They named him Lucky Outlaw or Little Outlaw, but we renamed him Tim. Twisty Porter and Mrs. Muriel Rousseau presented the dog to me before the game started. She said he was the first member of the Rabid Fans Club.

Mrs. Muriel Rouseau presents Lucky Outlaw to Jimmy Outlaw, fans' favorite. He is the first member of the rabid fans club.

Tim was some dog. He went with us when we moved to Jackson, Alabama, for the off-season. He would follow us to the Methodist church and run up into the balcony. Every time one certain lady sang a solo, Tim would join in with a gosh-awful howling. Someone would have to take him home. Usually me, I guess.

Playoff Against Buffalo

1938

The '38 season ended with an 87-67 and we were 2nd in the league. We played Buffalo in the playoffs: Buffalo won 4 straight. I ended up with the second highest season batting average of all the Syracuse players for all time. I still held that record when I went back there for the Wall of Fame induction.

I was named to the International League All-Star team as Center Field. Dick was named manager and in the coming months, I felt like a ping pong ball. Clarence Rowland of the Chicago Cubs and Harry Hinchman of Pittsburgh made offers to Jack Corbett of Syracuse for Ted Kleinhaus, left-handed pitcher, and me, either as a pair or individually

JIMMY OUTLAW, SYRACUSE, 1938

Detroit, Cleveland, and Chicago of the American league had rumored they were interested. The Cubs wanted an immediate deal, but the Pirates, who were in the lead in the National League at that time, were willing to wait until the end of the International League season to make the trade.

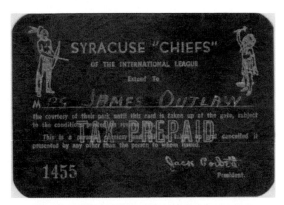

SYRACUSE"CHIEFS" OF THE NATIONAL LEAGUE
EXTENDS TO MRS. JAMES OUTLAW THE COURTESY OF
THIS PARK UNTIL THIS CARD IS TAKEN UP AT THE GATE,
SUBJECT TO THE CONDITIONS PRINTED ON THE
REVERSE SIDE. THIS IS A PERSONAL COURTESY AND
WILL BE TAKEN UP IF PRESENTED BY ANY PERSON
OTHER THAN THE PERSON TO WHOM IT IS ISSSUED.

In the off-season on Sept. 9, 1938, I had originally been purchased with Jake Mooty by the Brooklyn Dodgers from Cincinnati. But on September 14, 1938, that sale was nullified by Baseball Commissioner Judge Kennesaw Mountain Landis. Then on October 4, 1938, I was drafted by the St. Louis Cardinals from Cincinnati Reds in the 1938 Rule 5 draft. A couple of months later, on December 13, 1938, I was traded to the Brooklyn Dodgers for Lew Krausse and some cash. On the same day, Brooklyn traded me with Buddy Hassett to the Boston Bees for Ira Hutchinson and Gene Moore. So, I headed back to the Majors with the Boston Bees.

.

Inning Five
Boston Bees – National League
April 19, 1939 -September 28, 1939

In 1939 I went to Boston along with Buddy Hassett, pitcher, traded for Gene Moore and Ira Hutchinson. In 1936 Bob Quinn had become president of the Boston Braves. The 1935 team had finished last, 61½ games behind the first place Chicago Cubs, with a record of 38 wins and 115 losses.

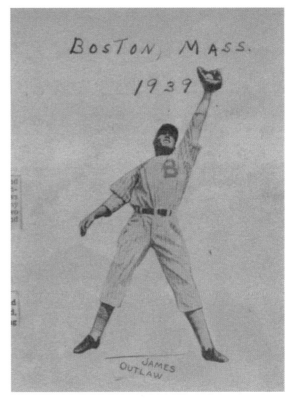

1939 Boston Bees, National League

Editor' Note: After Quinn became president, in an effort to remove the stigma of utter failure, he decided to change the name of the team. To do this, he invited fans to submit names. From the thousands of suggestions received, a final decision would be made by invited sports writers. The name selected was "Bees." To go with this name, Quinn had the ballpark called "The Beehive." (Images of Sports, Boston Braves by Richard A. Johnson, Arcadia Publishing, 2001) The team was called the Bees for only five years.

Jimmy Outlaw, Boston Bees. 1939

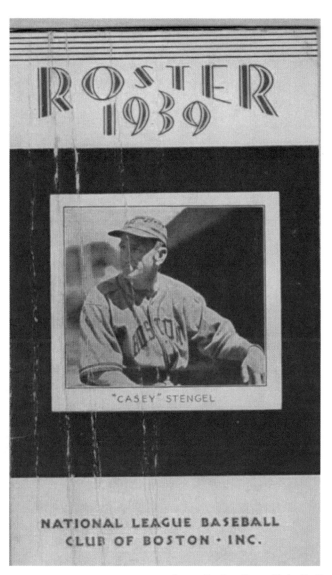

SPRING TRAINING HEADQUARTERS
HOTEL MANATEE RIVER
BRADENTON, FLORIDA
February 28th to April 6th

RETURN ITINERARY

Lv. Bradenton	Apr. 6th	9:00 A.M.	Seaboard Air Line
Ar. Sebring	Apr. 6th	12:15 P.M.	Seaboard Air Line

SEBRING HOTEL

Lv. Sebring	Apr. 6th	6:30 P.M.	Seaboard Air Line
Ar. Orlando	Apr. 6th	11:00 P.M.	Seaboard Air Line

COLONIAL ORANGE COURT HOTEL

Lv. Orlando	Apr. 9th	12:00 M.D.T.	Seaboard Air Line
Ar. Savannah	Apr. 10th	11:37 A.M.	Seaboard Air Line

DE SOTO HOTEL

Lv. Savannah	Apr. 10th	10:30 P.M.	Seaboard Air Line
Ar. Charlotte	Apr. 11th	11:25 A.M.	Seaboard Air Line

CHARLOTTE HOTEL

Lv. Charlotte	Apr. 11th	6:40 P.M.	Seaboard Air Line
Ar. Washington	Apr. 12th	7:35 A.M.	Seaboard Air Line

SHOREHAM HOTEL

Lv. Washington	Apr. 13th	9:00 P.M.	Pennsylvania R. R.
Ar. Boston	Apr. 14th	7:45 A.M.	N. Y.-N. H. & Hart.

BAGGAGE

All personal trunks will be sent direct to Boston from Bradenton. They must be packed and ready to ship by noon on April 5th.

HOTELS DURING CHAMPIONSHIP SEASON

Brooklyn	COMMODORE (N. Y.)
Chicago	EDGEWATER BEACH
Cincinnati	NETHERLAND PLAZA
New York	COMMODORE
Philadelphia	BENJAMIN FRANKLIN
Pittsburgh	SCHENLEY
St. Louis	CHASE

Cover Boston Bees Club, National League, 1939

I went to Spring Training with the Bees in Bradenton, Florida. Manager Casey Stengel told a news reporter, "We had our eyes on Outlaw all last season and when we had a chance of getting him from Brooklyn in a trade, we grabbed him. I was impressed by the fact that he won the center field position on an International League All-Star team. Anyone horning into that team who wasn't a Newark Bear had to be good."

I signed my contract with Boston on March 4, 1939, in Bradenton, the last member of the club to sign for the season. The coaches said they thought I had considerable value and put my tag at $20,000 and two players. I was fast and played a good deep field. In the early practice games against the "Yannnigans" (scrub team) I had a little hard luck but pulled out by the time the season started.

Photo taken by a fan at Boston

1939 Boston Bees team with manager Casey Stengel. Jimmy Outlaw, eighth from left, Casey Stengel standing far right.

I played for Casey before he got smart. The great pitcher Warren Spahn (363 wins) agreed. Casey became smart while managing the New York Yankees (1949-1960) where he won ten pennants and seven World Series. He then lapsed back into being not so smart while manager of the New York Mets (1962-1965) finishing last every year.

1939 Boston Bees fans pennant

The Braves (the Bees 1936-40) was the last team that had Babe Ruth on the roster. In 1935 he was part manager and was to share in profits, but his health was deteriorating, and he retired June 1, 1935, soon after his last three homeruns in pro ball history.

Bob Quinn made Casey Stengel manager in 1938. Neither the name change nor the new manager helped improve the team record. In the years Casey was there (1938-1943) the team finished out of the first division each year and dead last four times. Casey was part owner of the team, but when he was dismissed as manager, he sold his part to Lou Perins.

Casey Stengel with Boston Bees, 1939

WARREN SPAHN, FAR RIGHT

I think Grace enjoyed getting to know the other wives in Boston. We sort of hung out with John Hill and his wife. I am not sure why we called him John. His name was Oliver. Maybe that is why he went by John. He was from Georgia so we could understand each other real good. This was the celebration of 100 years of baseball – the Centennial year, so there were some extra things going on that included the wives. She saved nearly everything and put them in the scrapbook.

The Boston paper liked to run photos of the players off field – the fans loved it! Here Grace and Jimmy Outlaw are on an outing with Mr. and Mrs. John Hill

Wives and grilfriends of the 1939 Boston Bees are seated on the rail for a photo. Grace Outlaw is on the far left.

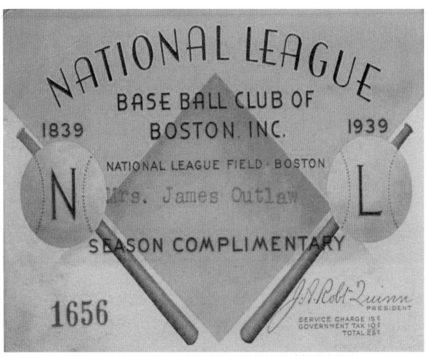

NATIONAL LEAGUE BASE BALL CLUB OF BOSTON, INC.

1839-1939

MRS. JAMES OUTLAW

Season Complimentary

J.H. Robt Quinn

Editor's Note: The Baseball Centennial year was celebrated in 1939 because most people considered that the first game was in 1839. 1839 is said to have been the year that Abner Doubleday invented the game, but there is no concrete evidence. A committee organized by Al Spalding in 1905 made the determination, but most people agree that baseball was not really invented on a certain date but evolved over a couple of hundred years. Boston had an official team way back in 1870, the Red Stockings, which had been the Cincinnati Red Stockings.

BRAVES FIELD, LARGEST BALL GROUNDS IN THE WORLD, BOSTON, MASS.

Braves Field, built 1915 home of the Boston Braves – also known as the Beehive, 1935-1939

Caption on postcard: Braves Field: Home of the Boston Braves Baseball Team of the National League. Braves Field is located just off Commonwealth Ave. (Allston) Boston at Gaffney and Babcock Streets. It has a seating capacity of 40,000. The park was built in 1915

Lighting equipment for night baseball was installed in 1946. The field was also the home gridiron of the Boston College Football Team. In 1936 Braves Field was renamed National Park but was called the Beehive Braves Field 1915-1952 [*now is Nickerson Field of Boston University.*] 1952 was the year the Boston team moved to Milwaukee, Wisconsin, and became the Milwaukee Braves, then on to Atlanta. The Braves still have the oldest baseball franchise in the nation.

Home of the Boston Braves under the lights

PLAYER ROSTER - 1939

CHARLES D. ("Casey") STENGEL, Manager

PLAYER	Address	Age	Height	Weight	Bats	Throws	Games	E. R. Av.	Won	Lost	Club in 1938
Pitchers											
Doll, Arthur	Chicago, Ill.	25	6' 1"	190	Right	Right	39	3.54	17	10	Hartford
Earley, Thomas	Roxbury, Mass.	21	6'	180	Left	Right	35	3.86	12	9	Hartford
Errickson, Richard	Vineland, N. J.	25	6' 1"	175	Left	Right	34	3.15	9	7	Boston
Fette, Louis	Alma, Mo.	32	5' 11"	180	Right	Right	33	3.15	11	13	Boston
Frankhouse, Fred	Port Royal, Pa.	34	5' 10"	165	Right	Right	30	4.02	3	5	Brooklyn
Hazel, Albert	Bloomington, Ind.	22	6' 1"	172	Left	Left	32	2.52	15	5	Evansville
Lanning, John	Asheville, N. C.	27	6' 1"	185	Right	Right	32	3.72	8	7	Boston
MacFayden, Daniel	Belmont, Mass.	32	5' 11"	170	Right	Right	29	2.95	14	9	Boston
Moran, Albert	Point Pleasant, N. Y.	21	6' 4"	185	Right	Right	33	3.61	12	9	Hartford
Pezzullo, John	Bridgeport, Conn.	27	5' 11"	180	Left	Left	47	2.88	26	9	Savannah
Shoffner, Milburn	New York Mills, N. Y.	33	6' 1"	184	Left	Left	26	3.54	8	7	Boston
Sullivan, Joseph	Bremerton, Wash.	28	6'	184	Left	Left	37	3.76	18	10	Toronto
Turner, James	Nashville, Tenn.	35	6'	185	Left	Right	35	3.46	14	18	Boston
								Bat. Av.		Fielding Av.	
Catchers											
Andrews, Stanley	Lynn, Mass.	21	5' 11"	175	Right	Right	120	.304		.970	Hartford
Lopez, Alfonso	Tampa, Fla.	30	5' 11"	165	Right	Right	71	.266		.989	Boston
Masi, Philip	Chicago, Ill.	22	5' 10"	175	Right	Right	127	.308		.975	Springfield-Ohio
Sutcliffe, Charles	Fall River, Mass.	22	5' 8"	165	Right	Right	50	.295		.953	Salisbury-Boston
Todd, Albert	Elmira, N. Y.	31	6' 1"	200	Right	Right	133	.264		.985	Pittsburgh
Infielders											
Cuccinello, Anthony	Flushing, N. Y.	31	5' 7"	170	Right	Right	147	.264		.974	Boston
Fletcher, Elburt	Wollaston, Mass.	23	6'	180	Left	Left	147	.272		.990	Boston
Hassett, John	New York City, N. Y.	26	5' 11"	180	Left	Left	115	.293		.974	Brooklyn
Hill, John	Douglasville, Ga.	26	5' 10"	170	Left	Right	142	.338		.952	Atlanta
Huber, Otto	Garfield, N. J.	22	5' 10"	165	Right	Right	123	.311		.955	Evansville
Kahle, Robert	Richmond, Ind.	23	6'	170	Right	Right					Boston
Majeski, Henry	Staten Island, N. Y.	22	5' 9"	174	Right	Right	151	.325		.974	Birmingham
Miller, Edward	Mt. Lebanon, Pa.	22	5' 9"	165	Right	Right	147	.290		.960	Kansas City
Rowell, Carvel	Citronelle, Ala.	23	5' 11"	170	Left	Right	114	.310		.917	Dayton
Warstler, Harold	No. Canton, Ohio	31	5' 8"	150	Right	Right	142	.231		.937	Boston
Outfielders											
Cooney, John	Sarasota, Fla.	37	5' 10"	160	Right	Left	120	.270		.981	Boston
Dickshot, John	Waukegan, Ill.	27	6' 1"	195	Right	Right	29	.228		1.000	Pittsburgh
Garms, Deba	Wichita Falls, Tex.	30	5' 8"	165	Left	Right	117	.315		.985	Boston
Hodgins, Ralph	Guilford College, N. C.	23	5' 10"	170	Left	Right	123	.323		.980	Evansville
McLeod, Ralph	No. Quincy, Mass.	23	6'	168	Left	Left	132	.332		.961	Hartford
Outlaw, James	Jackson, Ala.	24	5' 8"	165	Right	Right	115	.339		.966	Syracuse
Simmons, Al	Milwaukee, Wis.	35	5' 11"	190	Right	Right	125	.302		.993	Washington
West, Max	Alhambra, Calif.	22	6' 1"	186	Left	Right	123	.234		.985	Boston

1939 Boston Bees player roster at beginning of season.

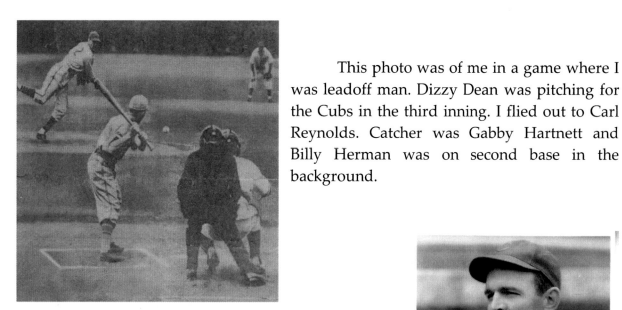

This photo was of me in a game where I was leadoff man. Dizzy Dean was pitching for the Cubs in the third inning. I flied out to Carl Reynolds. Catcher was Gabby Hartnett and Billy Herman was on second base in the background.

Up against Dizzy Dean

I especially remember a game where Claude Passeau was pitching for the Cubs. It was in August in Boston. I got three for five hits, but Chicago still won 6-1. Two days later I got another hit off him. Claude was from Waynesboro, Mississippi, not too far from my

Claude Passeau

hometown in Jackson. He was still pitching for the Cubs when I played with Detroit in the 1945 Word Series.

By the end of his career he had played 13 years and won 162 games with more than a thousand strikeouts. He lived in Lucedale, Mississippi, after he retired, and I was able to visit with him several times.

On June 27, 1939, in Boston the team played Brooklyn to a 2-2 tie in 23 innings. The game lasted 5 hours and 15 minutes. We would have won it in the thirteenth inning if Otto Huber had not tripped on his shoes. He was a pinch runner, and from then on, anytime Casey put in a pinch runner, he would check his shoes first. Casey called Huber the guy who put us in the Red Sox Book record. This happened again when I was in Detroit but not with the same player.

Jimmy Outlaw Boston Bees 1939

Photo taken by a fan

The back of the photo says, "Some woman took this on the first trip to Cincinnati and gave it to me the other day."

[*The photographer had written, "Ain't it just too cute."*]

84

I ended the year *[age 26]* playing 65 games with 136 times at bat; scored 15 runs, made 35 hits. Not my homerun season, though. Only stole one base, too. I did have a good eye, though. I walked ten times. Maybe not great pitchers. My batting average was .263.

Editor's Note: March 23, 1940 – purchased by the Detroit Tigers from the Boston Bees and sent to Buffalo NY Bisons AAA team for the Tigers

𝕴𝖓𝖓𝖎𝖓𝖌 𝕾𝖎𝖝
𝕭𝖚𝖋𝖋𝖆𝖑𝖔 𝕭𝖎𝖘𝖔𝖓𝖘
1940

Buffalo Bisons 1940

T he official purchase date is listed as March 23, 1940, by Detroit Tigers, but I was assigned to the Buffalo Bisons in New York. My purchase was actually announced by Manager Steve O'Neill in Plant City, Florida, in Spring Training. He said I was extra insurance for third base in case regular third baseman Smokey Joe Martin did not recover from a fractured ankle he had during off season that winter. He said I was expected to be there in time for an exhibition game against the Toronto Maple Leafs at Avon Park.

Until about this time, no major leagues had official farm teams except the St. Louis Cardinals. Other teams saw how successful that was and started their own farm system, actually owning the teams.

JIMMY OUTLAW, Infielder

Promo photo for Jimmy Outlaw, Bisons, 1940

The Bisons, International League, were the primary farm team for Detroit starting that year. In 1940, Buffalo had entered a non-exclusive working agreement with Detroit. This was a result of what took place in 1939 when late in the season, Cleveland (the team they had a working agreement with at the time) chose to recall Lou Boudreau and Ray Mack. At the time, Buffalo was very much in the race for the championship of the International League while Cleveland was going nowhere. Without these two players Buffalo finished third in the league. The results of this act by Cleveland was that Buffalo broke off the agreement with them.

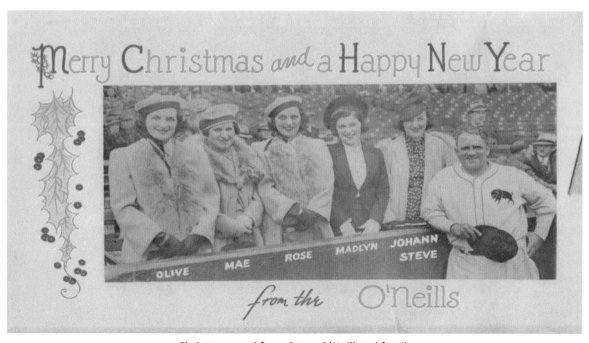

Christmas card from Steve O'Neill and family

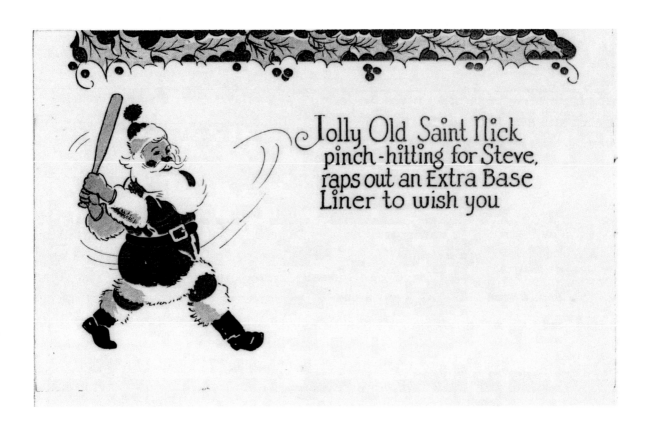

Jolly Old Saint Nick
pinch-hitting for Steve,
raps out an Extra Base
Liner to wish you

I will have to say that Steve O'Neill was my favorite manager of my whole career. He was catcher for 17 years with the Indians, the Red Sox, the Yankees, and the Browns. He managed in the Majors for 14 years. His brother, John Joseph "Jack" O'Neill, played five years of major ball with the Cardinals, the Cubs, and the Braves. Steve sent us this Christmas card with a photo of his wife and daughters.

"With only one veteran regular surviving from the 1939 year combination is the lineup, this quartet of players will guard the inner defense when the revamped Bisons take the field for their home debut against the Baltimore Orioles in Offerman Stadium this afternoon. Left to right, they are Johnny Kroner, second baseman; Jimmy Outlaw, third base guardian; Les Fleming, first baseman; and Danny Carnavale, shortstop."

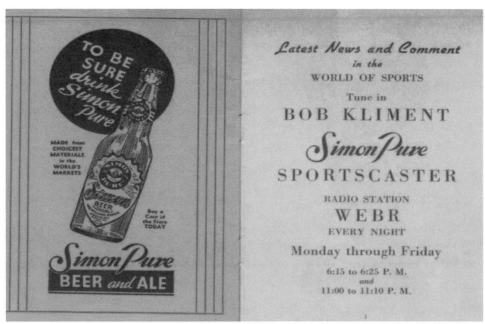

The booklet for the 1940 opening banquet

STEVE O'NEILL

Minooka, Pa.'s contribution to baseball. Played with Cleveland Indians 1911 to 1923. Greatest catcher in American League through most of that period; good defensive man, especially at blocking the plate; a fine handler of pitchers and ever dangerous at bat. Got start in pro baseball through break. While visiting his brother, Mike, who managed Elmira in 1910, both Elmira catchers were injured. Rushed into action, Steve caught 28 straight games and was drafted by Athletics. Purchased following year by Cleveland. Born July 6, 1892.

ROBERT F. "BOB" KLIMENT

Age 28. Born, Louisville, Ky. Married. Started in radio in 1932. Alumnus of Marshall College, Huntington, W. Va. First sports assignment in 1935. Football games. Has described baseball, Mid-Atlantic League; also Bison ball games. Biggest special event — handling description of 1937 Ohio River flood at Cincinnati, which was fed to the National network. His "wrestler's corner" is a regular feature on Friday night Simon Pure Sports Review. Available to speak at dinners, banquets, college and high school assemblies.

Steve O'Neill is in this program with Robert F."Bob" Kliment who was the sportscaster. Simon Pure was the sponsor of the broadcast and he was their spokesperson.

BISON SCHEDULE for 1940

●

WITH BALTIMORE

At Home	On the Road
May 2, 3, 4	April 18, 19, 20
June 13-13, 14-14, 15, 23-23x	June 6, 7, 8, 9-9x
July 29, 30-30, 31	July 22, 23, 24

WITH SYRACUSE

May 5x, 6, 7, 8	April 21-21x, 22, 23, 24
June 24, 25-25, 26	June 3, 4, 5
July 28-28x, Aug. 20, 21	July 25-25, 26-26, 27, Aug. 19

WITH JERSEY CITY

May 9, 10, 11	April 28-28x, 29, 30
June 10, 11, 12	June 20, 21, 22
Aug. 4-4x, 6, 22, 23, 24	Aug. 12, 13, 14, 15

WITH TORONTO

May 12-12x, 30-30pm	May 21, 22, 23
June 30-30x, July 19, 20	July 1-1pm, 2, 3
Aug. 7, 8, Sept. 8x	Sept. 4, 5, 6, 7-7

WITH NEWARK

May 13, 14, 15, 16	April 25, 26, 27
June 27-27, 28, 29	June 16-16x, 17, 18, 19
July 21-21x, Aug. 1-1, 2, 3	Aug. 16, 17, 18x

WITH MONTREAL

May 17, 18, 19x	May 24-24pm, 25
July 4-4pm, 6	July 11, 12, 13, 14-14x
Aug. 9, 10, 11-11x, 27, 28	Sept. 1x, 2-2pm, 3

WITH ROCHESTER

May 31, June 1, 2-2x	May 26x, 27, 28
July 7-7x, 8, 9, 10	July 16, 17, 18
Aug. 25x, Sept. 11, 12, 13	Aug. 29, 30, 31, Sept. 14, 15x

x Sunday   *pm Holidays*

4

BISON ROSTER for 1940

●

PITCHERS	HOME ADDRESS
Earl Cook	Stouffville, Ont.
Salvatore Maglie	Niagara Falls
Floyd Giebell	Wierton, W. Va.
Joseph Rogalski	Ashland, Wis.
Floyd Stromme	Fargo, N. D.
James Trexler	Richmond, Va.
Harold White	Utica
Quinn Lee	Phoenix, Ariz.
Fred Hutchinson	Seattle, Wash.

CATCHERS	
Frank Zubik	Lemont Furnace, Pa.
Clyde McCullough	Nashville, Tenn.

INFIELDERS	
Dan Carnevale	Buffalo
Lester Fleming	Beaumont, Tex.
William Martin	Oxnard, Cal.
Greg Mulleavy	Buffalo
Jimmy Outlaw	Jackson, Ala.
John H. Kroner	St. Louis, Mo.
Les Scarsella	Santa Cruz, Cal.

OUTFIELDERS	
Ollie Carnegie	Buffalo
Henry Nowak	Cleveland
Mayo Smith	Lake Worth, Fla.
Patrick Mullin	Grindstone, Pa.

5

Booklet listing all the players for the team at the beginning

Several of the players with the team in 1940 were not on the 1941 team. Here are the ones who were not with the team the next year, 1941:

FLOYD STROMME

Floyd Stromme, Pitcher

Earned 15 letters in high school in baseball, football, track and hockey. Attended Northwestern University. Fifth year in pro ball. Here on option from Cleveland. Just one-half inch under six feet; weighs 184. Bats and throws right. Born in Cooperstown, N.D., August 1, 1916. Won 11, lost seven for New Orleans last year. Won 19, lost six with 2.10, low for the league, for Fargo-Moorehead in 1937.

Les Scarsella, First Baseman

Purchased from Boston Bees outright. Formerly with Toronto and Newark. With Cincinnati last year. Batted .308 in 1938 for Newark, making 156 hits, including 14 homers. Played only 16 games for Reds last year. Batted .305 for Bees in 17 games this year. Born Nov. 23, 1913; weighs 190. Bats and throws left.

LES SCARSELLA, FIRST BASEMAN

SAL MAGLIE

Sal Maglie, Pitcher

Has been with Bisons since being picked up off Niagara Falls sandlots. Has great curve, fair speed, but lack of control has held him back. Born April 26, 1917, in Niagara Falls. Six feet, two inches; weighs 170 pounds. Bats and throws right. Appeared in 39 games last year, winning three, losing seven.

He became very good. We called him "The Barber" because he wasn't afraid of brushing the batters away from the plate. He never gave up. He had three tries with Buffalo, pitching 0-7 the first year. He became pitcher for the Giants, Cleveland, and the Dodgers in the 50s, for ten years in the majors.

William Joseph Martin, Third Baseman

Holds International League record of five homers in five successive times at bat. Made in 1937 with Baltimore. Two chances in Majors, with Giants and White Sox. Born Seymour, Mo., August 28, 1912, attended University of California. Bats and throws right. Five feet, 11 ½ inches tall, weighs 180. Lifetime batting average of .309, 104 homers. Hit .331 and .321 in two seasons for Bisons.

WILLIAM MARTIN, THIRD BASEMAN

FLOYD GIEBELL, PITCHER

Floyd Giebell, Pitcher

Here on option from Detroit. Only two years of previous pro experience. Won 18, lost six in first year for Evansville with earned run average of less than two runs per games. Won one, lost 10 for Toledo although having low average of 3.58. Born in Pennsboro, W. Va., Dec. 10, 1914. Throws right, bats left. Six feet two inches; weighs 172.

Joe Rogalski, Pitcher

Passed out of Detroit chain this year after four years. Part payment for Clayt Smith. Had three fine years in 1936-37-38, winning 45 while losing only 21. Fair success with Toledo and Detroit last two years. Born Ashland, Wis., July 15, 1915. Bats and throws right. Six feet two inches; weighs 187.

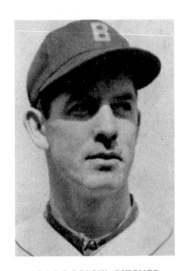

JOE ROGALSKI, PITCHER

FRANK ZUBICK

Frank Zubick

Out on option several years, Zubik is back with the Bisons to stay this season. Has learned tricks of trade and is valuable understudy to McCullough. Born Everson, Pa., June 18, 1914. Stands six feet, one inch; weighs 195. Bats and throws right.

Hank Nowak

Reserve outfielder, came to Buffalo with only one year of pro experience after graduation from John Carroll University, Cleveland. Bats left, throws right. Five feet, 10 ½ inches; weighs 168. Crack halfback in college. Still lives in Cleveland, where he was born Dec. 11, 1917. Lifetime batting average of .265.

HANK NOWAK, OUTFIELDER

GREG MULLEAVY, PLAYER-COACH

Greg Mulleavy

Player-coach is great favorite with fans. With Bisons since 1933. Batted over .300 four of seven years. Lifetime batting average of .301. Weighs 160, stands five feet nine inches. Bats and throws right. Born in Detroit, Mich., Sept. 25, 1907. With Chicago White Sox in 1930 and 1932, Boston Sox in 1933 before coming to Buffalo.

Dan Carnavale

Buffalo's only native son on team. Was picked off Muny diamonds while playing with Simon Pures where he had fine record. Started playing at St. Joseph's Collegiate Institute. Attended Canisius College. Throws and bats right. Batted .354 with Perth-Cornwall in Canadian-American League in 1937. Five feet, 11 inches tall and weighs 175. Born Feb. 8, 1918.

DAN CARNAVALE

Clyde McCullough, Catcher

Sparkplug of team since joining Bisons. Great catching prospect owned by Chicago Cubs. New York Yankees chain for four years. Rugged 180 pounder; five feet, 10 inches. Born Nashville, Tenn., March 4, 1917. Bats and throws right. Lifetime batting average of .277.

CLYDE MCCULLOUGH

LES FLEMING, OUTFIELDER

Les Fleming

Combination first baseman and outfielder. Has driven home 510 runs in the last five years. Lifetime batting average .290. Hit 27 homers for Toledo last year. Also 15 doubles and six triples. Five feet, 10 inches; weighs 185. Looks more like fighter with square jaw. Born Singleton, Tex., Aug. 5, 1915. Bats and throws left.

John Kroner, Second Baseman

Has been playing since 1928. Spent four years in American League, two with Cleveland, two with Boston. Also played with Baltimore and Syracuse. Secured in trade for Roy Johnson from Syracuse. Born in St. Louis, Nov. 13, 1909, bats and throws right. Five feet, 11 ½ inches; weighs 170. Has lifetime batting average of .238.

JOHN KRONER, SECOND BASEMAN

Pat Mullin, Outfielder

The speed merchant of team. Ran wild in Texas League in 1938, copping 40 bases. In 1937, first year in pro ball, led Evangeline League in batting with .384, including 16 homers, 17 triples, and 29 doubles. In three years has made 92 doubles. Born in Trotter, Pa., Nov. 1, 1916, now lives in Grindstone, Pa. Bats left, throws right. Six feet, two inches; weighs 185.

PAT MULLIN

QUINN LEE

Quinn Lee

Boyish looking right hander. Five feet, 9 ½ inches; weighs 163. Was cut loose by Detroit and signed as free agent. Picked up by Detroit after winning 22, losing only five for Alexandria in 1936. With Detroit's Beaumont farm through 1937-38-39 but failed to win consistently. Tough luck has dogged him through early season. Born in Paris, Ark., Nov.6, 1914.

Offerman Stadium, commonly known as Bisons Stadium, Buffalo, New York

Our home field was Offerman, but most people just called it the Bisons Stadium. We lived near there. It had lights and we played night games there until World War II caused a restriction on light, and there were only daytime games. It was only about 10 years old when I was there.

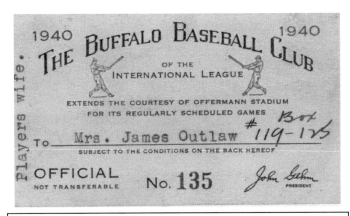

Mrs. James Outlaw, Players wife.

The Buffalo Baseball Club of the International League extends the courtesy of Offermann Stadium for its regularly scheduled games. Box 119-125

There was a series of newspaper interviews with the wives named "Meet the Missus." Grace was featured in one of the columns:

Mrs. James Outlaw

When Jimmy Outlaw was a high school baseball hero while playing for the Jackson, Alabama, high school team some ten years ago, his No. 1 fan was a fellow student of Jackson High, Grace Windham.

[I need to make a correction here. I did not get to play baseball in high school because I broke my arm two years in a row.]

Today, Grace is still the No. 1 booster for the mite infielder of the Buffalo Bisons, but her name is no longer Windham, having changed it to Outlaw three years ago.

Every time the Bisons play at home Mrs. Outlaw can be seen behind home plate, pulling for Jimmy to "hit it over the fence" every time he comes to bat.

Mrs. Outlaw loves baseball. She gets a big thrill out of every game, especially when Jimmy hits safely or makes a spectacular play in the field.

Possibly the reason Mrs. Outlaw likes baseball is that she was quite an athlete herself in high school. She played with the Jackson High girls' basketball team and also participated in minor sports.

The Outlaws live at 171 Linwood Ave. during the summer months, but in the off season spend their winters in their old hometown, Jackson.

The Outlaws have much in common. Both love to play golf, "but Jimmy always beats me," complains the Missus. Both also go strongly for hunting, "Jimmy never hits anything – either," Mrs. Outlaw laughingly stated.

The Outlaws were married three years ago while Jimmy was owned by the Cincinnati Reds.

He was sent to Syracuse the following year. Both were disappointed, but Mrs. Outlaw learned that baseball is a game of ups and downs.

Jimmy went up again the following year and remained with the Boston Bees all last year.

This year he is back in the International League with the Bisons.

"But we'll be back up again within the next year or two," predicts the Missus.

Outlaws' residence in Buffalo, New York

I was playing third base but would have to see what happened. It was a strange feeling to go back and face Syracuse at their home Memorial Stadium. The announcer welcomed me and said that I held the record for batting average for the Chiefs. He warned the pitchers to be ready for me.

Jimmy Outlaw, Buffalo Bisons

It was near the end of the season when I was hit on the wrist by a pitch by Bill Crouch in a game with Montreal. I didn't let them pull me out of the game, but I never did have the batting average I had before that injury. I was on the sick list just a week, but maybe should have taken more time off.

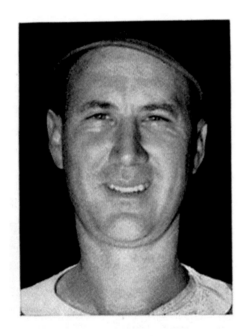

Bill Crouch

"Crowd Roars Welcome to Herd. Starting line-up: (left to right) Dan Carnavale, Jimmy Outlaw, Pat Muller, Ollie Carnegie, and Les Fleming."

(Left to right) Mayo Smith, John Kroner, Frank Zubik, Floyd Stromme, Steve O'Neill

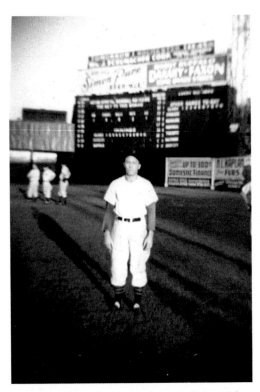

In 1940, I played in 145 games and was at bat 531 times with 164 hits. I had 14 homeruns and I had the second highest batting average on the team at .309. Final tally was 76 wins and 83 losses for 6th place in the league.

We did enjoy going to Niagara Falls. Every time we had company, we took them there. Here we are with the wire-haired terrier, Tim, that was given to us in Syracuse.

The fans were always interested in our families. This is Grace (seated in the automobile) with Mrs. Nowak. Her name was Rose. The Nowaks were a nice couple and we enjoyed being with them.

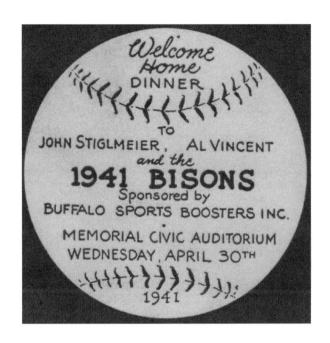

Roster of 1941
BISON PLAYERS

Al. Vincent,
Manager
John Stiglmeier,
Business Manager
Jimmy Hutch,
Trainer
Robert Boken
Henry B. Bunoski
Ollie A. Carnegie
Earl D. Cook
Charley Fuchs
Morris Hancken
Fred C. Hutchinson
James J. Levey
Eugene Markland

Joe Martin
Lambert D. Meyer
Patrick Mullin
Lynn Nelson
James Outlaw
Edward D. Parsons
Robert Patrick
Boyd G. Perry
Leo Pukas
Michael Rocco
Mike Roscoe
Mayo Smith
Jim Trexler
Virgil C. Trucks

1941 Home Games
SCHEDULE

MAY
May 1, 2, 3
Syracuse
May *4, 5, 6, 7
Baltimore
May 8, 9, 10
Newark
May *11, 12, 13, 14
Jersey City
May 16, 17, *18
Toronto
May 28, 29
Rochester
May *30, 31
Montreal

JUNE
June 1
Rochester
June 16, 17, 18
Baltimore
June 19, 20, 21
Jersey City

June 22
Syracuse
June 25, 26
Montreal
June 27, 28
Rochester

JULY
July 2, 3, *4
Toronto
July 5, *6
Montreal
July 7, 8, 9
Syracuse
July 10, 11, 12
Newark
July *13
Toronto
July 17, 18
Rochester
July 27
Syracuse
July 28, 29, 30
Baltimore

July 31
Syracuse

AUGUST
August 1, 2
Syracuse
August *3, 4, 5, 6
Newark
August 7, 8, 9
Jersey City
August 10
Baltimore
August 11, 12, 13
Rochester
August 25, 26, 27
Montreal
August 31
Toronto

SEPTEMBER
September 7
Rochester
*Denotes
Doubleheader

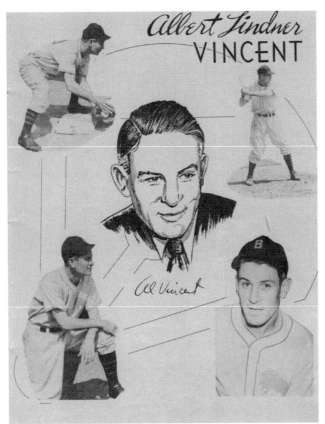

For the 1941 and 1942 seasons we were managed by Al Vincent. He was from Birmingham and had managed at Beaumont. They won the league championship in 1938. He was with the Bisons two years before he went on to Detroit. I played for him there, too. He was a nice guy. He continued to manage major league teams, then was at Lamar University. The stadium there is named for him and he is in their Hall of Fame.

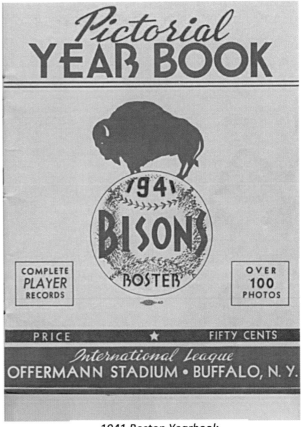

1941 Boston Yearbook

The following players were some of those featured in the 1941 Yearbook:

BOB BOKEN

Bob Boken:

Robert Anthony "Bob" Boken, Third Baseman: A real clutch hitter has a brilliant record for that important column, runs batted in....832 is the number up to the start of this season and before the end he hopes the figure will be over 950…Led the Southern Association last year with 118 and on two other occasions topped the 100 mark, with 124 in 1930 the high water mark…Played with Washington and Chicago in American League in 1933-34…Was obtained with Mickey Rocco in the Les Fleming deal…This is his 13th season in baseball…Is married and has two youngsters.

Ollie Carnegie:

And here is the highlight of Ollie Carnegie's brilliant career. He is shown accepting the Most Valuable Player award from International League President Shaughnessy for his great year in 1938. That season Ollie set a new all-time record for a Buffalo player with 45 homeruns, drove home 136 runs, and batted .330.

Ollie A. Carnegie, Outfielder:

Grand Old Man of the Bisons...One of the most popular players in Buffalo history...And for just reason....Just look at his homerun and runs batted in record...1069 runs knocked across the plate and 265 homers...Not counting this year...Record books list his age as 37....But general opinion is that he's over the 40 year mark....Has powerful shoulders, developed down around Pittsburgh...Has always been a powerful hitter right from the sandlots up....Played first pro ball with Flin in 1920...Then retired in 1931 when the Depression cost him his job....Played one season with Hazelton, then joined Buffalo late in 1931 and has been here since...Likes Pittsburgh very much and always figured on living there....But Buffalo made him change his mind and he now lives here all year around....Out on Linden Avenue with his wife and children...Can't cover outfield the way he used to, but he's still one of the most feared batters in the league.

OLLIE CARNEGIE

EARL DAVIS COOK

Earl Davis Cook, Pitcher:

"Iron-Man Earl" will be his nickname from now until he hangs up his glove and spikes...For his brilliant exhibition in Jersey City last year...One of the greatest in the history of baseball....Pitching two games in one day, and winning both, by shutouts...Score was the same in both games, 2-0...He failed to issue a pass in either game...Was obtained from Cincinnati in '39 for Art Jacobs...Was sold with Hal White to Detroit for $35,000...Here on option for season...Is sure he'll stick with Tigers next year...One of few Canadians in upper bracket of pro baseball...Ninth season in game...Is married, lives in Lemonville, Ont.

Earl was one of those Canadians. He pitched a double shut-out against Jersey City on August 15, 1940, 2-0 and 2-0. That was the only time in league history this had been done. Four days later he pitched a two-hit shutout against Syracuse.

Robert Ned Harris:

When Hank Greenberg was inducted into the Army, he was touted as the home run slugger's successor, but Hank's shoes proved too big...He is now getting needed experience with Bisons...This is only his third season of pro baseball...Graduate of Florida University...Packs plenty of power at the plate, is one of the fastest men on club, has fine arm...Needs more polish on defense, especially on ground balls, but is tabbed as a sure bet to make the grade with Detroit. ...is married

ROBERT NED HARRIS

CHARLEY FUCHS

Charley Fuchs, Pitcher:

The real tough luck pitcher of the Bison mound staff....Pitched as fine a ball as any member of the squad in early season but did not win a game until June...Won 19 games in tough Texas League last year, hurled 17 complete games, six shutouts and fanned 133....Pitched no-hit no-run games in 1939 and 1940...In 1939 he worked 20 complete games, fanned 171 batters....Is married

Morris M. "Buddy" Hancken, Catcher:

If hustle alone made a great baseball player, this peppy youngster would now be in the big leagues....in fact, he did start this season with the Philadelphia Athletics....After drawing his release from Connie Mack, Buddy signed with the Bisons...He has seen considerable service, catching regularly while Parsons was suffering a Charley Horse.....Is married.

BUD HANCKEN

FRED HUTCHINSON

Fred Charles Hutchinson, Pitcher:

One of the greatest pitching prospects in history of baseball…Pitched in Class AA in first year and won 25 games, five of them shutouts, and worked 29 complete games…After some of stiffest bidding in the history was sold to Detroit for $75,000…As could be expected, he failed to make the major league grade the first year, but he's still a brilliant prospect…After all, Bob Fellers come only once in a generation and Feller was here first…From his record this year, Hutch will be back with Detroit to stay next season…One of most feared batters in league, especially tough in pinch… He is the lone bachelor on the team.

Oh, I remember Hutch really good. We called him "Bear" and he went up to Detroit the year before I did. He was later manager for Detroit for eleven years.

James Julius "Jim" Levey, Shortstop:

He is a former United States Marine…As every former Canisius College football player probably knows…His long run through a muddy field for a touchdown to defeat the Griffins, 6-0, back in 1926, is one of the highlights of Canisius gridiron history….Rated one of the finest fielding shortstops ever to play in the American League…He was with St. Louis Browns for four years….Recently had biggest hitting day of his life, clouting three homers in a double header….Was secured from Dallas of Texas League in a trade for Johnny Kroner and Walt Ogiego…Is married

JIM LEVEY

DUTCH MEYER

Lambert Dalton "Dutch" Meyer, Second Baseman:

He is being groomed for one of the toughest assignments in baseball, that of taking over Charley Gehringer's duties as second baseman for the Tigers…As every baseball fan knows, Gehringer is rated the "perfect ball player." Dutch is a fine fielder and has a good arm…But his main asset is his power at the plate…He "hits 'em a mile" to left field and also gets enough hits to keep his average over the coveted .300 mark…He was a great football player at Texas Christian University….It was his assignment, as an end, to pull down Sammy Baugh's passes…..His father is the famed coach of the Texas Christian Football team…He originally signed with the Chicago Cubs and played his first game with them in 1937…..Was out of baseball in 1938, but came back strong with Knoxville in '39….Was purchased by the Tigers for $35,000 last year….He led the Southern Ass'n in homers with 22 and batted in 98 runs although missing over a month of the season….Is married.

Edward Dixon "Dixie" Parsons, Catcher:

If Old Man Jinx hadn't picked on Dixie through most of the season, he'd be right up with the leaders in the fight for the home run title. He hits as hard a ball as any player in the International League…..But you can't hit homers while on the bench with a very painful Charley Horse…Dixie is owned by Detroit…And the Tigers expect him to be their first string pitcher within the next two years. This is his sixth year in pro baseball…. Is married.

DIXIE PARSONS

Robert Lee Patrick, Outfielder:

A real prospect, owned by Detroit…He plays a brilliant game in the outfield, has a fine arm and speed to burn….Also packs plenty of power at the plate…Was making a strong bid for the league batting title when he suffered a broken ankle in an odd accident…While on third Bob thought the catcher was going to try to pick him off and he leaped into the bag…There was no play but Bob cracked a small bone in the ankle. He quickly recovered, but the long layoff dulled his eye and he lost many valuable points before regaining his real stride. Is married.

BOB PATRICK

JOHN 'PRETZELS' PEZZULO

John "Pretzels" Pezzulo, Pitcher:

There's no question about how he got his nickname once you see him pitch…Opposing batters say he has one of the best pickoff motions in nailing runners off first in the league….Was obtained from Syracuse in even trade for Lynn Nelson…Served two years with Philadelphia Phillies…Biggest year was 1938 when he won 26, lost nine and had earned run average of only 2.88 for Savannah…Led the league in percentage, victories, innings pitched, complete games, and strike-outs, including 17 in one game…Tried Iron-man stunt against Rochester last year, winning first, 5-2, losing second 0-1.

Michael D. "Mickey" Rocco, First Baseman:

Takes particular delight in beating Rochester…Always tries hard…But everything just seems to go right against the Red Wings….Which is O.K. with Bison fans…Who would rather see the Bisons defeat Rochester than any other club in the league…His three homers in succession against Rochester was the finest individual performance of the first half of the season in Offerman Stadium…Was obtained with Bob Boken from Nashville in trade for Les Fleming and a bundle of cash…Hit 21 homers, batted in 101 runs last year…Is married.

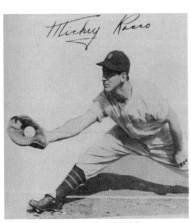

MICKEY ROCCO

I remember Rocco coming over to our house a lot. He loved Perry and would take him out playing in the train yard. He would bring him back covered in grease and oil.

Michael Robert "Mike" Rosco, Pitcher:

The only regular on the Bison team developed on the still young farm system…Selected from Winston-Salem near the tail end of the 1940 season…Has a fine curve, fair speed and a deceptive motion that results in picking plenty of runners off first base…Is coach of Seton Hall College…Won first six games before suffering defeat this season…Looms as a big winner for next few years….Is married.

MIKE ROSCO

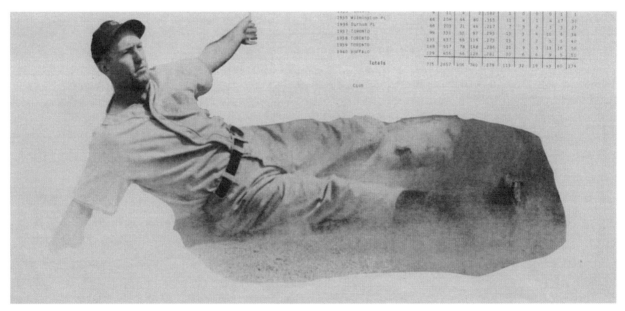

EDDIE MAYO SMITH

Edward Mayo Smith, Outfielder:

There is no finer defensive outfielder in the league…Can play left, right, or center field with equal ability…Has dropped only one fly ball in the last eight years, and that was this season…Was obtained from Toronto for Johnny Tyler…Played with Maple Leafs on and off for seven years…His homer that beat Newark early in the season will long be remembered by every fan who saw the dramatic climax to that thrilling game…Is married.

I played with him on the Detroit team.

JIM TREXLER

Frank James "Jim" Trexler, Pitcher:

No. 1 Fireman of the league, according to Manager Al Vincent…He has everything to make a great relief pitcher….A blazing fast ball, sharp breaking curve, and the one thing needed by firemen more than anything else, coolness under fire…Born in Richmond, Va., he spent six of nine years pitching for his home city….One with Atlanta….And this is his second with the Bisons….Hasn't finished under .500 in games won and lost since 1935…Is married, has a boy who hopes to follow in his dad's footsteps.

Virgil Oliver "Fire" Trucks:

Strikeout king of the league, whom his battermate, Dixie Parsons says will some nights "fan 20 to 24 batters". ..In three years before coming to Bisons he whiffed 712 batters, including 418 in 1938 when he won 25 games for Andalusia in the Alabama-Florida League…That year he pitched 26 complete games, allowed the sensational low earned run average of only 1.25 per nine innings….Only 22 years old he is rated a sure bet to clinch a regular berth with Detroit next year…Feels the same way and has gone so far as to have a Tiger tattooed on his arm….Pitched nine innings of no-hit, no-run ball against Montreal, but lost a game in 10th 0-1…Is part Indian, born in Birmingham, Alabama, and still lives there….Is married.

VIRGIL "FIRE" TRUCKS

Virgil and I stay in touch really regularly. I see him at the Alabama Sports Hall of Fame each year and sometimes in between. He played eleven years with Detroit. He was also with the Browns, the White Sox, and the Athletics for a total of 17 years in the Majors.

HAL WHITE

Harold George "Hal" White, Pitcher:

"Prince Hal" is one of the most popular players to wear a Bison uniform in years…Came up unexpectedly last year to lead the league with a 16-4 record, in shutouts with five, and also in earned run average with 2.43, despite the fact the Bisons finished in second division….Was sold with Earl Cook to Detroit for $35,000, but was returned for more seasoning….Looks like high school student on the mound…and also in street clothes…Is a great favorite with the ladies…Was born in Utica, still lives there….Was just married during last off-season.

Jimmy Hutch, Trainer:

JIMMY HUTCH, TRAINER

Bison players of the last quarter of a century claim that Buffalo has the finest trainer in baseball, major or minor, in Jimmy Hutch, who has been taking care of the pains and aches of Bison players since 1915, excepting for a short period during the World War when he was in charge of the Curtis Aeroplane Hospital.

Jimmy has patched up many Bison players who were supposed to be all through and made them good for many more years. One of his prize recent jobs was Al Smith's worn out arm and fixing it up where now he is winning games for Cleveland.

In addition to baseball Hutch also trains Canisius College football teams and the Buffalo hockey Bisons. He has been at Canisius for 19 years. He also trained many great fighters and bike riders years ago.

Hutch is married and has one son, Norbert. The Hutch family lives right across the street from Offerman Stadium.

"The Buffalo Bisons wrecking crew, Jimmy Outlaw, left, and Eric McNair, batted in six of the herd's seven runs Thursday night at Offerman Stadium, as buffalo turned back the Montreal Royals 7 to 6, in a ten-inning thriller to take a 2-to-1 game lead in the league playoffs."

This is me with Eric McNair; we called him "Boob" after a comic strip character. He was moved down from Detroit after 23 games there and a low batting average. We were neck and neck for team average for Bison 1941 season. He ended up with a .357 and I ended with a .261 – I was low that year.

1941-BUFFALO BISONS-1941

Lower row, left to right: Charley Fuchs, pitcher; Hal White, pitcher; Virgil Trucks, pitcher; Jimmy Outlaw, outfielder; Mike Roscoe, pitcher; Maurice (Buddy) Hancken, catcher; Dutch Meyer, second baseman; Ollie Carnegie, outfielder; Jim Trexler, pitcher. Standing, left to right: Jimmy Hutch, trainer; Mayo Smith, outfielder; Fred Hutchinson, pitcher; Bob Boken, third baseman; Dixie Parsons, catcher; Bob Patrick, outfielder; Joe Martin, infielder; Pretzels Pezzullo, pitcher; Mickey Rocco, first baseman; Earl Cook, pitcher; Jim Levey, shortstop; Al Vincent, manager.

1941 Buffalo Bisons: Left to right lower row: Charley Fuchs, pitcher; Hal White, pitcher; Virgil Trucks, pitcher; Jimmy Outlaw, outfielder; Mike Roscoe, pitcher; Maurice (Buddy) Hacken, catcher; Dutch Meyer, second baseman; Ollie Carnegie, outfielder; Jim Trexler, pitcher.

Standing left to right: Jimmy Hutch, trainer; Mayo Smith, outfielder; Fred Hutchinson, pitcher; Bob Boken, third baseman; Dixie Parsons, catcher; Bob Patrick, outfielder; Joe Martin, infielder; Pretzels Pezzullo, pitcher; Mickey Rocco, first baseman; Earl Cook, pitcher; Jim Levey, shortstop; Al Vincent, manager.

While I was playing ball for Buffalo, our son Perry was born in Jackson, Alabama, in August. Grace had come home to Alabama early in the season of 1941. I wanted her to be near extended family in case I was on a road trip when the baby was born. During that time, she also helped take care of her father who was quite ill. When Grace and Perry were able to come home from the hospital, one of my good friends, Police Chief of Jackson,

Grace, baby Perry, and Jimmy Outlaw at the family home in Jackson, Alabama. 1941

carried them from the hospital. His name was Stewart O'Neal "Lefty" Bolen. He played major league baseball 4 years: two with the Browns (1926-27) and two with the Phillies (1931-1932). He was a left-handed pitcher and batted left-handed. I always said that is why Perry throws and bats left-handed!

Jimmy Outlaw showing photo of his new son to teammates.

Ha, this shows me with a cigar. Here I am with Bob Boken and Dixie Parsons at a golf game at Meadowbrook Country Club, guests of a fan. I gave out cigars to announce Perry's birth. That was what fathers did back then. Of course, I didn't get to see him until later– he was about two months old by then. Our friends in Buffalo sent gifts and cards to Grace and Perry. She wrote them all down in his Baby Book.

The team ended the year with 88 wins and 65 losses, for third place in the league. I played in 146 games and was at bat 511 times with 135 hits. That was for 71 runs, 26 doubles and eight triples. I only had 2 homeruns that year and batted .264.

That was the same year that Grace's father died, so we spent the off season in Alabama. Her brother, Jim, was with the newspaper in Alexander City and her other brother, Ped, had enlisted in the army. All ball players had to find work during the winter to be able to pay bills. We certainly didn't make enough playing ball to support a family.

Talladega Daily Home newspaper front page announcement that the powder mill would be built in Childersburg, near Grace's mother's home in Alexander City.

I worked at gunpowder plant in Childersburg about 30 minutes away from Alex City. The Alabama Army Munitions Plant, four miles north of Childersburg, employed 25,000 people from all over. People flooded into town to get jobs. Still the tail end of the Depression. There were all sorts of trailers and shacks where families were living. It was run by Dupont and produced highly explosive materials (gunpowder) and also heavy water used in the Manhattan project. They tell me there are still areas around there that are contaminated.

This shows that the United States was preparing for war before Pearl Harbor was attacked. We were all ready to do our part.

1942 official Buffalo Bisons team photo

I was 29 years old, married and had a baby when World War II was declared in 1941. Large numbers of the nation's population became part of the military service of America. All three of my brothers were in the army, among the twelve million who saw service. They even took my brother, Mack, who had lost an eye. In order to get in, Mack had memorized the eye chart so they would not notice that he had one glass eye. Neither the army nor the Navy would take me as I had ankles that rolled in, making them unfit for long marches, and I was color blind, thus not satisfactory. I had to be content to do my effort for the war by working in war-related plants in the off-season.

Baseball was allowed to continue during the war as a way of keeping morale up on the home front and among those on overseas duty as well, but there were restrictions placed on the games. Some were put in place by the government and some by Judge Kennesaw Mountain Landis, the Commissioner of Baseball at that time. For example, all spring training had to be conducted north of the Mason-Dixon Line to save transportation expenses, and the format for the World Series was modified. The first three games would be played at the home field of one of the participating clubs, then moved for the remaining of the series to the other team's park. This was done to cut down on travel as the railroads were hard pressed to keep up with the demands of the military in the movement of troops and supplies. At least once during the war, the Detroit team returned home from an away game at Cleveland aboard a Great Lakes Ferry Boat. Night games were also prohibited.

The Stars and Stripes

September 3, 1943

As to the military personnel, baseball was a tremendous spirit booster. Where possible, games were broadcast, and the *Stars and Stripes* carried all the latest scores and stats. Navy personnel on ships got the news via teletype messages. Pro baseball players were among those first to enlist and each club lost valuable team members.

In 1942, I played in 136 games, at bat 486 times. I scored 56 times with 128 hits. My average was .263. I never did get back up to what I was hitting before my wrist was injured, but I did get five homeruns!! We ended the year in 7th place with 73-80 record

Jimmy Outlaw, number 27, coming in home congratulated by number 22

Grace wrote a note in the scrapbook in 1942. She said, "This article explains why I was too busy to keep this scrapbook up." She had a baby at home that kept her running. She was a good bridge player, dancer, roller skater, seamstress, and golfer. She was also a plumber. One day when I came home in Buffalo she had the commode off the floor and was trying to get Perry's shoes that he had put down the toilet. She put it back together. She got the shoes and the toilet worked, too.

Editor's Note: Dad talked about the entertainment they enjoyed while living in Buffalo. They went to plays, concerts, performances, and dined out at fancy places. They went to the Rainbow Room in New York City for afternoon tea dances and to the Cotton Club to hear Cab Callaway.

Grace, Jimmy, and son Perry
Outlaw, Buffalo, New York,

We were so happy to see my brother, Cornell, who was in the Army. He came up from his base in South Carolina to visit us. I remember having a dreadful feeling about him having to go overseas. When he was sent to England, he was assigned to a hospital corps and learned to do X-rays. I guess that was how he got into photography! He was quite an artist and could do anything. He took his saxophone with him when he went to England, he and his small band were invited to play with Glenn Miller in a USO show.

Cornell Outlaw, US Army, on visit to Buffalo, New York with baby Perry Outlaw, his first nephew.

Curtis-Wright Aircraft Company, Buffalo, New York, 1942, producing P-40 Warhawks

That year we stayed in Buffalo for the off-season, and I got a job at an aviation plant. The Curtis-Wright Aircraft Company was the largest aviation company in the world and they offered jobs to us at a good salary. The company produced more airplanes in 1941 (before the US was actually in the war) than any other manufacturer except General Motors. We built the P-40 Warhawks and my job was to deliver the .50 caliber machine guns for installation just before delivery of the planes to bases throughout the world. There was another airplane manufacturer in Buffalo, the Bell Company. Bell Aircraft had just completed a new plant named the Niagara Falls Wheatfield Plant. They hired about 3,000 employees for the production of the P-39 Aircobra. These two companies made the city the center of aircraft production for America from 1940-1945.

I always tell the story about one fellow who was building a metal box for his home use when an inspecting officer came by and asked him what he was making. He replied, "I am making a dollar and a half an hour. What are you making?"

I sure remember it being cold, very cold. In fact, when our shift was over, we all had to dust the snow off our cars to find which one was ours. That one winter was enough for us there. The other years we went back to Alabama for the off-season. I had jobs there during the winter, too.

1943

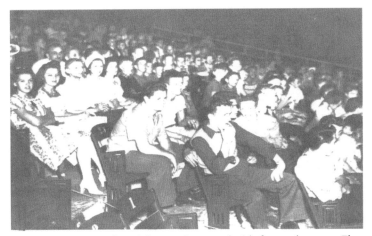

The club gave out free tickets to boys and girls for each game. The seating area was called the Knothole Gang.

Over 15,000 boys and girls were invited to see the Bisons every year. If every youngster in Western New York old enough to understand baseball didn't see at least one regularly scheduled game in Offerman Stadium each season, it wasn't the fault of the Buffalo Baseball Club. The club made special effort to distribute guest tickets through all schools, Boys Scout troops, YMCAs and churches, just to name a few of the groups.

They had a special section in the grandstand on the third base side, and they had special ushers to take care of them and they probably had to keep order and make some of them behave, too.

Radio quiz show for kids. Grace Outlaw is the special guest for this show.

The Knothole Gang was a name they would use to refer to the kids who were given free tickets to see a game, or just all youngsters who were fans of the Bisons. There was even a club named that. The local radio station WKBW had a weekly quiz show where some of the kids were asked questions. Each week they had a guest and one week Grace was on the show. She is on the far right in the picture.

The newspaper ran this photograph of me signing a baseball in the Bisons' dugout. It says the boy is 13 year old Richard Gallivan. I wish I knew where he is now and wish I knew if he has this picture.

I tell you, the fans helped make playing ball the best thing ever. Most guys were more than happy to sign autographs anytime and anywhere.

Jimmy Outlaw signing autograph for 13 year old Richard Gallivan

Manager Steve O'Neill, 1940
Buffalo Bisons

Steve O'Neill was called up to coach for the Detroit Tigers at the end of the 1940 season. He told me that as soon as he could do it, he would have me brought up to the Majors with him. He was true to his word when he was named manager. He became a coach in 1941 and manager in 1943. That's when he brought me to Detroit at the tail end of the season.

Inning Seven
Detroit Tigers
1943-1945 Regular
Season

Steve O'Neill was a coach in 1941 and 1942 with Detroit Tigers and became manager in '43. Officially, I signed with the Detroit team on September 9, 1943.

Naturally, I was thrilled to have a chance at the big boys. I already knew several of the Detroit players and the ones I hadn't yet met, I had certainly heard of them and kept up with them. Buffalo was the steppingstone to Detroit and we all hoped to get called up.

Jimmy Outlaw and manager Steve O'Neill in Detroit Tigers locker room

They were all very welcoming to me. Acted like they were glad to see me there. Steve O'Neill showed a lot of faith in me. He told reporters that he felt I would be an outstanding versatile player. I think that meant he planned to move me all over the field – which he did.

They gave me number 27 and I stayed with it my whole time at Detroit. I had played with several of the team members when we were on other teams.

Jimmy Outlaw, number 27, on far left, 1943

This roster includes everybody who played at some time in the 1943 season:

Pitchers

Tommy Bridges

Rufe Gentry

Johnny Gorsica

Roy Henshaw

Hal Neuhouser

Prince Oana

Joe Orrell

Stubby Overmire

Dizzy Trout

Virgil Trucks

Hal White

Catchers

Dixie Parsons

Paul Richards

Al Unser

Infielders

Jimmy Bloodworth

Pinky Higgins

Joe Hoover

Joe Wood

Rudy York

Outfielders

Doc Cramer

Ned Harris

Charlie Metro

Rip Radcliff

Don Ross

Dick Wakefield

Other

John McHale

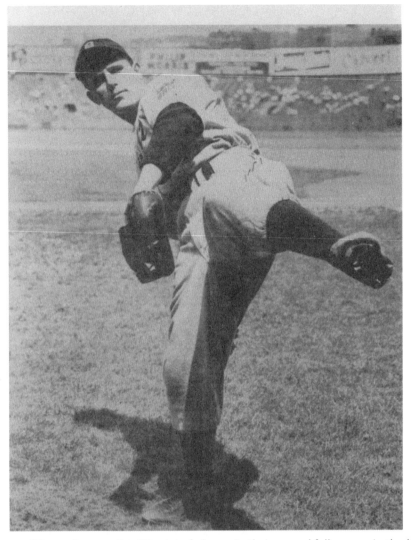

Virgil Trucks, pitcher, was with Detroit in 1943 – 1944 until he joined Navy in '44. I had played with him in Buffalo in 1941. He came back from the military right at the end of the '45 season. He did pitch one game in the World Series. Dixie Parsons and Rufe Gentry were also brought up that year from Buffalo.

"The sophomore jinx bit a lot of players in their second full season in the big leagues, but I avoided that for the most part and won 16 ballgames. But, I had to put my big league career on hold for two years following the season – I joined the U. S. Navy." - Virgil trucks

DOC CRAMER

Doc Cramer took me under his wing for some reason. I guess he just liked me is the only thing I can figure. He taught me how to watch the pitchers and the batters and learn where to position myself in the field. He actually taught me how to play outfield. In the outfield, he would watch the batter and give me a nod where I should be positioned in the field. He was a genius at that. He would look at me as each batter came up and motion his head to let me know if I should move closer in or further out, or to the right or left. He studied batters and pitchers and could tell by their stances what they were going to do.

Doc ended the 1943 year with a .300 and was one of the highest paid members at $8,000 year – so was Pinky Higgins. He was making more than Hal Newhouser who was making $7,500. I was probably in the $2000- $3000 range!

Briggs Stadium Detroit, 1943

127

The Tigers were going into a six-game series with the Cleveland Indians when Steve pulled me up on September 9. In the very first game I dressed in the uniform, the first of a double header at Briggs Stadium, Al Smith was pitching for the Indians. I used a lot of the strategy that Doc Cramer had already been schooling me on. Before that first game, he talked to me and gave me a heads-up on the pitcher. He told me how the left-hander pitched and what to look for.

I hit a homerun my second time up to bat, but the first one was not counted anyway, so this was my first official time at bat. That put us ahead 3-2 but we ended up losing the game 8-3.

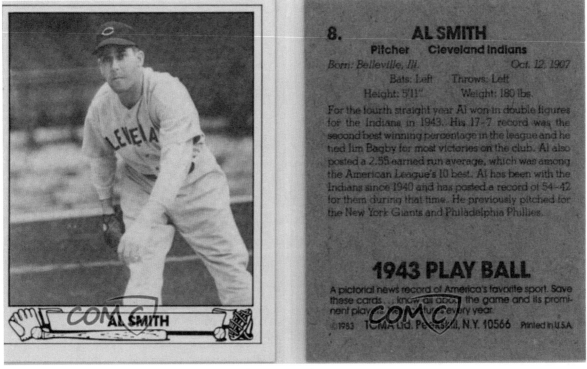

AL SMITH

Editor's Note: Smith's best season was in 1943, when he was named to the American League All-Star team and finished 15th in voting for the AL MVP Award for having a 17–7 win–loss record in 29 games (27 started), 14 complete games, three shutouts, two games finished, one save, 208⅓ innings pitched, 186 hits allowed, 74 runs allowed, 59 earned runs allowed, seven home runs allowed, 72 bases on balls, 72 strikeouts, 862 batters faced, a 2.55 earned run average and a 1.238 WHIP.

Jimmy Outlaw gets pointers on batting from Rudy York in the Tiger Dugout.

This is a photo of Rudy and me talking in the dugout after first game homerun. He was a great batter, but I tell you, he was not that good as a fielder. He was born in Alabama, but he was living in Georgia when he started playing ball. He stayed with Detroit from 1937 – 1945, playing first base most of the time. His first year he was bounced from one position to another, trying to find a place he could be good. They needed him because his batting was so good. On the last day of August in 1943, he hit two homeruns, making a total of 18 in one month. Babe Ruth had held that record at 17 until that day!

We won the second game that day but lost the other four in that series. Then we went to Chicago against the White Sox. We won two of the three games, then to Cleveland to face the Indians again. We only won one of the four at that ballpark. We headed to New York for a series of four with the Yankees – we only won one of those as well. Same results in the four at Boston with the Red Sox. We lost the first in Philadelphia against the Athletics, but won all the rest of the games in the season, including our last two with the Washington Senators. I learned as much about traveling as I did about baseball. It was different from the minors! Quite a bit better. We stayed in nice hotels and I learned that time in the lobby was a valuable strategy session as well as some time to get to know the players on a more personal basis. Wives did not usually go to away games.

1943 DETROIT

I played in 20 games out of the 26 remaining games in the season. I was at bat 67 times, for 18 hits with a .269. At the end of the season, Steve was looking at positions for the next year, knowing that wartime draft would make a difference. He knew he needed lots of options. He was looking at a temporary lineup and said I would likely fill the place vacated by Dick Wakefield who enlisted in the Navy. He projected that Don Heffner would fill in at second base where Jimmy Bloodworth had played. He was also thinking of converting Joe Wood to an outfielder. At that time, he said I would be in left, Doc Cramer in center. He was looking at Ned Harris, Don Ross, Charlie Metro, and maybe even Joe Wood for the right field spot.

Grace and Perry came to Detroit for the first games I played, which were at home. She is in this photo with Perry and she is next to Mrs. Jimmy Bloodworth and little Milan Bloodworth.

Perry and mother, Grace Outlaw, and Mrs. Jimmy Bloodworth and son Milan.

Bloodworth made his major league debut in 1937 and began to play regularly in 1939. In 1941, Bloodworth led American League second basemen in putouts and assists. That December, he was traded to the Detroit Tigers. He led the American League in grounding into double plays (29) in 1943. He served in the Army National Guard, and he missed the entire 1944 and 1945 seasons due to his military service. He returned to the Tigers in 1946.

JIMMY BLOODWORTH

1944

Contract April 18, 1944 – October 1, 1944

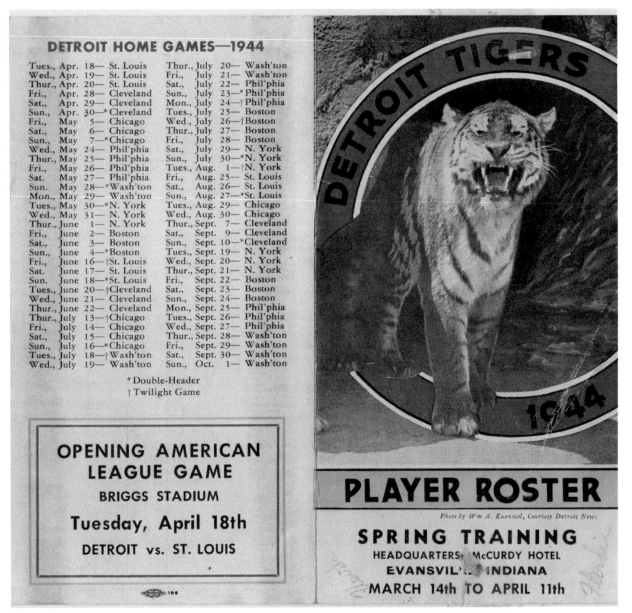

DETROIT HOME GAMES—1944

Tues., Apr. 18— St. Louis	Thur., July 20— Wash'ton
Wed., Apr. 19— St. Louis	Fri., July 21— Wash'ton
Thur., Apr. 20— St. Louis	Sat., July 22— Phil'phia
Fri., Apr. 28— Cleveland	Sun., July 23—*Phil'phia
Sat., Apr. 29— Cleveland	Mon., July 24—†Phil'phia
Sun., Apr. 30—*Cleveland	Tues., July 25— Boston
Fri., May 5— Chicago	Wed., July 26—†Boston
Sat., May 6— Chicago	Thur., July 27— Boston
Sun., May 7—*Chicago	Fri., July 28— Boston
Wed., May 24— Phil'phia	Sat., July 29— N. York
Thur., May 25— Phil'phia	Sun., July 30—*N. York
Fri., May 26— Phil'phia	Tues., Aug. 1—†N. York
Sat., May 27— Phil'phia	Fri., Aug. 25— St. Louis
Sun., May 28—*Wash'ton	Sat., Aug. 26— St. Louis
Mon., May 29— Wash'ton	Sun., Aug. 27—*St. Louis
Tues., May 30—*N. York	Tues., Aug. 29— Chicago
Wed., May 31— N. York	Wed., Aug. 30— Chicago
Thur., June 1— N. York	Thur., Sept. 7— Cleveland
Fri., June 2— Boston	Sat., Sept. 9— Cleveland
Sat., June 3— Boston	Sun., Sept. 10—*Cleveland
Sun., June 4—*Boston	Tues., Sept. 19— N. York
Fri., June 16—†St. Louis	Wed., Sept. 20— N. York
Sat. June 17— St. Louis	Thur., Sept. 21— N. York
Sun. June 18—*St. Louis	Fri., Sept. 22— Boston
Tues., June 20—†Cleveland	Sat., Sept. 23— Boston
Wed., June 21— Cleveland	Sun., Sept. 24— Boston
Thur., June 22— Cleveland	Mon., Sept. 25— Phil'phia
Thur., July 13—†Chicago	Tues., Sept. 26— Phil'phia
Fri., July 14— Chicago	Wed., Sept. 27— Phil'phia
Sat., July 15— Chicago	Thur., Sept. 28— Wash'ton
Sun., July 16—*Chicago	Fri., Sept. 29— Wash'ton
Tues., July 18—†Wash'ton	Sat., Sept. 30— Wash'ton
Wed., July 19— Wash'ton	Sun., Oct. 1— Wash'ton

* Double-Header
† Twilight Game

OPENING AMERICAN LEAGUE GAME

BRIGGS STADIUM

Tuesday, April 18th

DETROIT vs. ST. LOUIS

DETROIT TIGERS

1944

PLAYER ROSTER

Photo by Wm A. Kuenzel, Courtesy Detroit News

SPRING TRAINING
HEADQUARTERS McCURDY HOTEL
EVANSVILLE, INDIANA
MARCH 14th TO APRIL 11th

Spring training March 14-April 11, Evansville Indiana

Sam McCurdy hotel on the waterfront

Spring training was in Evansville, Indiana. We stayed at the Sam McCurdy Hotel on the waterfront on the Ohio River. It was a little old but was still one of the fanciest hotels in America. It was the base of the training, but we spent very little time in the lobby. It was the hotel where some famous movie stars stayed – Katherine Hepburn, Cary Grant, but I never did see one of them there.

Bosse Field, Evansville, Indiana

Girls' baseball team, Evansville, Indiana

A couple of years ago [1992], I enjoyed seeing a movie named *A League of Their Own* because it was filmed at Bosse Field where we had our training and games while we were there in Evansville. It looked about the same! Actually, the field really was really the home of a few girl leagues during the years. But, of course, not really the Racine Belles like in the movie.

It was built in 1915 and named for the mayor and was one of the first parks owned by a city. It has always been a minor league park and today I think the team is the Otters. The Evansville team was the Central League Champion in 1915, the year the park was built.

Girls' baseball team, Evansville, Indiana

We played exhibition games with Chicago White Sox and the Cubs, too, at Evansville in '44. We looked really good with both the Chicago teams. Rudy York hit .294 and I did a .278 at Spring Training. Two that came in a little after Spring Training, the "Wichita Twins" looked even better: Red Borom, just out of the service, and Chuck Hostetler from the Texas League.

After games with Pittsburgh on April 8 and 9, we went on the road to play exhibition games on our way back to Detroit. We left Evansville to play Rochester at Terra Haute, then on the road to Louisville to play their home team. Then to Muncie and to Detroit where we played Pittsburgh. The last exhibition game was April 16 and I was still on the team.

1944 Detroit Tigers official team photo

FIRST ROW: *left to right: Eddie Mayo, Paul Richards, Art Mills, Steve O'Neill, Al Vincent, Dick Wakefield, Frank Overmire.*

SECOND ROW: *John Gorsica, Dick Dresser, Jim Outlaw, Al Unser, Rufus Gentry, Hal Newhauser, Joe Orengo, Don Ross, Rudy York,*

THIRD ROW: *Roger Cramer, Jim Mooty, Michael Higgins, Bob Swift, Charles Metro, Walter Beck, Paul Trout*

FOURTH ROW: *Alex Okray (club house boy), Joe Hoover, Chuck Hostetler, Dr. Ray Forsyth (trainer), Rennie Okray (bat boy)*

DETROIT BASEBALL COMPANY
ROSTER OF THE TIGERS—1944

PLAYER'S NAME	POSITION	DATE OF BIRTH AND PLACE	HEIGHT	WEIGHT	BATS	THROWS	HOME ADDRESS	CLUB, 1943	Won—Lost	EARNED RUN AVERAGE
BECK, WALTER W.	Pitcher	October 16, 1908, Decatur, Ill.	6' 2"	200	Right	Right	1925 Forest, Decatur, Ill.	Knoxville	6 4	3.07
EATON, ZEBELON V.	Pitcher	February 2, 1920, Cooleemee, N. C.	5' 11"	175	Right	Right	13 Grove St., Cooleemee, N. C.	Honorable Discharge	.....	......
GENTRY, RUFFUS JAMES	Pitcher	May 18, 1918, Forsyth County	6' 1"	185	Right	Right	Route No. 3, Winston-Salem, N. C.	Buffalo-Detroit	20-16 1-3	......
GORSICA, JOHN	Pitcher	March 29, 1917, Bayonne, N. J.	6' 2"	175	Right	Right	112 E. Main St., Beckley, W. Va.	Detroit	4 5	3.38
HARE, JOE	Pitcher	June 22, 1910, Orange, Texas	6'	185	Right	Right	2740 Cafe St., Beaumont, Texas	Free Agent	.....	......
HENSHAW, ROY	Pitcher	July 29, 1911, Chicago, Ill.	5' 8"	168	Right	Left	Fennville, Mich.	Detroit	0 2	3.80
HRESKO, EMERY	Pitcher	June 16, 1926, Brownsville, Pa.	5' 10"	170	Right	Right	352 E. Stewart Ave., Flint, Mich.	Free Agent	.....	......
NEWHOUSER, HAROLD	Pitcher	May 20, 1921, Detroit, Mich.	6' 1¾"	182	Left	Left	18412 Asbury Park, Detroit 19, Mich.	Detroit	8 17	3.03
ORRELL, FORREST GORDON	Pitcher	October 6, 1918, National City, Calif.	6' 4"	210	Right	Right	1917 "I" St., National City, Calif.	Portland-Detroit	8-11 0-0	......
OVERMIRE, FRANK	Pitcher	May 16, 1919, Moline, Mich.	5' 7"	162	Right	Left	1154 Joosten St., S.W., Grand Rapids, Mich.	Detroit	7 6	3.18
TROUT, PAUL H.	Pitcher	June 29, 1915, Terre Haute, Ind.	6' 1"	195	Right	Right	1657 Hazelwood, Detroit 6, Mich.	Detroit	20 12	2.48
TRUCKS, VIRGIL O.	Pitcher	April 26, 1919, Birmingham, Ala.	5' 11"	195	Right	Right	760 Ninth Court, W., Birmingham, Ala.	Detroit	16 10	2.84
									BATTING AVERAGE	
PARSONS, EDWARD D.	Catcher	May 12, 1916, Talladega, Ala.	6' 2"	185	Right	Right	1384 Euclid St., Beaumont, Texas	Detroit		.142
RICHARDS, PAUL R.	Catcher	November 21, 1908, Waxahachie, Texas	6' 2"	182	Right	Right	Waxahachie, Texas	Detroit		.220
SWIFT, ROBERT	Catcher	March 6, 1916, Salina, Kansas	5' 11"	185	Right	Right	533 W. Ellsworth, Salina, Kansas	Philadelphia A's		.192
UNSER, ALBERT B.	Catcher	October 21, 1915, Morrisonville, Ill.	6'	185	Right	Right	2120 No. Union, Decatur, Ill.	Buffalo-Detroit	.287	.248
HEFFNER, DONALD H.	Infielder	February 8, 1911, Rouzerville, Pa.	5' 11"	155	Right	Right	416 No. Old Ranch Rd., Arcadia, Calif.	Philadelphia A's		.194
HIGGINS, MICHAEL F.	Infielder	May 27, 1909, Red Oak, Texas	6' 1"	195	Right	Right	4004 Southwestern Blvd., Dallas 5, Texas	Detroit		.277
HOOVER, ROBERT JOE	Infielder	April 15, 1916, Brawley, Calif.	5' 11"	175	Right	Right	6530 Colgate, Los Angeles, Calif.	Detroit		.243
MAYO, EDWARD J.	Infielder	April 15, 1913, Holyoke, Mass.	5' 11"	180	Left	Right	54 Vreeland Ave., Clifton, N. J.	Philadelphia A's		.219
ORENGO, JOSEPH C.	Infielder	November 29, 1916, San Francisco, Cal.	6'	190	Right	Right	943 Church St., San Francisco, Calif.	St. Paul		.286
YORK, RUDOLPH P.	Infielder	August 17, 1913, Cartersville, Ga.	6' 1"	209	Right	Right	Cartersville, Ga.	Detroit		.271
CRAMER, ROGER	Outfielder	July 22, 1905, Beach Haven, N. J.	6' 2"	185	Left	Right	Manahawkin, New Jersey	Detroit		.300
HARRIS, ROBERT "NED"	Outfielder	July 9, 1916, Ames, Iowa	5' 11½"	170	Left	Left	14879 Washburn, Detroit 21, Mich.	Detroit		.254
METRO, CHARLES	Outfielder	April 28, 1919, Heilwood, Pa.	5' 11½"	175	Right	Right	110 W. Water St., Mayfield, Ky.	Detroit		.200
OUTLAW, JAMES P.	Outfielder	January 20, 1913, Orme, Tenn.	5' 8"	165	Right	Right	Jackson, Alabama	Buffalo-Detroit	.276	.269
ROSS, DONALD R.	Outfielder	July 16, 1915, Pasadena, Calif.	6' 2"	200	Right	Right	416 S. Old Ranch Road, Arcadia, Calif.	Detroit		.267
WOOD, JOSEPH P.	Outfielder	October 3, 1920, Houston, Texas	5' 9"	160	Right	Right	3226 Prospect St., Houston, Texas	Detroit		.323

All players who played in 1944 (from data base MLB)

Pitchers

*Boom-Boom Beck

*Zeb Eaton

Rufe Gentry

*Bob Gillespie

Johnny Gorsica

Roy Henshaw

*Chief Hogsett

*Jake Mooty

Hal Neuhauser

Joe Orrell

Stubby Overmire

Dizzy Trout

Virgil Trucks

Catchers

*Hack Miller

Paul Richards

*Bob Swift

Infielders

*Red Borom

*Bubba Floyd

*Don Heffner

Pinky Higgins

Joe Hoover

*Eddie Mayo

*Joe Orengo

*Jackie Sullivan

*Al Unser

Rudy York

Outfielders

Doc Cramer

*Chuck Hostetler

Charlie Metro

Jimmy Outlaw

Don Ross

Dick Wakefield

Other

John McHal

The Spring Training book listed the following as Tigers in the Military at that time.

Benton, Al

Barry, Cornelius

Blackwell, Daniel

Bloodworth, James

Bridges, Thomas

Bumpers, Lemuel

Clark, Roy

Danahew, Abner

Eiautt, Joseph

Evers, Walter

Franklin, Murray

Gann, Clarence

Gehringer, Charles

Gray, Ted

Greenberg, Henry

Happac, William

Henny, Robert E.

Hirshon, Harold

Hitchcock, William

Hogue, Robert

Horton, Dennis

Howerton, Gordon

Hutchison, Fred

Johnson, John

Blake, George

Lipon, Johm

Madsen. Welby

Mayence, Robert

McCosky, William Barney

McHale, John

Meyer, Lambert D.

Moore, Anse

Mueller, John

Mueller, Leslie

Mullen, Patrick

Patrick, Robert

R'Adulovic, William

Riede, Harvey

Scott, Norman

Storie, Burl B.

Tabacheck, Martin

Tebbetts, George

Uhle, Robert

Wakefield, Richard

Wertz, Victor

White, Harold

PLAY BALL!

Because so many guys in their prime were serving in the military, the team players had a little age on them. The media guys had a heyday with that angle. I was 31 years old and felt like I was a newbie in more ways than just major league experience.

Opening Day was April 18, two days after the last exhibition game. It was at Briggs against St. Louis. There was a big to-do before the game to kick off the season. Owner Walter Briggs was there, and the Detroit Firemen brought a huge horseshoe made of flowers to wish us well. There were more than 500 servicemen there as guests of the club. Looked like every seat was filled, about 30,000.

"Heffner, 2b; Mayo, ss; Cramer,cf; York, 1b; Huggins, 3b; Outlaw, rf....this lineup which opposed St. Louis at Briggs Stadiium lists three newcomers."

The Yankees had won the series in '43. I remember one game in May, early in the '44 season with the Yankees in New York. We were in last place and had lost the last five games in a row. The Yankees had won six games in a row. Dizzy Trout was pitching a great game. He had a pretty good day. He got three hits, drove in one run and scored one himself. He limited the Yankees to seven hits. We were tied in the seventh. I followed two good hits and batted a single in the eighth inning, putting us one up. Outfield was fired up. We made four double plays. In the ninth, Trout hit a single, then went to third on a single by Doc Cramer. Next up the Yankees made a double play but Dizzy scored. Ending score was 4-2 and ended our five-game losing streak.

RED BOROM

Red was one of those guys that became a lifelong friend. He came to see our family in Jackson several times and everyone felt like he was an old friend of the family. He was just out of the Army in 1944, when Jack Zeller, general manager, called him to come to Detroit. He had played high school ball in Atlanta and pro and semi-pro ball since about 1935. He played most of 1944 and all of the 1945 season with the Tigers, all the way to World Championship.

By June, we still were not playing pennant-winning ball. Our percentage at the end of June was just .435. We had a really poor month, 10-16. We picked up some momentum in July and for that month we had a .548, making the season average at the end of July still below .500. We started playing real ball the last half of July and in August, we were on a winning streak. For the first time since May, we were in the winner's column. We kept at it until it came down to the pennant race. In August we averaged .704 and September was .750.

In September, my arm was in good shape. In right field I could peg the throw to third nearly every time. I also did some fancy fielding. In one game Gentry was pitching against Cleveland, I made at least six perfect catches. The next series was in Detroit with the Yankees, and we seemed to work together as a team. Finally learning to read each other. September 19 at Briggs, I got three hits, two were for extra

RUFE GENTRY

bases. My triple scored one of Detroit's four runs. In the third inning, the Yankees were in a good position to score and the Snuffy Stirnweiss single to center was followed by Frankie Crosetti's single to right.

My throw to third was too late to beat the fast Stirnwiess to third. But it was a good throw, which Pinkie Higgins relayed to second to nail Crosetti's try to stretch his hit to a double. Crosetti was not happy about the call, but he was the only one who thought he was safe. Yeah, there were some pretty rough fusses on the field.

SLIDING INTO HOME

OUTLAW SCORES IN CRUCIAL TIGER GAME: Detroit Tiger Jimmy Outlaw, left, slides in and rolls over to score in the second inning of the crucial Detroit-Philadelphia game in Detroit Sept. 25. Outlaw scored from first on a wild throw from third baseman Charlie Metro to Will McGhee at first. Catcher Frank Hayles makes a futile try. Umpire is Ernie Stewart. In losing the game to the Athletics, 2-1, the Tigers allowed the St. Louis Browns to tie them for the league lead.

Hal Newhauser was still king. On Sept. 27, 1944, he won his 27th game of the season. He ended with 29 for the year. Here he is joking with me about the Lucky Number 27.

Jimmy Outlaw, number 27 and Hal Newhauser, 1944

"TIGERS 1 ½ GAMES AHEAD   Cramer . Mayo, Higgins, York, Wakefield, Outlaw, Richards, Swift, Hoover"

By September 19, 1944, we were 1½ games ahead, but after playing 150 games the pennant race was to be decided in the last four game series of the two top runners: St. Louis Browns and Detroit Tigers. We played the last placed team, the Washington Senators at home, while St. Louis traveled to play the New York Yankees, who had won the American League Pennant the last three years. In 1941 the Yankees won 101 games, seventeen games ahead of second place Boston. They went on to beat Brooklyn Dodgers in the World Series. In 1942, they won 103 games and lost 51, nine games ahead of second place team, Boston again. In the World Series they lost to the Cardinals. In 1943 they earned the pennant with 98-56 record, and they won the World Series against the Cardinals. But, in 1944, they were behind St. Louis and Detroit. St. Louis was up against a very good team.

Editor's Note: The odds favored the New York Yankees to win the 1944 American League race. They had won the previous three races and were the defending World Champions. No one gave the St. Louis Browns any notice. Even the hometown newspaper could say only one good thing about this club: it had been in the American League for over 30 years.

As the season opened, the Browns swept the Tigers and went on to win 9 games in a row, a new record for the opening season consecutive wins. However, they won only five of their next fifteen games. No team was a consistent winner. Steve O'Neill, Tigers manager, commented toward the end of May that no team would run away with the pennant.

By May 25, Browns were in second place, 2½ games behind the Yankees and only three games ahead of the last place Chicago. It would be a very close race that lasted throughout the rest of the season.

The Tigers did not really become a contender until the last of June when they consistently played above a .500. Detroit had two of the league's best pitchers, Hal Newhauser and Paul "Dizzy" Trout, but there was a big gap in the pitcher corps after that. It was so big that the two often relieved each other. At one point, O'Neill approached old Roger "Doc" Cramer, a strong-armed outfielder to pitch. Seventh place Detroit got a big lift when Dick Wakefield was unexpectedly released from Navy service. By August 15, Detroit was in third place, eight games behind the Browns.

After leading the league since June 1, the Browns fell out of first place on Sept. 4. It was now the Yankees, Browns, Tigers and Red Sox that were only three games behind. It had become the tightest pennant race in the American League since 1908. By Sept 17, Detroit was on top. On Sept. 25, the Browns pulled into a tie with Detroit with five games left to play. The next day, the Browns lost and fell behind Detroit by one game with four games left to play.

The Browns would face third place New York in their final four games while Detroit would face last place Washington. Washington had won only three of their previous 18 games against Detroit. The Yankees still had a possibility of taking the pennant, being behind only three games, and they had beaten the Browns ten of the eighteen games in the season.

Even if the season ended in a Brown-Tiger tie, the Tigers would still have the advantage. By a flip of the coin, it had been determined that the game playoff would be in Detroit, where Hal Newhauser would be pitching. Hal had beaten the Browns every time they faced him at Briggs.

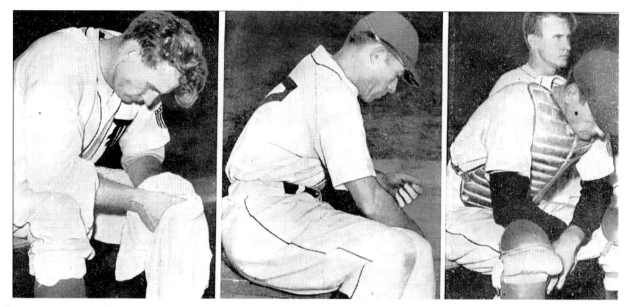

"Tigers out; new contract seen for O'Neill.   Paul Trout, Jimmy Outlaw, Paul Richards eliminated by the Senators yesterday. These Tigers like their hard-fighting teammates, are unable to hide their bitter disappointment.

St. Louis went into their last four games with an 85-65 record and beat the Yankees in all four games, ending with an 89-65 record. Detroit, at 86-64, was to play last place Washington Senators. They split with them two games to two. The first game in the series was rained out on Thursday night so we played a double header on Friday, one on Saturday and one on Sunday. We ended with 88-66 for a .571 just .007 behind St. Louis at .578. In the World Series, St. Louis lost to the Cardinals, 4 games to 2.

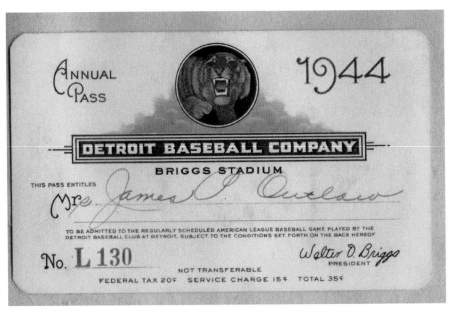

ANNUAL PASS. 1944. DETROIT BASEBALL COMPANY BRIGGS STADIUM

THIS PASS GRANTS MRS. JAMES OUTLAW TO BE ADMITTED TO THE REGULARLY SCHEDULED AMERICAN LEAGUE BASEBALL GAMES PLAYED AT THE DETROIT BASEBALL CLUB AT DETROIT, SUBJECT TO THE CONDITIONS SET FORTH ON THE BACK HEREOF. SIGNED WALTER O. BRIGGS, PRESIDENT

Jimmy and Perry Outlaw at home on Freida Street in Dearborn, Michigan

Grace and I found a great place to live in Dearborn near the train depot. Freida Street was in a wonderful neighborhood and we felt lucky. The family that owned the house, Mr. and Mrs. Britton, lived downstairs all year long, and in the winter, Mrs. Britton's parents lived upstairs. In the summer, her parents, the Drums, went to Lake Charlevoix. So, we used the upstairs while they were gone. The times worked out perfectly and we became good friends with the family.

My stats at the end of the season were 136 games, 535 at bat, 69 runs, 146 hits with a .273 batting average. I also had 57 RBIs. While we were living in Detroit, we spent off-seasons in Alabama, mostly in Alexander City, near Grace's mother.

"REAL McCOY! Rained out of yesterday's scheduled series with the White Sox here, several Detroit Tigers went to the circus and met a live replica of their nickname. In the above picture, Terrell Jacobs, the circus wild animal trainer, introduced his younger tiger cub to the visitors. The players, right to left, are Infielder Eddie Mayo, Outfielder Red Borom, Catcher Al Unser, Dr. R. D. Forsyth, trainer; Pitchers Zeb Earl Gentry, Stub Overmire, Outfielder Jimmy Outlaw, and Walter (Boom Boom) Beck. Photo courtesy of Herald American"

"OUTLAW SCORES IN CRUCIAL TIGER GAME. Detroit Tiger Jimmy Outlaw, left, slides in and rolls over to score in the second inning of the crucial Detroit-Philadelphia game in Detroit Sept. 25, 1944. Outlaw scored from first on a wild throw from third baseman Charlie Metro to Bill McGhee at first. Catcher Frank Hayes makes a futile try. Umpire Ernie Steward, in losing the game to the Athletics, 2-1, the Tigers allowed the St. Louis Browns to tie them for the league lead."

On the right, Zeb Eston is about to receive congratulations from Roy Cullenbine and me after Zeb hit his game-tying homer

ZEB ESTON HOME RUN

Zeb Eston hits a homerun

Tiger Stadium, Detroit

The three "old" men

At spring training in Evansville, it looked like we were going to have a little age on us. I was the baby of the group who would bear the brunt of the Detroit outfield duties. Chuck Hostetler would turn 40 on September 2, Roger Cramer, would be 40 on July 22 and I was already 32. The Evansville paper columnist Frank Kennesson ran a story about us.

Dick Wakefield was re-inducted into the Navy out of left field and Chuck came out of baseball retirement to play regular left field. Hostetler was playing for a Wichita industrial team when he was recruited at age 38. He was mostly pinch batter the year before and hit a .298 but was even better in center field. He handled 136 balls with only two errors. Doc was getting on up there in years, but you would never know it in a game. He threw 13 assists the year before, but my stats were actually a little better, thanks to his tutelage.

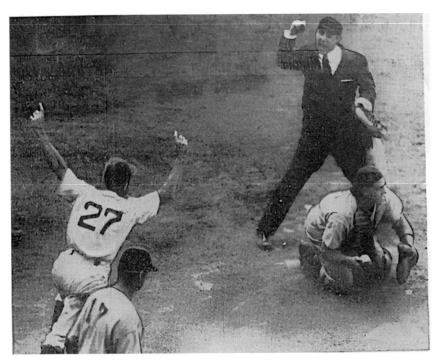

"Here I was really upset at the umpire calling me tagged out at home in a game at Briggs against the Yankees. That ump's name was Art Passarella. He was just wrong, and I let him know I thought so."

The newspapers lots of times called me quiet on the field. This one even says I was self-effacing, whatever that means. I guess I was, but it was because I was taught to be polite and have nice manners and I just couldn't get past that. I was never thrown out of a game and they talked like that was some kind of big deal. Now, I didn't like a strike called when it was close. One time I told the umpire, "A few more pitches like that one and I'll have to double my life insurance." I didn't talk much, but sometimes I just couldn't pass up a wise crack and then the whole bench would just double over.

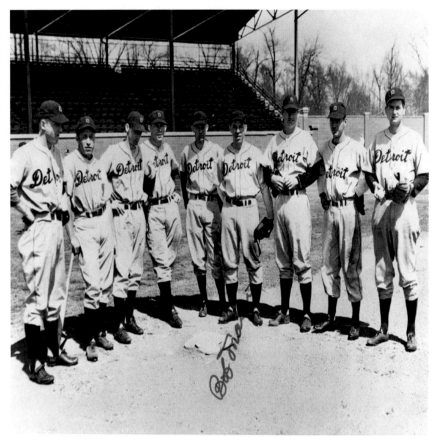

"TAKE YOUR CHOICE" The columnist here got all the players who had experience at third base. These were potential replacements for Pinky Higgins. L to R: Ed Mayo, Jim Outlaw, Jim Webb, Ed Borom, Carl McNabb, Bob Maier, Don Rose, Joe Hoover, and Paul Richards.

This list is of everyone who played any during the season. Not all were there at the first, and some were not there at the series

Al Benton	Zeb Easton	Bob Maier
Red Borom	Hank Greenberg	Eddie Mayo
Tommy Bridges	Joe Hoover	John McHale
George Caster	Chuck Hostetler	Pat McLaughlin
Doc Cramer	Art Houtteman	Carl McNabb
Roy Cullenbine	Russ Kearns	Ed Mierkowicz

Hack Miller

Les Mueller

Hal Newhauser

Prince Oana - from Hawaii

Joe Orell

Jimmy Outlaw

Stubby Overmire

Billy Pierce – kid from Chicago - got homesick so they had to trade him to the White Sox

Paul Richards

Don Ross

Bob Swift

Jim Tobin

Dizzy Trout

Virgil Trucks

Hub Walker

Skeeter Webb

Milt Welch

Walter Wilson

Rudy York

Wakefield was reactivated before the season; he was called back into the Navy. Pinky Higgins went off for military service, too. Pinky had an interesting personality like a loaded bomb.

"Outlaw rides back for his third stick-up effort"

"Greenberg in India, McCosky in Hawaii, and Wakefield in Iowa in the Navy Air Wing don't need to worry. The jobs they left behind are in the competent hands of little Jimmy Outlaw. Not in the same pay category, or size, but he could fill in for any one of these guys."

This is in an article in my scrapbook: *"Outlaw Rides Back for His Third Stick-Up Effort"* by Sam Greene, *"Detroit Jimmy Covers Wakefield Spot in Tiger Front; Placid in Temperament, He's Lively in Wit and Like Rabbit on Bases."* I was fast. They called me a jackrabbit more times than one. And my size - they kept comparing me to the giants on our team! Steve felt he could trust me in most positions. So, he moved me around some. In the field and third base.

Al Benton and Les Mueller were both fresh back out of service. Benton started the season strongly, gave up only one earned run in his first 45 innings. He was in the Navy for two years with no injuries, but then he was hit by a line drive for a broken ankle. Benton's first day back in the lineup was the same day Hank returned on July 1, and he went in to relieve Dizzy Trout. While Benton was out, Mueller took his place in the pitching rotation.

SKEETER WEBB

Skeeter Webb came from the Chicago White Sox in December 1944. He was about 4 years older than I was but I knew him from home. He was from Meridian, Mississippi, just across the state line from my hometown.

I liked the majors with no night games; I could get to bed early. I liked a good night's sleep and having breakfast with Grace and my son, Perry, who was four. I did like a good cigar after the games, but still don't like beer. I was determined to keep in shape.

A lady reporter in Chicago came up to some of us in the Del Prado Hotel. She wrote a column for the *Chicago Tribune* asking questions sent in by her readers. One question was "What advice would you give a boy who wanted to become a professional ball player?" They asked Hal, Joe Hoover, Dizzy, Don Ross, Milt Welch, and me. I told her, "I

Outfielder Jimmy Outlaw watches pitcher Hal Newhauser reach for a cigar while conversing with Dorothy Wenker, clerk at Del Prado Hotel cigar counte, as the Detroit Tigers were waiting to resume hostilities with the White Sox under the Cominsky Park lights last night.

151

think boys should start playing as early as they can on a small team somewhere – sandlots, high school teams, and organized clubs. Get on a team and play as often as you can. The more you play the better you'll get and when you are good enough, you will be discovered!"

When second baseman Eddie Mayo got hurt, Red Borom came in his place, and played the entire 1945 year. He batted over .300 in September when we were playing for the pennant. He told me he played 55 games in 1945 including two games in the World Series. I remember him hitting a ground ball up the middle right to the pitcher Hank Borowy, but it bounced off his glove. Shortstop Roy Hughes picked it up and threw him out. At least the ump called it out. It was awful close and to this day I think he was safe. He was also a pinch runner in game three in the series.

Red and I stay in real close contact with each other. I have been to see him several

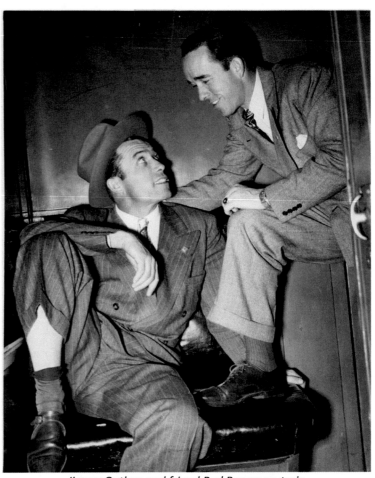

Jimmy Outlaw and friend Red Borom on train

times and when he is here, he is like one of our family. That year he ended with a .269 with a .307 on-base percentage. He is sure a good guy. A regular ballplayer.

Rudy York, oh yes, I remember him well. He joined the Tigers in 1941 when Hank Greenberg was on military duty. What a year with 27 home runs. That included a three-homer game. The next year he was still unbelievable with 21 homers, but 1943 was a lot better year. He had 34 and was one of those up for MVP. Before I got there, he had held the record for the most homeruns in one month; I think it was 18 in one month.

In '44 and '45 his total was down to 18 each year and didn't end up at his best for the series. After we won the '45 series, he was sent to Boston, but then he led the Red

Sox to the American League pennant that year when he had two grand slams against the Browns. He started off the '46 series with two homeruns to win Game One in a 10-inning game, and then had a three-run winner in game three. But St. Louis went on to win in seven games.

Steve said he was bombarded with questions about how to place me when the others came home from the war. He said he had a pile of letters on his desk from fans begging him not to replace me with Hank! He was the only manager with a problem of too many good players. He had always stuck up for me, and said he wished he had a whole team like me. He liked my willingness to do whatever he asked, and I sure respected him.

"These Tigers read with interest the Times story of the imminent discharge of Capt. Hank Greenberg and hope he'll soon be back with the team. Left right are Walter Wilson and Jimmy Outlaw. Tigers who know him say Hank will be in shape for baseball."

CAPT. HANK GREENBERG, US ARMY

Hank was already in the Army when I was pulled up, but I knew that in the 1940 season they had put Hank in outfield and moved Rudy from catcher to first base, and that worked pretty well. They won the pennant and went to the series, but they lost in seven games. Then Hank was off to war. He came back on July 1, 1945, to a crowd of almost 48,000. He homered against the As in the 8th inning in his first game.

I think Hank really appreciated all the time I helped him get back in shape. We stayed up many nights with him hitting my pitches until his hands were raw. I remember him wrapping his hands in bandages and then keep on hitting. Man, such determination. We became really good friends. Our wives got along good, too. The Greenbergs really enjoyed our son Perry.

HANK GREENBERG, US ARMY

July Marathon Games

In July, we played at Philadelphia for a four-game series. In the first game we were tied 1-1 and went into overtime – a lot of overtime. We played 24 innings before they finally called it a tie. Les Mueller pitched over 19 innings before Steve replaced him.

I got credit for saving the game in the 10th inning with a throw to catcher Bob Swift; Peck was out. Game lasted four hours and 48 minutes and was called due to darkness. The umpire said he could not see, and the rules prohibited turning on the lights to finish a daytime game. *(The 1945 Detroit Tigers: Nine Old Men and One Young Left Arm Win It All" by Verge Harmon Smith)*

The day after that we played a double header, split. Then we lost the fourth game. The second game of the double header was called in the sixth inning due to rain. We were losing 1-2 so that was the final score. Wish we could have finished.

At that time, they said I was the only active ballplayer to have played in two marathon games. Back in 1939, I played for the Braves (Bees) against Brooklyn in a game that went on for 23 innings.

Sept 12 Make up game

On Sept. 12 in Philadelphia, Detroit played the Athletics in a double header, in which the Tigers won the first game. The second game was to be the make-up game for the 24 inning one that earlier had ended in a tie when the game was called due to darkness.

In the 7th inning of a scoreless game Roy Cullenbine singled and stole second. I followed this with a single, scoring Cullenbine and giving the Tigers a 1-0 lead.

In the 9th inning, with two outs, runner on base, and a 3-2 count on the batter, Roberto (Bobby) Mendez Estalella hit a double that tied up the game.

In the 11th inning, Rudy York singled and my triple drove him in to give us the lead again, 2-1. With two outs in the inning the Athletics managed to push across another run to make it all tied up again, 2-2.

The 16th inning, with a man on, getting dark, Estalella knocked a double that gave the Athletics a 2-3 win. That totaled 40 innings before they won that game!

So, we were seriously in the pennant race. With seven games left to play, if Detroit would win six of those, then Washington couldn't win. Or any combination of Tiger victories plus Senator defeats totaling six (example Detroit wins five more, Washington loses one more; Detroit wins three more, Washington loses three more) would assure Tigers the pennant.

I always really liked Bob Feller. He was a hero in the Navy on the USS Alabama. He was pitching for the Indians in September when we were two games ahead of second place Washington. We lost that game, but Bob and I always greeted each other with the memory of that day! I robbed Feller of a no-hitter.

BOB FELLER. PITCHER, CLEVELAND INDIAN

He always remembered that. In the fifth inning, with one out, I hit a blooper, a rainbow between the outfield and the infield, and it went into right field just short of outfielder Les Fleming. I got to first. Then Paul Richards was walked. Red Borom was up next into a fielder's choice, forcing Paul to second. Red on first, me on third. Skeeter Webb, bounced his ball back to Feller for three away. We didn't even get anyone on base after that inning and never scored. Cleveland did not score again, but Detroit lost 2-0. But, Bob didn't get his no-hitter that day!

When we played Cleveland in Cleveland, that was when our pitching staff had some injured and the ones who were able to play were just too tired from being overworked, but Cleveland only got three hits in this game. That was enough to win, though.

Bob Feller always greeted Jimmy Outlaw with a joke about the day Jimmy robbed him of a no-hitter.

In the third inning when Jeff Heath hit a homerun with one man on (Cleveland) and that was enough to win the ballgame. When we lost it that put us only one game ahead of second place Washington. We had six games left to play.

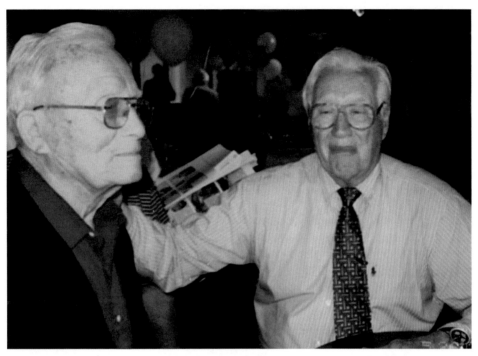

3JIMMY OUTLAW AND BOB FELLER AT BAYBEARS STADIUM IN MOBILE IN 2005.

Red and I often talk about the game that put us in the series. We were playing the Browns. Hank came up to bat with the bases loaded. We were 3-2 at the time. Red was on third. He said when he saw Hank's hit headed toward the stands that was the biggest thrill of his career. That hit meant we were going to the series. Red told Burge Smith, "Nothing could ever surpass that moment." I will have to say winning the series was the top for me.

BACK AGAIN - - - - By Jack Sords

THERE IS NOTHING FLASHY ABOUT OUTLAW'S PLAY BUT HE'S DOING A GREAT JOB OF OUTFIELDING

MAKE IT LOOK EASY!

JIMMY OUTLAW, FILLING THE BILL WITH THE DETROIT TIGERS IN HIS THIRD BIG LEAGUE EFFORT. HE HAD PREVIOUS EXPERIENCE WITH THE REDS AND BRAVES

Inning Eight
1945 World
Series

Editor's Note Detroit won the American Pennant on the last day of the season and Chicago won the National League Pennant on the next to the last day of their season.

WWII had recently ended but there were still restrictions on the use of fuel. Due to this, the World Series of 1945 would be played in a manner to limit the required travel arrangements. The first three games would be held in Detroit with the remainder of the games in Chicago.

So many people wanted to see the Series that hotel rooms in Detroit were next to impossible to secure. Some lake steamers were anchored in the Detroit River so they could serve as additional hotel space.

There were more people who wanted tickets than there were tickets available. Ballplayers could get 20 tickets each game. Thus, Dad was able to get members of his family who were able to come in the games. For rooms, all had to squeeze into his apartment.

The day before opening day was cold and windy and accompanied by rain. Both teams had to work out warm-ups they could get in between showers while also being miserable due to the cold. Except for absence of rain the day of the opening game on October 3 was just as miserable.

Despite the weather, well over 50,000 fans, dignitaries, and specially invited soldiers and sailors from all over the United States were in attendance.

Like the ball teams, the fans were anticipating a great game as both teams started their best pitchers: Hal Newhauser for the Tigers with a stat of 25-9, and Hank Borowy for the Cubs with an 11 and 2 with the Cubs, but had played the first part of that season with the Yankees where he was 10 and 5. Both pitchers had won over 20 games each during the season.

The World Series was set: the first three games would be at Tiger Stadium and the remainder would be in Chicago.

JIMMY OUTLAW, DETROIT TIGERS 1945 WORLD SERIES

The sports writers were trying to make us sound like neither team was any good, but I guess they were trying to drum up interest. One even called us "Stumblebums." That stung, but we were only thinking about the title. Fans didn't let the newspaper opinions get to them either. The excitement was in the air. Detroit was on top of the world.

There were strikes going on in the city that made transportation and housing hard to get. We had family staying at our house. Thank goodness we had room. My mother and father came for the Detroit games. They rode the train from Jackson, Alabama.

Jimmy's father, James Franklin Outlaw, Jackson, Alabama, with grandson Perry Outlaw preparing to depart for game one of the 1945 World Series in Detroit

Cubs Team

The Chicago team roster was pretty impressive:

Pitchers

Hank Borowy

Bob Chipman

Jorge Comelias

Paul Derringer

Paul Erickson

Ed Hanyzewski

George Hennessey

Claude Passeau

Ray Prim

Walter Signer

Ray Starr

Mack Stewart

Hy Vandenberg

Lon Warneke

Hank Wyse

Catchers:

Paul Gillespie

Mickey Livingston

Len Rice

Dewey Williams

Infielders:

Heinz Becker

Cy Block

Phil Cavarretta

Stan Hack

Roy Hughes

Pep Johnson

Lennie Merullo

Johnny Ostrowski

Reggie Otero

Bill Schuster

Outfielders:

Lloyd Christopher

Peanuts Lowrey

Bill Nicholson

Andy Pafko

Ed Sauer

Frank Secory

Other Batters:

Johnny Moore

Charlie Grimm

Coaches:

Roy Johnson

Red Smith

Milt Stock

GAME ONE

Wednesday, October 3, 1945

Detroit, Briggs Stadium

Length of game: 2:10

Chicago Cubs: 9   Detroit Tigers: 0

Time: 2:30 PM ET

Attendance: 55,000

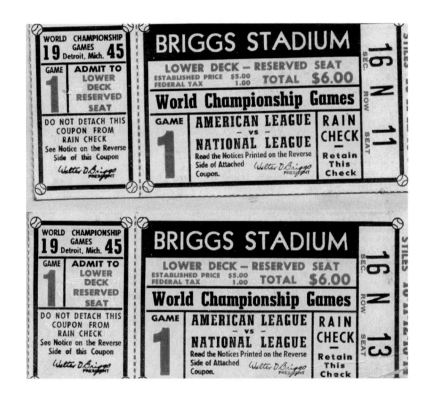

·This was the first series for the new Commissioner of Baseball Happy Chandler. Landis had died that year and the series was dedicated to him. Owner Walter Briggs and his son, "Spike," were there, of course, and Connie Mack, President of the American League was present.

Opening ceremonies were exciting, but we could only think about getting on that field and winning. We were all freezing even before the first pitch. One of our players had brought warm bricks for his feet.

When Commissioner Chandler threw out the first pitch to Richards, it actually looked pretty good. Maybe a knuckleball which only reminded us that the Cubs had four knuckleball pitchers.

Unfortunately, the only thing worse than the weather was the play of the Tigers. It was a terrible day for us. Our play was off, way off, while the Cubs seemed to do everything right. After two outs, Newhauser was tagged for four runs in the first inning aided by not-so-good defensive support from the team.

A couple of years ago, a man named Burge Smith came to see me for information to put in a book he was writing. He talked to a lot of us old guys – I hope he gets to publish it.

> *Editors Note:* **The 1945 Detroit Tigers; Nine Old Men and One Young Left Arm Win It All** *was authored by Burge Carmon Smith who spent months in Cooperstown for research and interviewed all players who were still alive. His research for his Masters' Degree Thesis was published in book form in 2010. It is an invaluable resource for details of each game of the series.*

I really hate to even remember that first game – the first inning, especially. I did ok for the whole game, but some others had a really tough time.

- Smiley Hack was the first up and I got right on his grounder to third base and made a good throw to first. So, I made the first out against the Cubs in the series. When Don Johnson stole second, his cleats cut Mayo's hands on the slide. Funny thing, those two second basemen got along just fine. They even shared the same pair of sunglasses. You know, we all got along with everybody. We loved the game. Lowery flied out to Doc Kramer and then Cavaretta hit a slow ball right to Mayo. Mayo always played deep, but that time he was too deep and didn't make it in time. When Richards allowed a pass ball, Johnson came in to start the scoring spree. O'Neill came out to chat with Hal but went back to the dugout. With Povitch, Pafco, and Cavaretta on base, a fly ball to Cullenbine looked like it was in the stands. By the time he caught up with it, it was too late. We finally got in, but Livingston had the only really good hit for the Tigers. So, the four to nothing score hung heavy over our heads.

- In the bottom of the first, we started to make some headway. Webb and Mayo both got on base, then Cramer hit into a double play. Greenberg and Cullenbine both walked, but then York popped up – the last out.
- We held the Cubs for the next inning. Newhauser struck out the first three. In the bottom of the inning, my hit popped up, Richards walked, then Newhauser hit into a double play and that was that.
- In the third inning, Hal gave the sports writers something to talk about. The Cubs were hitting and we weren't catching. The Cubs scored three more runs, making the score 7-0. Hal was sent to the dugout and what we heard was not pretty. The crowd was booing, and he grabbed a bat and kept going right past us into the tunnel to the club room. We could hear pounding and yelling all the way. He was hitting the wall and lightbulbs with a passion. Benton came in to close out the top; I got the last out of the inning when I snagged a ground ball by Johnson. Borowy was still pitching for the Cubs. He could get on a wild streak sometimes and once he hit Greenberg's hat and knocked it off his head.
- Tobin took over pitching in the fifth and got the Cubs out with his flutter ball. In the bottom, when Greenberg hit a hard drive to center, Mayo tried to outrun centerfielder Pafco's pitch to third. I can still hear the sound of that throw hit Hack's glove – a long time before Mayo slid in. Sportscaster Povitch couldn't resist his sarcastic style, "The darndest thing just happened. Eddie Mayo, the smartest guy on the Tigers, tried to go from first to third on Greenberg's single at a time when the Tigers were seven runs behind and was thrown out. The Cubs will be glad to learn that Mayo represents the Tigers' best baseball brains. They will assume they have nothing more to fear from the Tigers."
- Cubs scored twice more in the seventh inning. Nine to zip was awful. 'The score is 9-0 finish, the same score by which forfeited games go into the record. It's obvious that the Tigers could have achieved the same result by not showing up. The fans finally had enough of our sloppy playing, and we tried to ignore the booing coming from the stands.

However, the Detroit fans were quiet leaving the game. Arthur Daley of NY Times wrote, "With the incomparable Newhauser beaten, Detroit's hopes were lower than the mercury in the thermometer. And, brother, that was pretty low."

We were pretty depressed that night. Doc Cramer, the only one who tried to be positive, said, "They are still a long way from home." He also commented that the ground was still slippery from all the rain – that caused his mistakes.

We had gone through four pitchers that game. Newhauser for 2 and 2/3 innings, Benton for 1 and 1/3, Tobin for 3, and Mueller for 2. But we were pumped up and ready to come back the next day.

GAME TWO

Thursday, October 4, 1945   **Chicago Cubs: 1   Detroit Tigers: 4**

Detroit, Briggs Stadium   **Time: 2:30 PM ET**

Length of game: 1:47   **Attendance: 53,636**

I remember that the game brought out a lot of patriotic spirit. Trucks and Greenberg were called Bluejacket Trucks and Captain Greenberg. The bands played a lot of marching songs, too. These guys played a great game.

- Wyse was doing good for the Cubs until the fifth inning. Doc and I had the only two singles until then, and he had walked Cullenbine twice.
- Then in the fifth with two outs, Webb singled to left and Mayo walked. Cramer hit a single to score Webb. Score was now 1-1, two outs with Mayo on third and Cramer on first. That first run of the series gave us a lot of spunk then. Then when Grimm decided not to walk Greenberg, we were on fire. I had worked with Hank a lot and knew how well he hit under stress. Maybe that was the Army Air Force in him. Anyway, with a one and one count, the ball that Wysse threw as a fast ball had slowed down over the plate and Hank hit one into the stands. With bases loaded Hank Greenberg's homerun put us up 4-1. Hank said that Tobin had coached him on pitcher Wyse. You know, he had been with the National League a long time and knew Wyse pretty good.

- I remember a hit that York made in the sixth. It was way up, but Pafko climbed up that fence like a monkey and grabbed it. It was sure to be a homerun.

Every time I see Virgil we replay that game. He was one fine pitcher that day. He always gave a lot of credit to the Navy Great Lakes manager, Mickey Cochrane: "Mickey taught me a lot about pitching and helped me improve my curve ball." Virgil had come on so late in the season he didn't even know all of us on the team. After the game, Steve O'Neill was in his caged office and we could hear him humming the *Army Navy Together* song. "Hooray for the red, white, and blue."

GAME THREE

Friday, October 5, 1945   **Chicago Cubs: 3   Detroit Tigers: 0**

Detroit, Briggs Stadium   **Time: 2:30 PM ET**

Length of game: 1:55   **Attendance: 55,500**

Our last game of the series at home; no matter who won that one we would be going to play in Chicago for the rest of the series. The weather was still gloomy. They had a tarp on the infield they took off about half an hour before the game, but it was still very wet. Commissioner Chandler stepped out and said the game would go on. The stands were a sell-out. I knew there was a section of wounded war vets there from the hospital at Battle Creek. Really got to all of us.

Claude Passeau pitched record-setting game. I think I already told you about Claude. We grew up right across the state line. Him in Lucedale, Mississippi. He was 6'3" – we were quite a pair in photographs, like Mutt and Jeff. He had been playing pro ball for about 11 years by that time. He had really good years in 1940 and 1942, with 20 and 19 games each. He had an elbow problem, extra bone in it. Grimm called him "Mr. Chips" because of that. Most ball players had superstitions or good luck charms. Claude's was the number 13. He also really roughed up a ball before he used it. In one bad game he blamed it on a smooth ball. There was a rumor that Claude used sandpaper in his glove to rough up the ball, but I don't think he would have done that.

Rudy York got the only hit off of him. Stubby Overmire was pitching for us, and Steve put Benton in for him in the seventh to finish up the game. Red Borom was sent in to run for Swift who had walked to first in the sixth inning. Johnson got Walker's hit and thought he tagged him. So did the ump, evidently, because he called him out. Tough break.

So we were headed to Chicago with a 1-2. O'Niell said he would pitch Trout, Newhauser and Trucks to win the series. Ha, he predicted that. Anyway, the newspapers called them T.N.T. – good name.

We got on a special train at 4:30, then the Cubs had their own train, and the newspaper people were on a third one. They had rooms for us at the Hotel Stevens that looked out over Lakeshore Drive.

GAME FOUR

Saturday, October 6, 1945   **Chicago Cubs: 1   Detroit Tigers: 4**

Chicago, Wrigley Field   **Time: 1:30 PM CT**

Length of game: 2:00   **Attendance: 42,923**

Chicago was all pumped up. The train stations had been full of fans the night before when we came in.

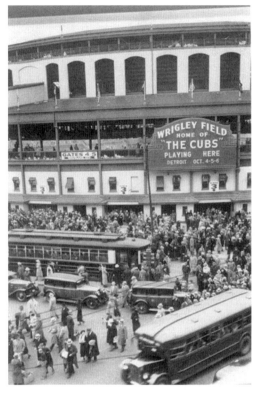

I was glad I was on third – I really felt at home there and especially I was glad I wouldn't be searching for a lost ball in the ivy. That was embarrassing when that happened. But by then it had turned brown. The rains kept coming and we couldn't have batting practice for the second time. The infield tarp stayed on until the game. There was a little stir when a couple of famous people came on the field and into the dugout. One was movie star June Haver. She was going around kissing all the guys. Red Borom was one of them and he still complains that he never got one of the photos. Then Phil Silvers came in and told us he had some money riding on us.

Later on we heard about the whole billy goat thing. The crowds in Chicago were all sell-outs just like at Briggs. We were in the dugout and some doing some practice when we saw a man and a goat walking all around the field. The man was waving, and the goat had a blanket on his back that said, "We got Detroit's Goat." Come to find out, the man was Billy Sianos and the goat Murphy was his pet. Billy owned a tavern near the stadium, and he had been bringing the goat to all of the Cubs' games for years. He had bought two box seat tickets. The story we heard was about the field manager, Andy Frian, and his crew of more than 500 who were hired that day to usher, and there were policemen, Army MPs, and Navy Shore Patrolmen there.

When Billy and his billy goat took their seats, it wasn't long before people were complaining of the smell of the goat and the ushers tried to get Billy to take the goat out, saying the tickets were not meant for goats. Billy demanded that they contact Mr. Wrigley, and sure enough, Wrigley said, "No smelly goats." They went back to the tavern, and he declared that the reason the Cubs lost the series was that Murphy was not allowed in the park. He reportedly said, "The Cubs will suffer because of what they did to us." The tavern business boomed after that, anyway. It is still there today, but in a different place, the incident became famous as the Billy Goat Curse on the Cubs. It is still not broken.

Dizzy Trout was our pitcher. An old friend from back home, Ray Prim, was pitching for the Cubs. Trout went the whole game and had a five-hitter, but they only scored one run in the sixth. He had been under the weather with a cold and he had suffered a back injury during the season. When we were on the train, I heard Steve O'Neill arguing with a report who thought Trout wasn't ready. Steve finally lost his temper and told him to get away from him, "Trout is my man!" That day, Trout told Steve he was ready to pitch the game of his life.

- Neither team got any hits for a couple of innings and the outfielders were up to speed with every play. Dizzy enjoyed being the center of attention. Sometimes, he'd leave the mound and go the wall and kick the mud off of his shoes. Lots of times, he used his bandana to clean his glasses, making everyone just wait.
- We got two runs in the top of the fourth and Grimm took Ray out and put Paul Derringer in. He didn't do much better. I hit a ball to third that could have been a double play, but I made it to first. Greenberg went home. We scored one more, then Dizzy's ground ball to Johnson got me out.
- In the bottom of the fourth, after two hits, Caster and Bridges both started to warm up, getting ready to replace Trout, but he struck three out and still had a no-hitter.
- We let them get one run in the sixth. Dizzy was really show-boating. He would taunt the fans by doing all sorts of things. Tying his shoes, adjusting his belt buckle, repositioning his cap, or calling time to bring the catcher out to the mound for a chat. Steve did go out once at least and looked like he was frustrated with Dizzy as well.
- The Cubs tried out three more pitchers, but the game ended at 4-1; so there we were ready for game five with 2-2!

GAME FIVE

Sunday, October 7, 1945   **Chicago Cubs: 4   Detroit Tigers: 8**

Chicago, Wrigley Field   **Time: 1:30 PM CT**

Length of game: 2:18   **Attendance: 43,463**

Hal Newhauser was the winning pitcher – the whole game. Exciting game – lots of action. Manager wanted me to fly out to get runners on first and third around. Paul Derringer was pitching by then. He had replaced Hank Borowy. We had 'em 8-3 until the last inning and Phil Cavaretta hit a leadoff double and then scored with Nicholson's single. Then Hal got rid of the next two batters. One of our better games.

Hal Newhauser had been doing just what he should have been doing. Resting and taking care of that arm. And remember there was that lump on his shoulder he tried to keep hidden. He was up against Hank Borowy again and was determined to go more than the 2 and 2/3 innings he had in game one. He felt ready and felt the field was ready to back him up better this go around.

The weather was much better – warm even, so we could have batting practice for the first time in three days. But, during practice Rudy York hit a line drive just when the Cubs shortstop Roy Hughes was crossing the field. He had to be taken off the lineup.

- Top of the third, we had two come in on Cullenbine's hit, but no one had heard the umpire call it a foul ball, so they all went back, and Cullenbine struck out. I tell you, Pafco made of couple of spectacular catches, but Webb tagged up and came in on one of them. In the bottom of the third I didn't have a chance to reach a hit by Borowy. It flew by me just out of reach. Doc Cramer wasn't quite smooth enough to get Hack's hit to center and Borowy scored a run.

- We were 1-1 until the sixth inning, when we scored four. It was on Cramer's hit that Pafco made an error – really rare for him. Then after Greenberg and York both had hits, the Cubs put Hy Vandenburg on the mound. He walked Richards so now the bases are loaded. Cullenbine was like dancing over on third. He kept taunting the pitcher and started stealing a couple of times. This was when Newhauser came to bat and he was walked, bringing in Cullenbine for run number four.

- Inning seven: Hank was first up to face Derringer. His hit to left fell between shortstop and Lowery taking Hank to second. Cullenbine's sacrifice bunt actually got him to first and Hank to third. I then hit hard to center field and brought Hank in. We were 5-1 when the Cubs got two in the bottom. Boy, the wind that gave Chicago the nickname Windy City, earned its reputation that day. I had never seen the wind move balls around so much.

- They almost tied us in the seventh when Pafco was on base, and Livingston hit a ball that acted crazy. It was in foul territory, then blew back in to fair, then bounced into the stands. So, Livingston got two bases on the ground-rule double and Pafco scored.

- In the eighth inning we went three up and three down and in the bottom Hack grounded out and I snagged a bunt and got it to first. Then a pop-up threw catcher Richards into a tailspin. The wind blew it out over the mound, but Richards did bag it behind the pitcher. Three outs.

- Right at the first of the ninth inning, Cramer got hit on the ankle. The Cubs had put in another pitcher, Erickson. Greenberg hit a double that put Cramer on third. We knew it had to happen at least once: Cullenbine's hit got lost in the ivy wall. Pafco looked but couldn't find it, so the two base ground rule was invoked and we got our last two runs. The Cubbies' Cavaretta hit one and I heard Cullenbine yelling, "All right, All right." Cramer backed off and the ball hit the ground. Cullenbine was not able to get it to the infield in time. We could hear Cramer yelling, "What the hell did you mean, 'All Right?'" Cullenbine was meaning it was all right for Cramer to get the ball. Two players were hot. The Cubbies got one. Now the series is 3-2 and we had confidence we would win the title the next game.

GAME SIX

Monday, October 8, 1945	**Chicago Cubs: 8 Detroit Tigers: 7**
Chicago, Wrigley Field	**Time: 1:30 PM CT**
Length of game: 3:28	**Attendance: 41,708**

What a game. Lost it by one run and we should have won it, no question about that. It was exciting, to say the least. We led 1-0 until the fourth inning, then they had a lucky streak in the fifth that started them rolling. It is the game that sticks in my memory more than any of the others, so I seem to talk about it the most. It was the one that went 12 innings and lasted 3 and a half hours. It was so cold I remember Virgil Trucks blowing warm air on his hands. He said, "This is too cold for me. This Alabama boy is going home tonight." Well, he had to stay two more days before he got to go home.

- That first inning was a pitcher's game. It was actually a record breaker for Claude Passeau – another hitless inning to add to his record. Trucks held the Cubs for the first one, too.

- In the second, Claude walked me to put me on first with the bases loaded, then he walked Richards, and Cullenbine came in for our first run of the game.
- In the Cubs' half, Livingston got real upset with the umpire calling him out on second for the third out. He ran toward the umpire and ripped his jacket open, yelling his head off. He gave the ump a hard shove and the umpire shoved him right back. Funny, back then, the series had a rule that no player could be kicked off by the umpire. He would have been out of the game today. I think he had to pay a fine later on. The third inning went three up and three down for both teams.
- In the fourth we had another one of those outs with the bases loaded. I had hit a good grounder with Cullenbine on first, then Trucks was walked. Too bad Webb's fly ball to center busted that bubble. Claude was still pitching for the Cubs. Trucks gave up a couple of hits in the bottom, but Greenberg jumped way up to catch Pafco's fly. That was unbelievable. You can see it on the video of the series. Looked impossible to me, but he was a lot taller than I am.
- The fifth we didn't do anything. The Cubs had a good inning. Trucks always blamed first baseman York for waving him off to try to cover first on his own, but York was just too big to be fast enough. He slipped down and threw a wide ball to second to allow the bases to fill up. Passeau bunted straight toward Virgil. Virgil started to first, but then turned and threw it to me. It was too wide, but he always said I was too far off base. We argued about that play every time we were together after that. Next, catcher Richards stumbled over a bat that messed up his timing to catch a throw from center field, and let the second run come in. Two still on base when Lowery walked and loaded the bases with Cavaretta up to bat. His single scored two and then Steve pulled Virgil out of the game. He had done a good job considering all the mess up in the field. The fans weren't happy with that. George Caster went in. That was his first time to pitch in a World Series.
- Top of the sixth in game six: Claude Passeau and I share a laugh every time I see him, he holds up his middle finger. Most people just think he is being rude, but when they know the whole story it is different. He was pitching swell, but Cullenbine got a hit to the center, York hit a short fly and got out. Then I was up to bat and hit that ball hard right to Claude. He tried to stop it or catch it with his pitching hand and stopped it. He got it in time to get me out at first, but then he started jumping all around and yelled, "Time out." His finger was hurt so bad it took off the fingernail and started to turn blue right then, but he wanted to keep on pitching.

Bobby Maier came in to pinch hit for Richards and he did almost the same thing I had – right up the middle. Claude tried to catch it with his glove, but it bounced off and Maier got to first. Then Caster struck out.

- The next inning was a crazy one, too. Chuck Hostetler was about the fastest on our team and he was heading for home from second. O'Neill was waving all around and Chuck thought he meant for him to keep going. When he heard O'Neill yelling, he stumbled and fell face down, got up, but was caught in a run-down. Cramer had advanced to second, Greenberg walked, Cullenbine hit a single, and Cramer scored. That did it for Claude. Grimm took him out and Wyse came in and gave up a hit to York that brought Greenberg in. So, there we were at 5-3. Hostetler tried to hide how much that bothered him, but you could tell it did; he thought that is what people would remember him for. He always said he tripped on a cigarette butt.

- Actually, I know how he felt. I got caught in the ninth. Could have won the game. Borowy was pitching for the Cubs; Pafco was left on base. We were 7-7 at the end of the ninth and really all hepped up. Greenberg had hit one that bounced off the railing in the stands to tie the score.

- We played 12 innings. Another bad thing happened in the twelfth. Murello had replaced the Cubs shortstop and when Hoover tried to steal second, he slid into Murello with spikes in the air and cut Murello's arm in two places. He was still tagged out. The game was over when Greenberg ran to field a ground ball by Hack. Hank was on one knee, just like he 'should'a' been, but that ball hit a sprinkler head and bounced way over his left shoulder. Bad place to go with no one to back him up. By the time he recovered it, the Cubs had the winning run. 8-7

"But it ain't over 'til it's over."

GAME SEVEN

One day break on Tuesday

Wednesday, October 10, 1945	**Chicago Cubs: 3 Detroit Tigers: 9**
Chicago, Wrigley Field	**Time: 1:30 PM CT**
Length of game: 2:31	**Attendance: 41,590**

Everybody could tell that both teams had about worn out their pitchers, but Passeau's injury had put a hole in the Cubs' cage. I tell you what. Let's look at this old film for the seventh game. I could watch it all day. Hard to believe this was filmed 65 years ago!

Well, here we are at the seventh and deciding game, the crucial one, the first after the Victory. Even the band here at Wrigley Field has caught the spirit of the game. Just look at those drum majorettes. Now over here we see Borowy, anchorman of the Cubs, warming up. He'd like to make it three victories over the Tigers and the clinching game at that.

Hal Newhauser, the ace left-hander has his own ideas about that. And we will know the answer very shortly. The Tigers are not to be denied as Webb opened the game with a base hit. His teammate Mayo followed with a base hit to right sending Webb to third, Cramer loops a safe on into left field scoring the first Tiger run.

And here comes Charlie Grimm to remove Borowy from the ball game, and replace him with Derringer with one run home and Tigers on first and second. Greenberg crossed up the Cubs by advancing both runners on a sacrifice bunt, Caparetta handling the play unassisted.

Cullenbine was intentionally passed filling the bases. After York popped to Hack it looked like the trouble was over, but Derringer walked Outlaw forcing in Mayo. Catcher Paul Richards bobbed a healthy double to left field, scoring Cramer, Cullenbine, and Outlaw, giving the Tigers five big runs in the first inning of the final World Series game.

Newhauser was really bearing down in the fifth with a six to two lead as both Hughes and Sauer were strike out victims. In the Tiger seven with Erickson pitching, Cullenbine on first and two outs, Richards doubled to right center, scoring Cullenbine, driving in his fourth run of the game. The score, Tigers 7 Cubs 2.

The Tigers added two more to their total in the eighth with Passeau pitching, making it nine to two. And here we are in the ninth and final inning of the last World Series game of 1945.

Hughes singles off of Newhauser. McCullough came to bat for the pitcher Wyse but he became Newhauser's tenth strike out victim of the game. Hack flied to Cramer in center field for the second out. And when Don Johnson forced Hughes at second, the Detroit Tigers became the 1945 Champions of the baseball world.

After losing his opening assignment, Newhauser captured his second victory of the series, a highly important one. The Tigers had the batting power and pitching strength to win.

The capacity crowd lifted the total attendance at all World Series games to 8 million. No wonder baseball is called our national game. And all other sports help keep America fit. Help keep American youth fit in the bigger game of life the world over.

Oh, yeah. There was some excitement after that game. We all hugged each other, our wives, and anyone else that was there. Lots of jumping and whooping it up that is for sure.

The train ride back to Detroit was a little quieter, but lots of reporters were on the train, too, and we were all kept pretty busy giving them our personal reactions. Our wives and families were all excited and happy, too. Grace was bouncing all over the train. We were all mostly in the club car and I'm sure there was plenty to eat and drink. When we got back to Detroit, what a crowd was there waiting! Some fans were on the train with us, but it looked like all of Detroit came out the station in Dearborn to wave pennants and flags and cheer us as we got off the train. We lived close to the station, so we were home with just a short drive. I know I slept well that night.

"OUTFIELDER OUTLAW/ JIMMY OUTLAW, TIGER VETERAN: JIMMY HAS SAVED MANY A BALL GAME FOR THE TIGERS BY HIS FINE FIELDING"

Detroit Jubilant as Tigers Win World Championsh

HERE IS PART OF THE HUGE CROWD THAT JAMMED AROUND THE UNION STATION ON FORT STREET AFTER MIDNIGHT TODAY TO WELCOME THE TIGERS ON THEIR RETURN FROM CHICAGO

UNION DEPOT, DETROIT, MICHIGAN   2010

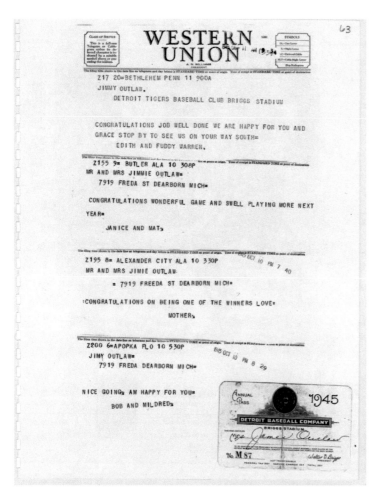

Mother and Father were at the Detroit games but were not able to go to Chicago. We got lots of telegrams, but the one from her was special. I wish she and my father could have been there. They were so proud of me it made me feel good.

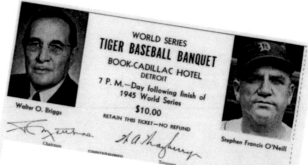

They had already made plans for the banquet. This ticket says it was for the night following the last game of the World Series. It was some whoop-de-doo. I guess they would have held it even if we had lost but this was a real celebration night.

PROGRAM. 1945

DETROIT TIGERS

WORLD CHAMPIONS

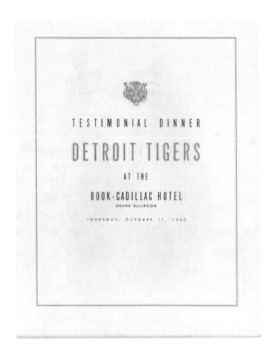

TESTIMONIAL DINNER

DETROIT TIGERS

At the Book Cadillac Hotel Grand Ballroom

WALTER O. BRIGGS

ROBERT BRIGGS, JR. VICE PRESIDENT, DETROIT BASEBALL CLUB

BANQUET COMMITTEE

Fourth Game

4

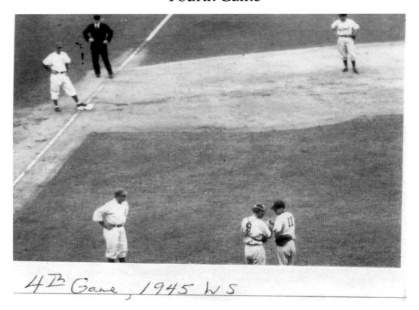

4ᵗʰ Game, 1945 WS

The following note was attached to this photo; author unknown:

Charlie Grimm (Cubs manager on field "perhaps" protecting against what he believed to be a "quick pitcher" Paul Dizzy Trout-Tiger Pitcher. Runner on third is probably Cavarretta or Stan Hack – each had 11 hits in the series. Tiger 3rd base is Jimmy Outlaw; catcher is Paul Richards

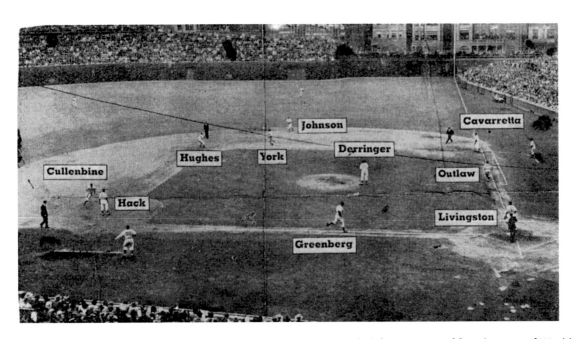

PATHS JAMMED-Jimmy Outlaw of Tigers batted with bases loaded fourt inning of fourth game of World Series at Wrigley Field yesterday and forced Rudy York at second. Hank Greenberg scored from third on play and Roy Cullenbine moved from second to third. It was the high point of series scoring action yesterday.

LIVINGSTON HITS THE DIRT: MICKEY LIVINGSTON SLIDES SAFELY IN TO THIRD BASE AS JIM OUTLAW STRETCHES FOR VIRGIL TRUCK'S HEAVE OF CLAUDE PASSEAU'S GROUNDER IN FIFTH INNING OF WORLD SERIES GAME NUMBER 6 AT WRIGLEY FIELD

INNING THAT WON THE SERIES: HAIL TO JIMMY OUTLAW WHO TOOK OVER AT THIRD BASE LATE IN THE SEASON AND TURNED IN A CAPABLE JOB,THEN TOPPED IT OFF WITH A SUPERB SHOWING IN THE SERIES. JIMMY DIDN'T MAKE AN ERROR IN THE SEVEN GAMES.

Stan Sianis, proprietor of the Billy Goat Tavern on North Michigan Avenue, explains why you never cross a Greek-or his goat. The story revolves around William "Billy Goat" Sianis, Sam's uncle and the joint's original owner:

"Back in 1945 my uncle tried to take his goat to Wrigley Field for the World Series between Detroit and the Chicago Cubs. He had two tickets and they refused to let him in. My uncle says, 'i've got two tickets. The goat has a yicket. Why not?' and they said they can't have animals in the ballpark. So my uncle says, "ask Mr. Wrigley.

"Somebody went up there, told Mr. Wrigley that my uncle was down there, a billy goat was down there. They have tickets, and they want to get in the game. Mr. Wrigley says, 'No goat allowed. The goat smells. We don't want any smelly goat in there.'

"My uncle went back to his tavern at 1855 West Madison. That was the Billy Goat then. He stayed there, and the Cubs lost the game. Later on, he sent a telegram to Mr. Wrigley after the Cubs lost the series. It says, 'Who's smelly now?' I've got the telegram right over there behind the bar.

"Then people say that my uncle said, 'As long as I live, the Cubs, they're not going to win any World Series here.' But my uncle, he never told me that. He always told me, 'The Cubs are going to suffer because of what they did to me and my goat.' That I remember.

"Nobody calls me from the Cubs. Nobody invites me. It's too late now. But you know what? If they asked me, I'd go out and find me a goat and take it with me right up there to Wrigley Field."

SEATED LEFT TO RIGHT, JIMMY OUTLAW, MAYOR JEFFERS,PAUL RICHARDS, K.T. KELLER, HANK GREENBERG,
WALTER BRIGGS, W.O. BRIGGS, JR., FRED MATTHEIS, STEVE O'NEILL, JACK ZELLER, HAL NEWHAUSER, LYLE
YFE,BUCK O'NEILL, DIZZY TROUT, AND C.E.WILSON. THIS WAS THE GENERAL SCENE AT THE VICTORY BANQUET
IN HONOR OF THE WORLD CHAMPION TIGERS AT THE BOOK-CADILLAC HOTEL THURSDAY NIGHT. SOME 1,500
WERE PRESENT AT THE FESTIVE EVENT. THE ENTIRE TIGER TEAM WAS AT THE SPEAKER'S TABLE, IN THE CENTER
OF WHICH SAT WALTER BRIGGS, THE PROUD TIGERS OWNER. THE HEAD OF THE TRIUMPHANT TIGER AND A
PORTRAIT OF BRIGGS WERE PROMINENT DECORATIONS BEHIND THE TABLE

191

Some of the stuff I have here on display was given to us at different times and ceremonies. There was a big banquet where they gave us the trophies. We had to buy our own rings, though. It cost a whopping $100!

Louisville Slugger bat company made a commemorative bat in black lacquer with all our autographs printed in gold ink. Well, most are autographs. Some I guess they didn't have autographs, so they printed them in.

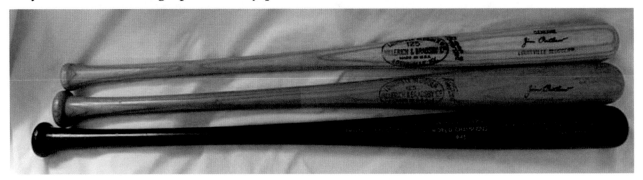

TOP: LOUISVILLE SLUGGER BAT WITH NAME ENGRAVED

Middle: Actual bat used in 1945 World Series

Bottom: Commemorative bat with all players' names in gold.

I signed a contract with Louisville Slugger Bats during my first year in pro ball. They used my name and provided bats for me. I used about 8 different models during my career. During the World Series I was using the McQuinn model which had the Ernie Vik V19 specs. It was 34" long and weighed 33 oz.

THIS IS THE DIAMOND CREW THAT WHIPPED ALL COMERS TO BRING THE WORLD TITLE HOME TO DETROIT. THEY WON THE FOURTH GAME WEDNESDAY, 9-3
Stellar pitching, batting, leadership and teamwork made the Bengals the champion ball club of the world for another season

We had our official photograph made, and then we had a time we all met at the hotel and signed each other's prints. We also signed bats for each other then.

193

1866 Kenesaw Mountain Landis **1944**

BASEBALL'S first Commissioner, who directed its destinies from 1920 until his death, November 25, 1944.

The annual player award by the members of the Baseball Writers' Association of America was voted a memorial to the late Commissioner at a joint session of the major leagues held in 1944.

Winners of the Kenesaw Mountain Landis Memorial plaque for the year 1944 were Harold Newhouser, of the Tigers, in the American League, and Martin Marion, shortshop of the St. Louis Cardinals, in the National League.

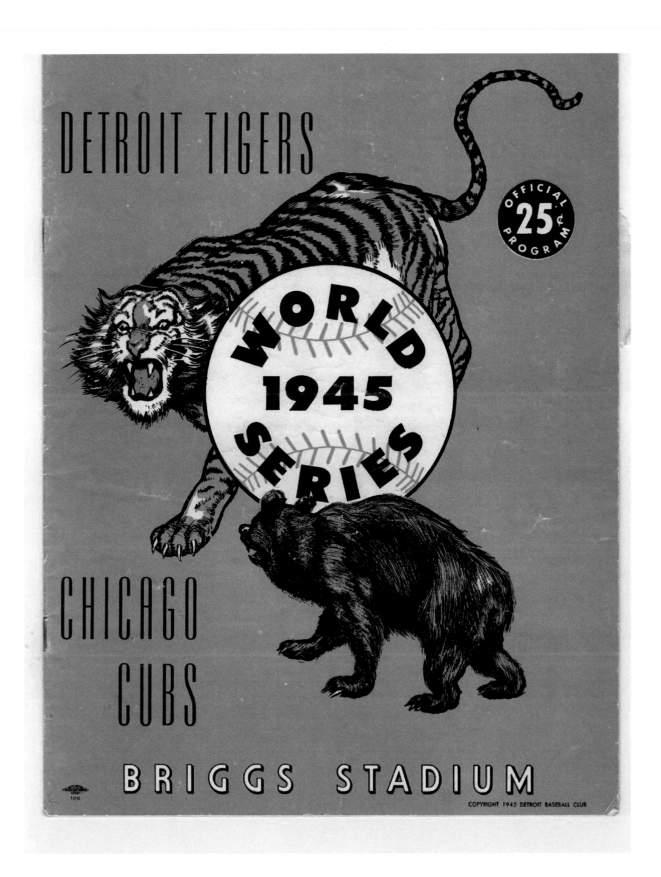

DETROIT TIGERS

OFFICIAL 25¢ PROGRAM

WORLD 1945 SERIES

CHICAGO CUBS

BRIGGS STADIUM

COPYRIGHT 1945 DETROIT BASEBALL CLUB

1945 TIGERS

ROBERT "JOE" HOOVER

Shortstop. Came to Detroit from the Hollywood club after having played with Indianapolis. He is a good ground coverer and in his career has played every position on the diamond. He lives in Los Angeles.

EDWARD J. MAYO

Trustworthy second baseman, whose aggressiveness and timely hitting as much as anything else were responsible for club's success, this year. Of Polish extraction, Eddie began his career in 1932, was turned over to Louisville by the Athletics late in 1943, and came to the Tigers in the draft. With Huntington, in 1943, and came to the Tigers in the draft. His play this year was of even better quality. He is extremely popular with Detroit fans. Resides in Clifton, N. J.

ZEBELON V. EATON

Pitcher, also an impressive pinch-hitter. On two occasions, this year, he has delivered with homers in emergencies. He was the leading pitcher in the Evangeline League, where he won 23 games for Alexandria, with 256 strikeouts and an earned-run average of 1.77. After going to Beaumont he entered the army from which he was honorably discharged. He spent most of the 1944 season with Buffalo and was recalled to Detroit in 1945. His home is in Cooleemee, N. C.

ALTON BENTON

Won eleven games and lost but two, with an exceptionally low earned-run average, early this season. Suffered broken ankle in May and found his effectiveness lessened after return to game several weeks later. The big fellow came to the Tigers in 1937 from Memphis. Had previously been with Oklahoma, Philadelphia Americans, Albany and Chattanooga. Was an efficient relief pitcher for Tigers in 1940. Returned to Club this year after honorable discharge from Navy. Twice nominated for All-Star participation.

RUDOLPH PRESTON YORK

First baseman. A Tiger since 1934, coming up from Fort Worth. After being sent out on option, to Milwaukee, he returned to Detroit where he became one of the game's leading sluggers. With Hank Greenberg, was principal factor in winning of pennant in 1940, when he hit 33 homers. Chosen for All-Star honors four times. Among leaders this year in home runs and runs batted in. Lives in Cartersville, Ga.

JAMES E. MILLER

Catcher, is a native of Celeste, Texas, and entered pro baseball in 1929. He joined the Tigers in 1944, but has seen little service with the club. His home is in McKinney, Texas.

CHARLES C. HOSTETLER

Alternated in the outfield for the club in 1944, but has been used principally as a pinch-hitter, this year. He is one of the oldest members of the squad, having been born in Uniontown, Pa. in 1905. He lives in Wichita, Kans.

ADVISORY COUNCIL OF BASEBALL

WILLIAM HARRIDGE
President, American League

HON. A. B. CHANDLER
Commissioner

FORD C. FRICK
President, National League

At their joint meeting, held in April, of this year, representatives of both major leagues chose for the important post of Commissioner, a man who had received the highest honors in his native state of Kentucky.

Starting his political career as a State Senator, Mr. Chandler served as Lieutenant Governor, and as Chief Executive of his state between 1935 and 1939. On October 30, 1939, he resigned as Governor to accept appointment as United States Senator, a position which he still holds.

WORLD SERIES FACTS

THE 1945 World Series is the 42nd to be played since 1903. There was no meeting of league Champions in 1904.

American League clubs have been victorious in 25 of the contests played and National League clubs in 16.

In only six instances has the series ended with the playing of four successive victories.

Attendance has ranged from the low of 1907 (78,068), when the Cubs trounced the Tigers, in four straight, to a high of 328,051 set in the 1926 seven-game series between the Cardinals and Yankees.

The most profitable series was the 1940 joust between the Cincinnati Reds and the Detroit Tigers when a total of $1,322,328 was received. Included in the amount was a $100,000 contribution for broadcasting rights.

From the players' standpoint, the 1935 series between Detroit and Chicago was the most profitable. Each Tiger share amounted to $6,544.76 while the losing Cubs each drew down $4,198.53 in prize money.

In the 41 series played to date, the New York American League club has the best record with ten victories and four defeats.

Detroit has participated in six World Series clashes previous to the present one—in 1907, 1908, 1909, 1934, 1935, and 1940. It was victorious in only the 1935 contest against the Cubs.

1945 TIGERS

WALTER W. WILSON

Six-foot, four-inch, pitcher, came to the club from Buffalo, where he won 18 and lost 14. Entered baseball in 1939 as member of Concord, N. C. club. Was with Wilmington and Hagerstown. Received honorable discharge from army before going to Buffalo. Lives in Glenn, Ga.

THOMAS D. BRIDGES

One of the most popular players ever to appear in a Detroit uniform, Bridges returned to the club and a royal welcome a few days before Labor Day, after having been in the army for two years. He celebrated the Holiday with a victory in a double-header. Tommy joined the club in 1931, and is appearing in his fourth World Series. A great curve-ball pitcher, he holds several records and was chosen for six All-Star lineups. Though of slight build, he has won 193 games in the A. L. His home is in Detroit.

ARTHUR J. HOUTTEMAN

Youthful member of the pitching staff, Houtteman showed great promise in local prep and American Legion circles in 1944. He has alternated this season between pitching assignments for Buffalo and relief work for the Tigers. He is a resident of Detroit.

JAMES TOBIN

Obtained from the Boston Braves, in August, after seven other American League clubs had waived on him, Tobin has confounded the opposition with his "butterfly" pitching and his long-ball hitting. Twice before crowds of more than 50,000, in Briggs Stadium, this season, he has responded with telling homers into the stands. He was with Oakland and Pittsburg between '35 and '39. Traded to Boston, he remained there until purchased by the Tigers.

GEORGE JASPER CASTER

Pitcher. Like Jim Tobin, a late arrival, this season, Caster was obtained from the Browns in time to do some effective relief pitching. After playing on the coast, in the late twenties, he was with the Athletics until 1940, when he was claimed for the waiver price by the Browns. His home is in Long Beach, Cal.

18 Overmir,
15 Mueller,
10 Bridges, P
P ...ce, P

WALTER W. PIERCE

Youthful southpaw. A product of the Detroit sandlots who became a Tiger late in 1944, after distinguishing himself in the All-American Boys' game in New York. A likely prospect, he has spent most of this season with Buffalo, where he won five and lost seven. His home is Highland Park, Michigan.

ARTHUR MILLS

Coach. Entered baseball with Pittsfield in 1924. Was also with Boston Nationals. At the start of the 1944 season, he succeeded Charlie Gehringer as first base coach.

VIRGIL (FIRE) TRUCKS

Fast ball pitcher. Granted a medical discharge from the Navy in late September, after two years service, had a record of 16 won and 10 lost, for the Tigers in 1943. In 1941, pitching for Montreal, he lost a no-hit game. Pitching for Great Lakes a year ago, he performed brilliantly, and only recently struck out 17 batters in a game at Norman, Okla. Trucks came to the club via Beaumont in 1941.

1945 TIGERS

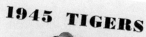

FRANK OVERMIRE

Southpaw. Is a Michigan product, five feet, seven inches in height, who came to the Tigers in 1943, after having pitched for Muskegon, in the Michigan State league. Last year he won 11 and lost 11. While with Beaumont, he struck out 58 batters in 204 innings. He attended Western Teachers College, at Kalamazoo, and makes his home in Grand Rapids.

ROGER CRAMER

Center fielder, who joined the club in 1942, in a player trade with Washington, has a throwing arm highly respected in American League circles. Although 39, he is an exceptional ground coverer, a crafty judge of fly balls and a dangerous long-distance hitter. An A. L. veteran, he contributed greatly to the winning of the 1945 pennant. His home is in Manahawkin, N. J.

EDWARD BOROM

Infielder, came to the Tigers in 1944, after receiving an honorable discharge from the Army. He began his career in baseball in 1936 and played with the Indianapolis club. Was with Buffalo in 1944 and part of 1945 season. He has furnished satisfactory relief for Eddie Mayo at second base. His home is in Wichita, Kans.

JAMES P. OUTLAW

Was the Tigers regular left fielder before Greenberg's return in July. Has since relieved in the outfield and at third base. One of the club's top hitters and a splendid fielder. Jimmy was once a member of the Boston Nationals and was with Buffalo for several seasons. Played spectacularly in the crucial, late season series with the Senators. He is a resident of Alexander City, Ala.

ROY CULLENBINE

Right fielder, a switch hitter, one of the club's leaders in home runs and runs batted in, this season. Roy returned to Detroit in 1945, in a player trade with Cleveland. Came up originally in 1938, via Beaumont and Toledo. Signed with Brooklyn for a reported bonus of $25,000, when declared a free agent by Judge Landis, in 1940.

JOHN J. McHALE

Recently brought up from Buffalo, Johnny was born in Detroit and makes his home here. Attended Notre Dame. Was with Muskegon club in 1941 and later with Beaumont. Received an honorable discharge from Navy's V-12 program and was sent to Buffalo where in 91 games, this season, he had 21 homers and drove in 71 runs with an average of .313.

LESLIE MUELLER

Won fame in the One-to-One thriller in Philadelphia, July 21, of this season, when he pitched nineteen and two-thirds innings of twenty-four inning game. In doing so, he came within one-third inning of tying the Tiger record for long distance pitching set by George Uhle in 1929. Like Trout, Mueller wears spectacles while on the mound. He won 18 games for Buffalo in 1940. He entered the army in 1942 and received an honorable discharge. He resides in Belleville, Ill.

EDWARD MIERKOWICZ

Outfielder, hit 22 homers and had an average of .304 in 131 games for Buffalo, this year, before being recalled by the Tigers in late August. Ten days later he was sent into the outfield, when Greenberg retired because of injuries and hit a double in a game with Boston which drove in the winning run.

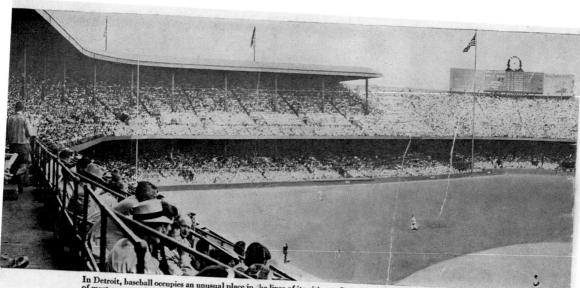

In Detroit, baseball occupies an unusual place in the lives of its citizens. It is the subject of most conversations. Support of the club is generous and loyal in victory or adversity.

In 1944 Detroit led the cities of both lea exceeded last year's figure by nearly 350,0

CHICAGO		1	2	3	4	5	6	7	8	9	10	11	R	H	E
6 Hack	Third Base														
20 Johnson	Second Base														
47 Lowrey	Left Field														
44 Cavaretta	First Base														
48 Pafko	Center Field														
43 Nicholson	Right Field														
11 Livingston 10 Gillispie	Catcher														
21 Merullo	Short Stop														
	Pitcher														

UNIFORM NUMBERS

6 Hack, IF	12 Williams, C	23 Hughes, IF	31	
7 Becker, IF	13 Passeau, P	25 Bifhorn, P	33	
8 Rice, C	20 D. Johnson, IF	26 Borowy, P	34	
10 Gillespie, C	21 Merullo, IF	27 Signer, P		
11 Livingston, C	22 Schuster, IF	30 Derringer, P	36 Warneke, P	

7 Erickson, P	42 R. Johnson, Ch	48 Pafko, OF
Starr, P	43 Nicholson, OF	49 Secory, OF
Prim, P	44 Cavaretta, IF	52 Smith, Coach
Grimm, Mgr.	45 Sauer, OF	53 Block, IF
41 Stock, Coach	47 Lowrey, OF	

CUB BATTING AVERAGES

	G	AB	R	H	RBI	HR	Pct.		G	AB	R	H	RBI	HR	Pct.
Starr	12	3	1	2	1	0	.667	Prim	39	49	4	13	1	0	.265
Otero	12	22	1	9	5	0	.409	Livingston	66	210	17	54	23	2	.257
Cavaretta	123	464	91	163	89	5	.351	Sauer	45	87	8	22	11	2	.253
Hack	144	571	104	185	39	2	.324	Nicholson	143	531	78	131	88	13	.247
Johnson	133	540	90	164	54	2	.304	Rice	31	98	11	23	5	0	.235
Pafko	136	501	61	151	101	11	.301	Merullo	114	381	38	89	36	2	.234
Becker	66	132	25	39	26	2	.295	Hughes	62	201	30	47	8	0	.234
Gillespie	70	153	9	45	23	2	.294	Chipman	22	15	1	3	1	0	.200
Lowrey	136	493	66	140	83	6	.284	Schuster	42	42	8	8	2	0	.190
Williams	54	96	15	27	5	2	.281	Secory	31	50	4	9	3	0	.180

Figures are approximate, being those available at Press Time.

UMPIRES—William Summers, A.L., Art Passarella,
Charles Berry, A.L.
OFFICAL SCORERS—Martin J. Haley, St. Lou
Edward Burns, Chicago Trib

GROUN

Foul poles are outside of playing field.

A batted ball striking facing or any part of upper stands on fair territory and bounding back on field: HOME RUN.

Ball striking flag pole above the base and bounding into stands: HOME RUN.

Ball striking BASE of flag pole in center field and bounding into stands: TWO BASES.

Ball striking foul line in left or right field on or below black marker and bounding into stands in foul territory: TWO BASES.

A packed stadium is a common sight. The view on these pages was taken on Labor Day, 1945, by Wally Steiger of the Detroit Free Press photographic staff.

ues in paid attendance. This year the attendance
) and set an all-time high for the game in this city.

DETROIT		1	2	3	4	5	6	7	8	9	10	11	R	H	E
7 Hoover, 28 Webb	Short Stop														
3 Mayo, 30 Borom	Second Base														
8 Cramer	Center Field														
5 Greenberg	Left Field														
6 Cullenbine	Right Field														
4 York	First Base														
22 Maier, 27 Outlaw	Third Base														
9 Richards, 1 Swift	Catcher														
	Pitcher														

17 Eaton, P   23 Miller, C   01 Mills, Ch
21 Houiteman, P   29 Kerns, C   32 O'Neill, Mgr.
25 Caster, P   2 Mierkowicz, OF
14 Tobin, P   12 McHale, OF
35 Trucks, P   26 Hostetler, OF

UNIFORM NUMBERS

7 Hoover, SS   5 Greenberg, LF   9 Richards, C   18 Overmire, P
28 Webb, SS   6 Cullenbine, RF   1 Swift, C   15 Mueller, P
3 Mayo, 2B   4 York, 1B   19 Benton, P   10 Bridges, P
30 Borom, 2B   22 Maier, 3B   16 Newhouser, P   20 Pierce, P
8 Cramer, CF   27 Outlaw, 3B   11 Trout, P   24 Wilson, P

.L., Louis Jorda, N.L., John Coulan, N.L.—Alternates:
Lee Ballanfant, N.L.
s Globe-Democrat., H. G. Salsinger, Detroit News,
ne, Fred Leib, Sporting News

RULES

Ball going through or sticking in screen on fair ground: TWO BASES.

A pitched ball sticking or remaining on back stop screen: ONE BASE.

A thrown ball: TWO BASES.

Photographers' dugout is part of home players' bench.

With no spectators in the field boxes in left and right field, the bull pen benches will be in their proper places. Whenever it becomes necessary to place spectators in these boxes, the bull pen benches will not be occupied and pitchers will warm up under the grandstand in center field.

TIGER BATTING AVERAGES

	G	AB	R	H	RBI	HR	Pct.		G	AB	R	H	RBI	HR	Pct.
Miller	3	4	0	3	0	0	.750	Swift	93	274	18	64	23		0.234
McHale	4	5	0	2	2	0	.400	Newhouser	38	105	6	26	17		0.234
Greenberg	75	258	43	80	53	11	.307	Mierkowicz	4	10	0	2	2		0.222
Mayo	131	489	71	142	53	10	.291	Webb	114	391	41	75	21		0.194
Outlaw	129	435	56	117	34		0.274	Mueller	24	43	5	8	3		0.179
Cullenbine	148	527	82	145	86	17	.274	Caster	28	17	2	3	1		0.176
Borom	52	131	18	35	9		0.269	Hostetler	42	44	3	7	2		0.163
York	151	578	69	155	88	18	.268	Overmire	32	56	5	8	3		0.145
Eaton	17	30	2	8	9		2 .266	Tobin	57	102	11	14	12	5	.137
Maier	131	488	58	129	34		1 .264	Benton	28	63	3	7	6		0.111
Hoover	73	225	33	57	17		1 .257	Wilson	25	20	1	1	0		0.044
Trout	39	102	11	26	12		2 .255	Bridges	2	1	0	0	0		0.000
Richards	80	225	26	57	26		3 .251	Houtteman	11	5	0	0	0		0.000
Cramer	138	528	59	143	55		6 .243	Kerns	1	1	0	0	0		0.000

Figures are approximate, being those available at Press Time.

CHICAGO
BASEBALL
CLUB
OFFICERS

JAMES T. GALLAGHER
*Vice-President—
Business Manager*

PHILLIP K. WRIGLEY
President

MARGARET DONAHUE
Secretary

THIS is the third time Grimm has led the Cubs in a World Series, the clubs of 1932 and 1935 being the previous contenders. The Chicago leader, who was a star performer at first base in his playing days and has a lifetime batting average of .291, began his baseball career as a pitcher and outfielder nearly thirty years ago.

He joined the Chicago club in 1929 after six years with Pittsburgh and remained as player or pilot until the summer of 1938. In 1941 he returned as coach but left to become the manager of the Milwaukee Brewers. He led the latter club into a championship in 1943 and was called back to be the boss of the Cubs after the start of the 1944 season.

CHARLES J. GRIMM
Manager

1945 CHICAGO CUBS

CHICAGO PITCHING STAFF

Left to right—DERRINGER, ERICKSON, WARNEKE, WYSE, VANDENBERG, CHIPMAN, PRIM, STARR, PASSEAU, SIGNOR, BOROWY.

PHILIP CAVARRETTA

First baseman. Leading batsman in National League this season. A brilliant fielder, one of three present members of Chicago club who were in lineup against Tigers in 1935. Was then only 18. Is appearing in third post-season Series. Hit .462 in World Series of 1938. Chosen for All-Star lineup in 1944. Lives in Evanston, Ill.

STANLEY HACK

Third baseman. Will be remembered by Tiger fans as Chicago player who tripled with no one out, in ninth inning, of sixth and deciding game, in 1935 Series. Was left on third by Bridges' fine pitching. Came to Cubs in 1932 and has appeared in four World Series clashes and as many All-Star games. A capable performer around the hot corner. Lives in Sacramento, Cal.

LEONARD MERULLO

Shortstop. A Cub since 1941. Played with Moline, Tulsa, Los Angeles and Toronto. A splendid defensive player who is making his first appearance in post-season games. Lives in East Boston, Mass.

PHOTOS COURTESY CHICAGO DAILY NEWS

1945 CHICAGO CUBS

WILLIAM NICHOLSON

Right fielder. Hit 33 homers and batted in 122 runs in 1944 to become National League's leading slugger. Also led League players in home runs, in 1943. A member of the club since 1939, he began his career with Oklahoma City in 1936. Has appeared in four All-Star games. Had no small part in club's success this year. Resides in Chestertown, Md.

HENRY WYSE

Pitcher, chalked up his twentieth victory for the Cubs in mid-September. Has been a member of the club since 1942. Previously he had been with Moline and Tulsa, starting his career with the former in 1940. Hank had the distinction this summer of stopping the Braves' Tommy Holmes after the latter had set a modern National League record for hits in 37 consecutive games. His home is in Tulsa, Okla.

HENRY BOROWY

Until July of this season, Borowy was a member of the Yankees' pitching staff. Purchased by the Cubs for a reported price of $100,000, he aided greatly in keeping the club out in front down the stretch. A graduate of Fordham University, where he pitched brilliantly, he began his professional career with Newark, Yankee farm club. He joined the Yankees in 1942 and up to his departure for Chicago had a record of 56 victories and 30 defeats. His home is in Bloomfield, N. J.

CHICAGO CATCHING STAFF
*Left to right—*WILLIAMS, LIVINGSTON, RICE, GILLESPIE.

PHOTOS COURTESY CHICAGO DAILY NEWS

1945 CHICAGO CUBS

CHICAGO INFIELDERS

Left to right—HUGHES, CAVARRETTA, HACK, BECKER, SCHUSTER, JOHNSON, MERULLO.

CLAUDE PASSEAU

Obtained in a trade from the Phillies in 1939, Passeau is next to Hank Wyse on the Cub's staff, in games won. He entered organized baseball in 1932 with the Decatur, Three-Eye club, and was with eight other organizations before going to the Philadelphia Nationals in 1936. In no season, since joining the Cubs, has he won fewer than 14 games. Claude has appeared in three All-Star games but this is his first time in a World Series line-up. He resides in Lucedale, Miss.

ANDREW PAFKO

Center fielder. Feared by National League clubs as Doc Cramer is in American League, for his throwing ability. An accomplished fielder and a dangerous hitter who joined the Cubs late in 1943. Was previously a member of Los Angeles club. Lives in Boyceville, Wisc.

THOMPSON (MICKEY) LIVINGSTON

Catcher. Received a medical discharge from the army and joined the Cubs late in 1944. He first came to the club in a trade with the Phillies for Bill Lee. Given a tryout by the Cardinals in 1935, Livingston was with Washington before going to Philadelphia. While in service, he hit four home runs on one afternoon for Camp Atterbury, 106th Infantry Nine. His home is in Newberry, S. C.

PHOTOS COURTESY CHICAGO DAILY NEWS

1945 CHICAGO CUBS

ROY HUGHES

Infielder. Played most of 1944 season at shortstop position where he performed acceptably. Had second call at position this year because of Merullo's fine play. Was previously with Indians, Browns and Phillies. Lives in Los Angeles, Cal.

RAY PRIM

Left-hander, got off to a late start but as the season progressed rendered effective assistance to the National League champions. One of the older members of the Chicago club, Prim won 22 games for Los Angeles in 1944. He has played with the Phillies, Senators and Minneapolis. His home is in Pico, Cal.

HARRY (PEANUTS) LOWREY

Left fielder. Has played both left and center this season. Was released from service in 1944. Joined Cubs, in 1942, following period with Moline, Tulsa and Los Angeles. Has been a mighty factor in surge of Cubs to first place. Makes his home in Los Angeles, Cal.

DONALD JOHNSON

Second baseman. Spent ten years in minors before signing with Chicago in 1944. Chosen for All-Star lineup of that year. Resides in Laguna Beach, Cal.

CHICAGO OUTFIELDERS
Left to right—NICHOLSON, SECORY, PAFKO, LOWREY, SAUER.

PHOTOS COURTESY CHICAGO DAILY NEWS

DETROIT'S RECORD IN PREVIOUS WORLD SERIES

SINCE the World Series games have been conducted under National Commission or Advisory Council auspices, Detroit has been the American League contestant seven times, beginning with 1907.

In that year, led by the peppery Hughie Jennings, the Detroit club failed to win a game after tying the first one with the Chicago Cubs, led by Frank L. Chance. In contrast to the huge crowds in attendance at the present Series, it is interesting to observe that the first game in Detroit, that year, attracted only 7,370 fans, while the second one drew an over-flow crowd in Bennett Park, on the site of the present stadium, consisting of 11,306 persons.

The year 1908 brought the same teams together in combat, led by the same colorful men. A fellow by the name of Cobb got seven hits in the Series but the result was not much more pleasing to local fans than the 1907 meeting, for Detroit won but one of the five games played.

It took seven games to decide the 1909 Series, in which Detroit again was a contestant against the Pittsburgh club, of the National league, led by Fred Clark. Each team had in its lineup, the premier batter in its League, if not two of the greatest players of all time—Tyrus Raymond Cobb and the great John P. "Honus" Wagner, the Pirate shortstop. The Series was a see-saw affair with "Babe" Adams, the youthful pitcher for Pittsburgh, getting credit for three of his club's four victories.

It was not until 1934, when Detroit purchased Mickey Cochrane, star catcher, from the Athletics, for $100,000, for its manager, that the Tigers were able to get into another championship battle. Cochrane's fiery leadership had enabled virtually the same club which had finished fifth the year before, to land on top in 1934.

In the play-off series with the St. Louis Cardinals, the Dean brothers, "Dizzy" and "Daffy", proved too much for the American League club. The count stood three to two in favor of the Tigers, after five games had been played, but St. Louis won the next two and the Deans, who had appeared in five of the games, were credited with victories in four. Mickey Cochrane and Frankie Frisch, were the rival leaders.

The 1935 Series, like the preceding one, was played in Navin Field but this time it was the Chicago club, led by Charlie Grimm, which opposed the Tigers. It marked Detroit's only victory to date in the contests between the rival leagues.

It was in this Series that Tommy Bridges endeared himself to Tiger fans, with his heroic performance in the 9th inning of the sixth game, played on October 7th, in Briggs Stadium. With the Series standing three to two, in Detroit's favor and the score tied at 3 to 3, there was a despondent groan as Hack, Cub third-sacker, and first man up, hit a triple over Walker's head in center. With no one out, at least one Chicago run seemed inevitable.

It was then that Bridges delivered one of the finest exhibitions of pitching under pressure, ever seen at Michigan and Trumbull Avenues. Leaving Hack waiting impatiently on third, with the needed run, he fanned Jurges, forced French to bounce an easy ball to the pitcher's box and then tossed him out at first. He finished gloriously by retiring the side when Galan, head of the batting list, flied to Goslin.

Detroit's first World Championship, as a member of the American League, was won in the Tiger half of the ninth, when with one down, Mickey Cochrane got his third hit of the day, a single off Herman's glove. He reached second when Gehringer grounded to Cavarretta, at first.

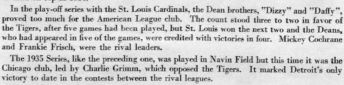

No Tiger favorite ever received a warmer welcome than did "Goose" Goslin as he strolled from the dugout to the plate. A "money hitter", the "Goose" acknowledged the greeting with a single to right, which sent Mickey Cochrane home with the needed run, gave the Tigers the Series honors and this city of a million and a half frenzied baseball addicts, such a night as it will never forget.

It is interesting to note that only two players, Bridges and Greenberg, who were members of the 1935 team which battled the Cubs, are members of this year's outfit.

Three of the Chicago players, Warneke, Hack and Cavarretta, who participated in the 1935 contest, are in the lineup for Chicago today.

Del Baker led the Tigers in 1940, in their last World's Series, previous to the present one. This one was the first to be played in the handsome new Briggs Stadium, with the Cincinnati Reds as opponents.

Like the contest of 1909 it went seven games but Detroit had to take second money when the Reds, led by William B. McKechnie, captured four of the seven games.

TURNING BACK THE CLOCK

Some interesting scenes of other World Series encounters in which the Tigers have engaged. The views were taken by William A. Kuenzel, veteran photographer of the Detroit News staff.

A clubhouse scene immediately following the winning of the only World Championship by a Tiger club to date. It shows Mickey Cochrane, Goose Goslin and Tommy Bridges in joyful embrace after the Cubs had been routed in the sixth game of the Series October 7, 1935.

Cochrane, who had made his third hit of the game, in the 9th inning, was advanced to second when Gehringer grounded to Cavarretta. He scored on Goslin's single to right, with the winning run.

In the Cub's half of the same inning, Hack first up tripled but Bridges bore down and left him stranded on third while the next three batters were retired.

This scene, taken in 1907, was not of a World Series game, but it shows the incomparable Tyrus Raymond Cobb, who was setting the baseball world afire, with his spectacular playing, in one of his famous slides. It also reveals the contrast between the facilities afforded Bennett Park fans at that time and those of Briggs Stadium today.

View of the grandstand in old Bennett Park, in 1907, when the Detroit and Chicago clubs met in the first of the four post-season series in which they have engaged. Although the fans in this scene appear to have something to cheer for, the Tigers lost the Series without winning a game. In 1908 when the two teams clashed again, Detroit won but one game out of five played.

The 1934 pennant was the first one which Detroit won in twenty-five years and the old town became quite hysterical. The view above shows a group of fans who sat up all night outside of Navin Field so that they might be in line for the day-of-game tickets in the first encounter with the St. Louis Cardinals.

Charles Gehringer, a Tiger favorite for many years, whose smooth, precision-like performance ranked him as one of the greatest second basemen in the history of the game. He was a participant in the 1934, 1935 and 1940 World Series games in which the Tigers appeared.

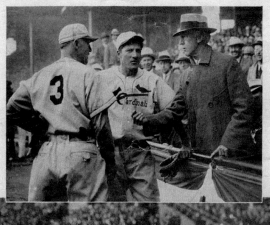

The supreme court of baseball, Commissioner K. M. Landis, handing down a decision from his box in Navin Field, on October 9, 1934, when Ducky Medwick angered the fans by charging Marvin Owen, at third base and was led off the field by an escort of police. The Commissioner explained that he was ordering Medwick out of the game because he feared retaliation by the fans in left field.

View of an incident in one of the games in the hard fought Series of 1909, between the Tigers and Pittsburgh Pirates. The great Hans Wagner has run over from short to put the ball on a Tiger going into third. Matty McIntyre, Tiger outfielder, is shown in the foreground.

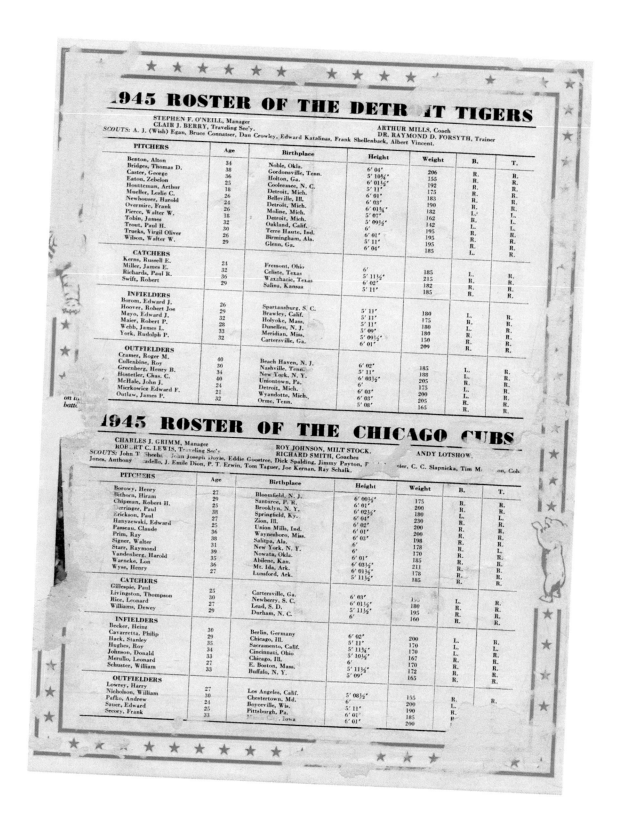

1945 ROSTER OF THE DETROIT TIGERS

STEPHEN F. O'NEILL, Manager
CLAIR J. BERRY, Traveling Sec'y. ARTHUR MILLS, Coach
       DR. RAYMOND D. FORSYTH, Trainer
SCOUTS: A. J. (Wish) Egan, Bruce Connatser, Dan Crowley, Edward Katalinas, Frank Shellenback, Albert Vincent.

PITCHERS	Age	Birthplace	Height	Weight	B.	T.
Benton, Alton	34	Noble, Okla.	6' 04"	206	R.	R.
Bridges, Thomas D.	38	Gordonsville, Tenn.	5' 10¾"	155	R.	R.
Caster, George	36	Holton, Ga.	6' 01½"	192	R.	R.
Eaton, Zebelon	25	Cooleemee, N. C.	5' 11"	175	R.	R.
Houtteman, Arthur	18	Detroit, Mich.	6' 01"	183	R.	R.
Mueller, Leslie C.	26	Belleville, Ill.	6' 03"	190	R.	R.
Newhouser, Harold	24	Detroit, Mich.	6' 01¾"	182	L.	L.
Overmire, Frank	26	Moline, Mich.	5' 07"	162	R.	L.
Pierce, Walter W.	18	Detroit, Mich.	5' 09½"	142	L.	L.
Tobin, James	32	Oakland, Calif.	6' 01"	195	R.	R.
Trout, Paul H.	30	Terre Haute, Ind.	5' 11"	195	R.	R.
Trucks, Virgil Oliver	26	Birmingham, Ala.	6' 04"	195	R.	L.
Wilson, Walter W.	29	Glenn, Ga.		185		R.
CATCHERS						
Kerns, Russell E.	24	Fremont, Ohio	6'	185	L.	R.
Miller, James E.	32	Celiste, Texas	5' 11½"	215	R.	R.
Richards, Paul R.	36	Waxahacie, Texas	6' 02"	182	R.	R.
Swift, Robert	29	Salina, Kansas	5' 11"	185	R.	R.
INFIELDERS						
Borom, Edward J.	26	Spartansburg, S. C.	5' 11"	180	L.	R.
Hoover, Robert Joe	29	Brawley, Calif.	5' 11"	175	R.	R.
Mayo, Edward J.	32	Holyoke, Mass.	5' 11"	180	L.	R.
Maier, Robert P.	28	Dunellen, N. J.	5' 09"	180	R.	R.
Webb, James L.	33	Meridian, Miss.	5' 09½"	150	R.	R.
York, Rudolph P.	32	Cartersville, Ga.	6' 01"	209	R.	R.
OUTFIELDERS						
Cramer, Roger M.	40	Beach Haven, N. J.	6' 02"	185	L.	R.
Cullenbine, Roy	30	Nashville, Tenn.	5' 11"	188	R.	R.
Greenberg, Henry B.	34	New York, N. Y.	6' 03½"	205	R.	R.
Hostetler, Chas. C.	40	Uniontown, Pa.	6'	175	L.	R.
McHale, John J.	24	Detroit, Mich.	6' 03"	200	L.	R.
Mierkowicz Edward F.	21	Wyandotte, Mich.	6' 03"	205	R.	R.
Outlaw, James P.	32	Orme, Tenn.	5' 08"	165	R.	R.

on the
batt...

1945 ROSTER OF THE CHICAGO CUBS

CHARLES J. GRIMM, Manager
ROBERT C. LEWIS, Traveling Sec'y ROY JOHNSON, MILT STOCK.
      RICHARD SMITH, Coaches ANDY LOTSHOW
SCOUTS: John T. Sheehy, John Joseph Doyle, Eddie Goostree, Dick Spalding, Jimmy Payton, F...
Jones, Anthony Cadello, J. Emile Dion, P. T. Erwin, Tom Taguer, Joe Kernan, Ray Schalk, ...ier, C. C. Slapnicka, Tim M... ...on, Cub...

PITCHERS	Age	Birthplace	Height	Weight	B.	T.
Borowy, Henry	27	Bloomfield, N. J.	6' 00½"	175	R.	R.
Bithorn, Hiram	29	Santurce, P. R.	6' 01"	200	R.	R.
Chipman, Robert H.	25	Brooklyn, N. Y.	6' 02½"	180	L.	L.
Derringer, Paul	38	Springfield, Ky.	6' 04"	230	R.	R.
Erickson, Paul	27	Zion, Ill.	6' 02"	200	R.	R.
Hanyzewski, Edward	25	Union Mills, Ind.	6' 01"	200	R.	R.
Passeau, Claude	36	Waynesboro, Miss.	6' 03"	198	R.	R.
Prim, Ray	38	Salitpa, Ala.	6'	178	R.	R.
Signer, Walter	31	New York, N. Y.	6' 01"	170	R.	L.
Starr, Raymond	39	Nowata, Okla.	6' 03½"	185	R.	R.
Vandenberg, Harold	35	Abilene, Kan.	6' 01½"	211	R.	R.
Warneke, Lon	36	Mt. Ida, Ark.	5' 11½"	178	R.	R.
Wyse, Henry	27	Lunsford, Ark.		185	R.	R.
CATCHERS						
Gillespie, Paul	25	Cartersville, Ga.	6' 03"	195	L.	R.
Livingston, Thompson	30	Newberry, S. C.	6' 01½"	180	R.	R.
Rice, Leonard	27	Lead, S. D.	5' 11½"	195	R.	R.
Williams, Dewey	29	Durham, N. C.	6'	160	R.	R.
INFIELDERS						
Becker, Heinz	30	Berlin, Germany	6' 02"	200	L.	R.
Cavarretta, Philip	29	Chicago, Ill.	5' 11"	170	L.	L.
Hack, Stanley	35	Sacramento, Calif.	5' 11¾"	170	L.	R.
Hughes, Roy	33	Cincinnati, Ohio	5' 10½"	167	R.	R.
Johnson, Donald	27	Chicago, Ill.	6'	170	R.	R.
Merullo, Leonard	33	E. Boston, Mass.	5' 11½"	172	R.	R.
Schuster, William		Buffalo, N. Y.	5' 09"	165	R.	R.
OUTFIELDERS						
Lowrey, Harry	27	Los Angeles, Calif.	5' 08½"	155	R.	R.
Nicholson, William	30	Chestertown, Md.	6'	200	L.	
Pafko, Andrew	24	Boyceville, Wis.	5' 11"	190	R.	
Sauer, Edward	25	Pittsburgh, Pa.	6' 01"	185	R.	
Secory, Frank	33	Mason City, Iowa	6' 01"	200	R.	

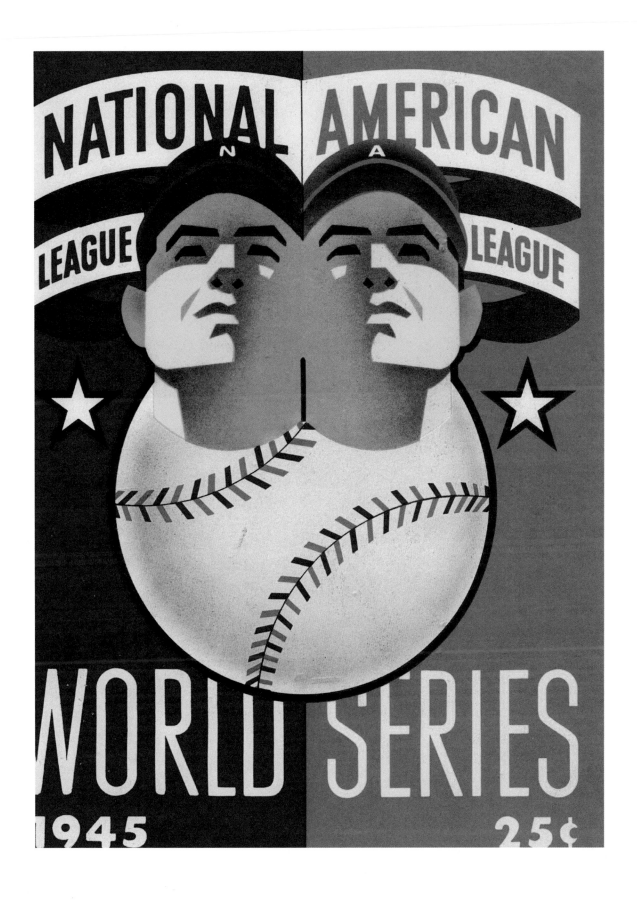

CHICAGO CUBS

CHARLES GRIMM
Manager

ROY JOHNSON
Coach

RICHARD "RED" SMITH
Coach

MILTON STOCK
Coach

ANDY LOTSHAW
Trainer

CHICAGO CUBS

HANK BOROWY
Pitcher

PAUL DERRINGER
Pitcher

RAY PRIM
Pitcher

CLAUDE PASSEAU
Pitcher

HENRY WYSE
Pitcher

HY VANDENBERG
Pitcher

MICKEY LIVINGSTON
Catcher

DEWEY WILLIAMS
Catcher

PAUL GILLESPIE
Catcher

CHICAGO CUBS

STANLEY HACK
Infielder

PHIL CAVARRETTA
Infielder

DON JOHNSON
Infielder

LEONARD MERULLO
Infielder

ANDY PAFKO
Outfielder

HARRY "PEANUTS" LOWREY
Outfielder

BILL NICHOLSON
Outfielder

HEINZ BECKER
Infielder

ROY HUGHES
Infielder

DETROIT TIGERS

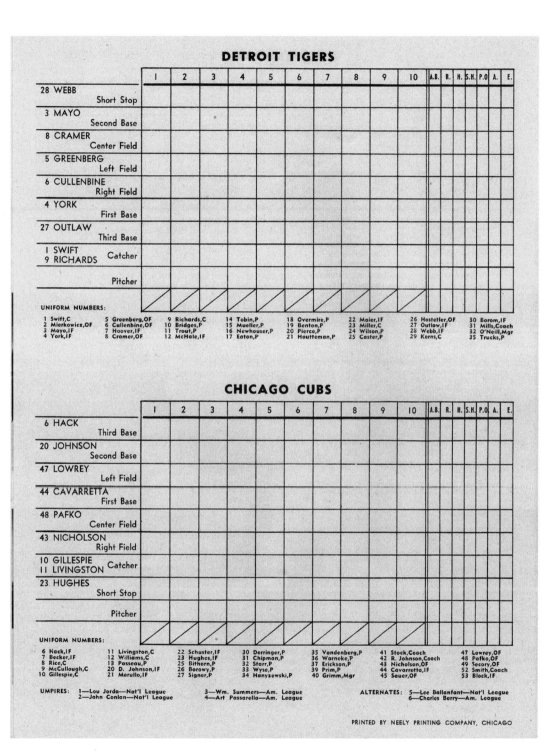

	1	2	3	4	5	6	7	8	9	10	A.B.	R.	H.	S.H.	P.O.	A.	E.
28 WEBB — Short Stop																	
3 MAYO — Second Base																	
8 CRAMER — Center Field																	
5 GREENBERG — Left Field																	
6 CULLENBINE — Right Field																	
4 YORK — First Base																	
27 OUTLAW — Third Base																	
1 SWIFT / 9 RICHARDS — Catcher																	
— Pitcher																	

UNIFORM NUMBERS:

1 Swift,C	5 Greenberg,OF	9 Richards,C	14 Tobin,P	18 Overmire,P	22 Maier,IF	26 Hostetler,OF	30 Borom,IF
2 Mierkowicz,OF	6 Cullenbine,OF	10 Bridges,P	15 Mueller,P	19 Benton,P	23 Miller,C	27 Outlaw,IF	31 Mills,Coach
3 Mayo,IF	7 Hoover,IF	11 Trout,P	16 Newhouser,P	20 Pierce,P	24 Wilson,P	28 Webb,IF	32 O'Neill,Mgr
4 York,IF	8 Cramer,OF	12 McHale,IF	17 Eaton,P	21 Houtteman,P	25 Caster,P	29 Kerns,C	35 Trucks,P

CHICAGO CUBS

	1	2	3	4	5	6	7	8	9	10	A.B.	R.	H.	S.H.	P.O.	A.	E.
6 HACK — Third Base																	
20 JOHNSON — Second Base																	
47 LOWREY — Left Field																	
44 CAVARRETTA — First Base																	
48 PAFKO — Center Field																	
43 NICHOLSON — Right Field																	
10 GILLESPIE / 11 LIVINGSTON — Catcher																	
23 HUGHES — Short Stop																	
— Pitcher																	

UNIFORM NUMBERS:

6 Hack,IF	11 Livingston,C	22 Schuster,IF	30 Derringer,P	35 Vandenberg,P	41 Stock,Coach	47 Lowrey,OF
7 Becker,IF	12 Williams,C	23 Hughes,IF	31 Chipman,P	36 Warneke,P	42 R. Johnson,Coach	48 Pafko,OF
8 Rice,C	13 Passeau,P	25 Bithorn,P	32 Starr,P	37 Erickson,P	43 Nicholson,OF	49 Secory,OF
9 McCullough,C	20 D. Johnson,IF	26 Borowy,P	33 Wyse,P	39 Prim,P	44 Cavarretta,IF	52 Smith,Coach
10 Gillespie,C	21 Merullo,IF	27 Signer,P	34 Hanyzewski,P	40 Grimm,Mgr	45 Sauer,OF	53 Block,IF

UMPIRES: 1—Lou Jorda—Nat'l League 3—Wm. Summers—Am. League **ALTERNATES:** 5—Lee Ballanfant—Nat'l League
2—John Conlan—Nat'l League 4—Art Passarella—Am. League 6—Charles Berry—Am. League

PRINTED BY NEELY PRINTING COMPANY, CHICAGO

BATTING AVERAGES

DETROIT PLAYERS	G	AB	R	H	TB	2B	3B	HR	SH	SB	RBI	PCT
James Miller, c	2	4	0	3	3	0	0	0	1	0	1	.750
Henry Greenberg, of	78	272	46	84	147	18	3	13	0	3	60	.309
Eddie Mayo, 2b	134	501	71	143	201	22	3	10	13	7	51	.285
Roger Cramer, of	141	542	62	149	203	20	8	6	15	3	59	.275
Eddie Borom, if	55	128	19	35	39	4	0	0	7	4	9	.273
Roy Cullenbine, of	154	536	84	146	238	28	5	18	5	2	92	.272
James, Outlaw, of	132	445	57	121	147	16	5	0	3	6	33	.272
Rudy York, 1b	155	595	71	157	246	25	5	18	0	5	89	.264
Robert Maier, 3b	132	486	58	128	170	25	7	1	5	7	34	.263
Harold Newhouser, p	40	109	8	28	35	5	1	0	8	0	12	.257
Paul Richards, c	83	234	26	59	82	12	1	3	2	4	30	.252
Zeb Eaton, p	26	32	2	8	14	0	0	2	0	0	10	.250
Joe Hoover, ss	73	217	32	54	77	10	5	1	6	6	17	.249
Paul Trout, p	42	101	11	25	38	3	2	2	0	1	12	.248
Robert Swift, c	95	279	19	65	70	5	0	0	5	1	22	.233
George Caster, p	32	14	0	3	3	0	0	0	2	0	1	.214
Jim Webb, ss	118	407	43	81	95	10	1	0	12	8	21	.199
Frank Overmire, p	31	54	5	10	14	2	1	0	6	0	3	.185
Les Mueller, p	26	44	5	8	14	3	0	1	1	0	4	.182
Charles Hostetler, of	42	44	8	7	10	3	0	0	0	0	2	.159
John McHale, if	19	14	0	2	2	0	0	0	0	0	1	.143
Ed Mierkowicz, of	10	15	0	2	4	2	0	0	0	0	2	.133
Jim Tobin, p	17	25	2	3	9	0	0	2	1	0	5	.120
Alton Benton, p	31	63	2	4	6	2	0	0	8	0	3	.063
Walter Wilson, p	25	20	1	1	1	0	0	0	2	0	0	.050
Arthur Houtteman, p	13	5	0	0	0	0	0	0	0	0	0	.000
Virgil Trucks, p	1	2	1	0	0	0	0	0	0	0	0	.000
Walter Pierce, p	5	2	0	0	0	0	0	0	0	0	0	.000
Thomas Bridges, p	4	3	0	0	0	0	0	0	0	0	0	.000

CUB PLAYERS	G	AB	R	H	TB	2B	3B	HR	SH	SB	RBI	PCT
Ray Starr, p	13	3	1	2	3	1	0	0	1	0	1	.667
Phil Cavarretta, 1b	132	498	94	177	248	34	11	5	3	7	95	.355
Stanley Hack, 3b	149	591	111	192	242	30	7	2	5	12	42	.325
Don Johnson, 2b	138	559	94	168	201	23	2	2	21	9	56	.301
Andrew Pafko, of	144	533	64	159	241	22	12	12	21	6	111	.298
Paul Gillespie, c	75	163	12	47	60	7	0	2	0	2	25	.288
Heinz Becker, 1b	67	133	25	38	54	6	2	2	0	0	27	.286
Harry Lowrey, of	145	523	71	148	205	22	7	7	11	10	90	.283
Dewey Williams, c	59	100	16	28	40	2	2	2	2	0	5	.280
Roy Hughes, inf	69	222	33	58	67	7	1	0	8	6	8	.261
Edward Sauer, of	49	93	8	24	36	4	1	2	3	2	11	.258
Ray Prim, p	42	51	4	13	13	0	0	0	6	0	1	.255
Thompson Livingston, c	71	224	19	56	71	4	2	2	6	2	23	.250
Bill Nicholson, of	151	559	82	136	209	26	4	13	3	4	89	.243
Len Merullo, ss	121	396	40	94	118	18	0	2	6	9	37	.237
Len Rice, c	32	99	11	23	26	3	0	0	3	2	5	.232
Paul Derringer, p	35	73	3	15	18	3	0	0	9	0	6	.200
William Schuster, if	44	47	8	9	13	2	1	0	2	2	2	.191
Claude Passeau, p	34	91	10	17	25	2	0	2	3	0	9	.187
Robert Chipman, p	25	17	1	3	4	1	0	0	3	0	2	.176
Henry Borowy, p	15	41	5	7	8	1	0	0	7	0	0	.171
Henry Wyse, p	38	101	7	17	19	2	0	0	8	0	7	.168
Frank Secory, of	34	58	4	9	10	1	0	0	3	0	3	.155
Paul Erickson, p	28	33	2	5	7	2	0	0	4	0	0	.152
Cy Block, if	2	7	1	1	1	0	0	0	0	0	1	.143
Harold Vandenberg, p	30	32	4	4	6	0	1	0	1	0	2	.125
Walter Signer, p	6	1	0	0	0	0	0	0	0	0	0	.000
Lon Warneke, p	9	2	1	0	0	0	0	0	0	0	0	.000
Edward Hanyzewski, p	2	1	0	0	0	0	0	0	0	0	0	.000

PITCHING RECORDS

DETROIT	G	W	L	PCT.
Bridges, Thomas D.	4	1	0	1.000
Newhouser, Harold	40	25	9	.735
Benton, Alton B.	31	13	8	.619
Caster, George J.	32	6	3	.667
Eaton, Zebulon V.	17	4	2	.667
Trout, Paul	41	18	15	.545
Overmire, Frank	31	9	9	.500
Tobin, James	14	4	5	.444
Mueller, Leslie	26	6	8	.429
Wilson, Walter	24	1	3	.250
Houtteman, Arthur	13	0	2	.000
Pierce, Walter W.	5	0	0	.000
Trucks, Virgil	1	0	0	.000

CHICAGO	G	W	L	PCT.
Borowy, Henry	15	11	2	.846
Wyse, Henry	38	22	10	.688
Vandenberg, Harold	30	7	3	.700
Passeau, Claude	34	17	9	.654
Erickson, Paul	28	7	4	.636
Prim, Ray	33	13	8	.619
Derringer, Paul	35	16	11	.593
Chipman, Robert	25	4	5	.444
Starr, Ray	13	1	2	.333
Warneke, Lon	9	0	1	.000
Hanyzewski, Edward	2	0	0	.000
Signer, Walter	6	0	0	.000

STEPHEN O'NEILL
Manager

ARTHUR MILLS
Coach

HANK GREENBERG
Infielder

THOMAS BRIDGES
Pitcher

DETROIT TIGERS

HAROLD NEWHOUSER
Pitcher

JAMES TOBIN
Pitcher

PAUL H. TROUT
Pitcher

ARTHUR HOUTTEMAN
Pitcher

WALTER W. PIERCE
Pitcher

ZEB V. EATON
Pitcher

WALTER WILSON
Pitcher

LESLIE MUELLER
Pitcher

GEORGE CASTER
Pitcher

CUBS' ROLL OF HONOR

IN this year of Victory, the Chicago Cubs pay tribute to the 347 members of the organization who served in their country's uniform—and most especially to these four who made the supreme sacrifice of their lives:

★ ROMAN WANTUCK, Los Angeles ★ LOUIS ELKO, Los Angeles ★ ALAN GRANT, Portsmouth
★ WILLIAM NIEMEYER, Elizabethton

CUB PLAYERS

Dale Alderson	*Pete Elko	*Paul Gillespie	Russell Meers	Mizell Platt	Robert Sturgeon
*Hiram Bithorn	Marvin Felderman	Alban Glossop	*Russell Meyer	Marvin Rickert	Eddie Waitkus
*Seymour Block	Leslie Fleming	Emil Kush	John MacPartland	Robert Scheffing	Ben Warren
Dominic Dallessandro	Cecil Garriott	*Mickey Livingston	Clyde McCullough	John Schmitz	
	Charles Gilbert	*Harry Lowrey	Vern Olsen	Lou Stringer	

CUB EMPLOYES

Arthur Ades	*Herman Cohen	Yosh Kawano	Gordon McKavanagh	*Oscar Roettger	Ray Warner
*Al Balder	*Harry Gonciar	James Ketzer	*Wm. McKavanagh	*Mitchell Seidenberg	*Chester Wojcik
Roy Bogren	Phillip Grossman	John LaPorta	Chuck Meyers	*Phillip Tomasevich	Walter Wojcik
*James Caputo	Abe Kandel	*Francis J. McFarland	Allan Moss	Robert Virgo	*Emmett Workman

PLAYERS ON CUB MINOR LEAGUE AFFILIATES

Clifford Aberson	William R. Daniels	Everett Johnson	Garman Mallory	Ted Pawelik	Roy Smalley, Jr.
Robert Adams	Pete Deem	George W.	William Manning	Albert Perillard	Francis Smith
Robert Anderson	Robert	Johnson	Roy Marion	Robert Peterson	John J. Smith
Howard Anman	Delameilleure	Sidney Johnson	Fred Marsh	Roy Peterson	Wm. Robert Smith
Lee Anthony	Joe Dickinson	Thomas Johnson	Ambrose Martell	*Russell Peterson	Robert Snyder
*Richard Aylward	Don Dietz	Gene Joselane	Perry Martin	Jodie Phipps	Bruno Somenzi
Ernest Baber	A. J. Dobernic	Vernon Kailey	*Stuart Martin	John Pileckas	Ray Sowins
Joseph Baker	Maurice Donovan	Robert Kapinus	Warren Martin	Gerald Poltrock	Stanley
Oren Baker	Fred Dreyer	Jerry Katherman	Adolph Matulis	M. M. Pontarelli	Stempkowski
Walter Balash	Willie Duke	Donald Kauppi	John P. Matyas, Jr.	Harry Potts	Charles Stock, Jr.
Roman Bartkowski	Charles Etherton	Edmund Keehan	Wallace Mehrens	Coleman Powell	Harvey Storey
Oliver Bass	*Charles Fitzgerald	Edward Kelley	Augustine Messuri	Louis Prempas	William Stratton
Lou Bekeza	Billy Flaugher	Richard Kemper	Robert Meyers	Jim Prince	Joe Stringfellow
Leonard Berry	Glenn Flory	Don Kepler	Guy Miller	George Purcell	Andrew Swota
Clair Bertram	James Forbes, Jr.	Robert Kezely	Eugene Mills	Wellington Quinn	Lewis Tabor
Kinnon Black	Leon Foulk	Anton Kindl	Martin Minogue	Ray Radovich	Allen Tacha
Glen Blackwood	Raymond French	James King	Melvin Mode	Paul Rankin	Vito Tamulis
Joe Blake	Harry Gallatin, Jr.	Albert Kinsey	Earl Moore	Joe Raso	John Taylor
Robert Blondi	Clayton Gardner	Bill Kleist	John Moore	Billy Rautsaw	Foster Thornton
Howard Boles	George Gatto	Edward Kosan	Charles Morrison	Stencel Reno	Wayne Timm
Woodrow Bottoms	Paul Gehrman	Walter Kowalski	Joe Moss	Herbert Rhodes	Frank Totaro
J. T. Boynton	Robert L. George	Paul Kral	Joe L. Murff	William Richards	Albert Toth
*William C. Brenner	Bill Gibson	*Albert Kreitner	Doyle Murnahan	Carl E. Ricks	Steve Tramback
*Orbie Brewer	Eugene Goforth	Robert Kuhlman	Eddie Murphy	Joel Ridings	Julian Tubb
Stanley Brinkerhoff	Harold Gold	George Kwasniewski	Michael Nacey	Leonard Riley	Leo Twardy
Leland Brown	Max Goldsmith	Cliff Lacy	Thomas Nagle	Raymond	Sindo Valle
Donald Bryant	Reid Gowan	Harry Land	Hilliard Nance	Robichaud	Eugene Vaughan
Ed Bucz	Eugene Granberg	Arthur E. Larsen	Harold Nerino	Harold Robinson	James Vaughn
Nelson Burbrink	Alan Grant	Harlan Larsen	Frank Nezgoda	Walter Robitski	Paul Varner
F. H. Burgess	Richard Groberg	Lavern Lather	William Niemeyer	Dick Ronovsky	Paul Vickery
Robert Burtis	Robert Grueter	Costa Lazarou	George Nieters	Francis Roquette	*Robert Vittoz
Nick Butcher	Hugh Gustafson	Albert Leitz	Ed Van Nordheim	Ted Rosa	John Vrablik
Proctor Cabaniss	Gene Guth	John Levitsky	Louis Novikoff	Walter Rospond	Roman Wantuck
Tom Cafego	Richard Hall	Milford Link	*Ralph Novotney	J. B. Ruark	John Warsaw
William Campeau	John M. Hanson	Robert Lyle, Jr.	P. J. O'Brien	Robert Rush	Don Watkins
Donald Carlsen	Edward Hartness	Lewis Macrinotis	*Robert O'Connell	Frank Rutkowski	Ted Wendt
Charles Carman	Robert Henriksen	Robert McCall	*Win Oliverio	Ralph Sabatiño	Richard Williams
H. W. Carter, Jr.	*Kenneth Hicks	John McCardell	Bernard Olsen	Robert Sawyer	Clarence Willis
Clifford Chambers	Walter Higgins	T. R. McClelland	Leonard Okrie	William Sawyer	Lee Roy Wilson
Calvin Chapman	Bertrom Hill	Lyle McFall	Charles Osgood	John Saxer	Max Wilson
John Childers	Lynn Hoffner	James McGrory	Furman Owens	Ted Scandurra	Porter Witt
Herbert Chmiel	Carroll Hoffman	James McGuire	Robert Owles	Henry Schenz	Lee Wortman
Robert Churchill	Charlie Hoffman	Lloyd McGuire	Richard Pace	Richard Schulefand	Mitchell Wozniak
Charles Clifford	Claude Horton	George McKinnon	Charles Paetz	George Schumann	William Wright
Richard Clouse	Jodie Howington	*Frank McMillan	Albert Pahr	John Sebastian	Walter Yonchuk
Richard Conger	Robert Huffman	James McMullin	Vincent Palumbo	Will Sellergren	Earl York
James Connors	Ed Hurley	*John McNicholas	Raymond Parello	James T. Sharpe	E. G. Zamecnek
Billie Cooke	Edward Jasper	Clarence Maddern	Clarence Parker	James Shilling	Bruno Zelasko
John Cosentino	*Frank Jelincich	Ed Malone	Ray Partee	Wilmer Skeen	Ed Zydowsky
Joseph Damato	Don Jameson	Elmer E. Mallory	*Leroy Paton	*Joseph Slotter	John Zydowsky

*Honorably Discharged

DETROIT TIGERS

FRANK OVERMIRE
Pitcher

ALTON BENTON
Pitcher

JAMES E. MILLER
Catcher

PAUL R. RICHARDS
Catcher

ROBERT V. SWIFT
Catcher

RUSSELL E. KERNS
Catcher

ROBERT P. MAIER
Infielder

JOHN J. McHALE
Infielder

EDWARD J. BOROM
Infielder

DETROIT TIGERS

RUDY YORK
Infielder

JAMES L. WEBB
Infielder

CHARLES HOSTETLER
Outfielder

EDWARD MAYO
Infielder

JOE HOOVER
Infielder

ED MIERKOWICZ
Outfielder

ROY CULLENBINE
Outfielder

JAMES P. OUTLAW
Outfielder

ROGER CRAMER
Outfielder

Inning Nine
Post Series Professional Ball
1946-1950

Detroit 1946

Perry was four years old by the time of the '45 Series and sometimes Grace left him at home for the games. He was a favorite of all the guys, though. He loved to dress up in costumes and cowboy was his favorite. Steve brought him into the dugout sometimes just for fun.

Jimmy Outlaw with four year old son Perry in Detroit dugout. 1946

Mr. and Mrs. Hank Greenberg

Hank was one of the guys who really got attached to our son Perry. His wife, nee Cara Gimbel, and Grace got along great, too. That Christmas they gave Perry a complete set of Lionel electric trains. You know, metal was still very hard to come by – I guess he got it through the Gimbel's stores. Perry played with it hours on end and always put it right back into the box, all neat and orderly. It is still in perfect condition even though well-used.

223

Barnstorming trip to Victoria, British Columbia, Canada

After the series we went back to Alexander City for the winter, but I was gone a lot with exhibition games. We went out to the northwest on a barnstorming tour. It was so cold, rainy, and snowy, I was ready to come home. Here we are in British Columbia in front of the Princess Hotel in Victoria. There was me, Bob Swift, and Doc Cramer from the Tigers on the tour. After that trip, Doc went on back home to New Jersey, Swift went back to his job selling ties at a Pontiac haberdashery, and I went home to Alexander City.

"Jimmy (the) Outlaw (right), who as robbed many a man around the third base sack of the World Champion Detroit Tigers, is presented at the bar of justice by J.T.Greene, Superintendent of the Alex City Schools, to show the judges (left to right), T.D. Kimbrough, Superintendent of the Avondale Mills School, and S.H. Lyon, Coach of Alex City High, a successful athletic product from Alabama."

Alex City ran a photo announcing that local Jimmy Outlaw was leaving for spring training in Lakeland Florida, in March 1946

We played an exhibition game in Mobile, near my home in Jackson. A lot of hometown folks came to see the Tigers play the Boston Braves at Hartwell Field. There were quite a few of us players who had our roots near Mobile. The papers called Skeeter Webb, from Hattiesburg and me the stars of the World Series.

"BOSS AND STARS OF WORLD CHAMPIONS" IN EXHIBITION GAME AT HARTWELL FIELD, MOBILE, ALABAMA

Skeeter Webb, Steve O'Neill, Jimmy Outlaw

Other players whose faces were familiar to locals were: Virgil (Fire) Trucks, Dizzy Trout, Paul Richards, Hammerin' Hank Greenburg and Dynamite Dick Wakefield. We won 2-0.

"Manager Steve O'Neill and Jimmy Outlaw, look things over at Hartwell Field where the Tigers defeated the Boston Braves 2-0 in an exhibition contest."

We played the Braves at Rickwood Field during that exhibition series, too. They tell me that Rickwood is the oldest professional pro park still around. It was built in 1910 for the Birmingham Barons and it is still their home park.

Opening Day at Briggs was April 16 against the St. Louis Browns. There were three day games. Outfielders Doc (Cramer) and Roger (Cullenbine) were still with us even though about 16 players left for one reason or the other. After spring training, Steve was still using the three of us as he needed but we were considered "spare outfielders."

Three old-timers who became invaluable: Outlaw, Cramer, and Cullenbine

We were all three regarded as alternate outfielders and had been replaced by Dick Wakefield, Walter Evers, and Pat Mullin. Soon in the season, there were some injuries and batting slumps and we were once again working all over the place. I did play in the opening game at third and Webb was at second.

Banner Day Ceremonies were held June 15, 1946, when the official Championship Flags were raised at Briggs Stadium.

Chriysler pipe and drum corps leads the championship team back across the field after the official flag amd banner raising ceremony. The Washington team was led by Bill Fenzel's band.

First there was a procession led by military banner bearers, Bill Finzel's band led the Washington team and the Chrysler Pipe and Drum Corps led Detroit players to the flagpole. There they raised the official banners for the American League and World Series Championships. Those flags were 15 feet by 10' and cost $100 each.

Baseball officials and owner Walter Briggs were seated in their reserved seats on he baseline.

We marched back to Homeplate where they first gave O'Neill a silver bowl given by Lyle Fyfe of the Detroit Board of Commerce. Spike Briggs introduced Happy Chandler and he called us up one at a time to give us our official Championship rings. That day there were 19 of us including Steve and Coach Art Mills. It also included two who had dropped out of baseball: Chuck Hostetler and Hub Walker. They said there were 16 others who had left the club and those would be mailed. The rings cost $100 each and each player was charged for them!

1945 World Championship bowl presented to Steve O'Neill

Manager Steve O'Neill presents his personal World Championship ring to Walter Briggs.

Then something really nice happened. Steve O'Neill asked Commissioner Chandler if he could have permission to give his ring to owner Walter O. Briggs. He then walked over to the third base box and Steve took the ring he had just been presented and gave it to Briggs. The photo makes it look like Briggs has a bandage on his eye, but that was adhesive tape he used to tape two pair of glasses together to help him see!

Team Stats for 1946

Played 154 games W 92 L62 finished in second place. .597 ave

Jimmy Outlaw Stats for 1946

5'8". 168 lbs. bat right. I was at bat 299 times for .261

Team salaries for top:

Hank Greenberg. $55,000

Hal Newhouser. $40,000

Dizzy Trout. $28,000

Al Benton. $13,000

Doc Cramer $12,000

Pinky Higgins $12,000

Paul Richards $12,000

Eddie Lake $10,000

Bob Swift $10,000

George Caster $8,000

This means I was pretty low on the pay scale. Probably about 5 or 6 K.

I have clear memories of a few people and events from that year:

- **May 19, 1946:** Home game 14 vs Boston Red Sox. Hal's sixth victory of the year. Trout pitching for Sox. Hank hit a homerun in second inning, Dick Wakefield and I hit two in the sixth for a 3-1 win. This game set a record attendance for Briggs – 353,077 in 14 games so far that year.
- **July 11-21:** We were on the road in the east: Boston, New York, Washington, and Philly; played 12 games. I played in all but two of those games and led the team with a .370 for that trip.

- **Diamond Classic:** Passeau pitched a foxy game – one hitter in third game of the Diamond Classic

Pat Mullen: Outfielder Pat Mullen and I had spent most of 1941 on the Buffalo team. He had been in majors with Detroit for part of both the '40 and the '41 seasons. In 1940 he played only 4 games with Detroit and played 54 games in '41 in the majors. He joined the army and was there while I was at Buffalo. He spent the prime time of his athletic years there. When he came back in 1946, he took right back up where he had left off with Detroit. Too bad he had to miss the series year. He said he followed every game word for word all he could.

PAT MULLIN, Outfielder

"Everything Fine on this Play, But Then-
Horrors!"

Jerry Priddy: Priddy was quite a character. Seemed to make enemies wherever he played. He was on Senators team then went into Army Air force, but he played baseball for the military in Hawaii so he stayed in good shape. He came back in 1946 and I remember a game when he threw away a double play in the fifth inning. I had been forced at second, but his feet were in the air and he threw wild to first. Pat Mullin scored on that play

Eddie Mayo: We were always doing stuff to please the fans. A radio show called *Quizdown* was really popular. You have to remember that hardly anyone had television sets those days. Once time Eddie Mayo and I were the guest contestants. Different people asked us questions and we tried to answer them. If they stumped us, they would win. I am sure this young man won that day.

Eddie Mayo and I were on a radio quiz show called Quizdown

Bob Feller: I should always be one of Bob Feller's favorite people because I struck out to give him a record to tie with the one held since 1904 by Rube Waddell. My strike made his total 343. Some people said that Rube really struck out 348.

Bob Feller fired it right past Jimmy Outlaw on this pitch

Jimmy Outlaw, number 27, historic record breaking strike for Bob Feller, pitcher

Bob and I always laughed when we saw each other since then, because I also broke up one of his no-hitters. Bob pitched for the Cleveland Indians. Waddell played for Philadelphia As, who were owned and managed by Connie Mack. Bob at that time held the record for most strike outs in one game, 18 Tigers in October 1938.

Jimmy Outlaw and Eddie Lake, 1946

Eddie Lake: Eddie and I roomed together on road trips. He was with Boston Red Sox for three years and came to Detroit in '46. He batted in 155 games for .254 in 1946. His wife and Grace were great friends, too. He stayed with Detroit until 1950. He got old, like I did.

EDDIE LAKE

TIGER TEAM PLAYERS ENJOY A CHINESE MEAL.

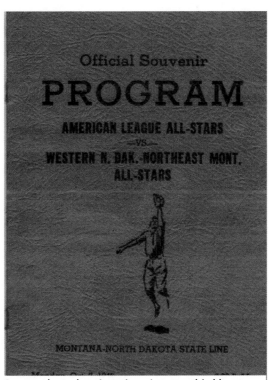

*I was selected as American League third baseman
for this match.*

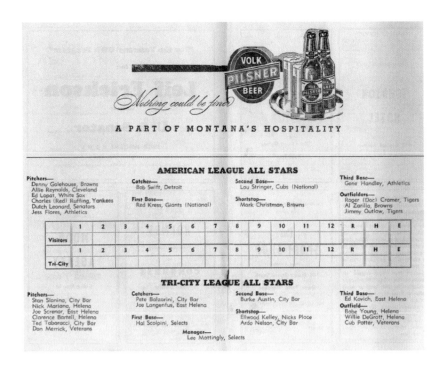

AMERICAN LEAGUE ALL STARS

Pitchers—
Denny Galehouse, Browns
Allie Reynolds, Cleveland
Ed Lopat, White Sox
Charles (Red) Ruffing, Yankees
Dutch Leonard, Senators
Jess Flores, Athletics

Catcher—
Bob Swift, Detroit

First Base—
Red Kress, Giants (National)

Second Base—
Lou Stringer, Cubs (National)

Shortstop—
Mark Christman, Browns

Third Base—
Gene Handley, Athletics

Outfielders—
Roger (Doc) Cramer, Tigers
Al Zarilla, Browns
Jimmy Outlaw, Tigers

	1	2	3	4	5	6	7	8	9	10	11	12	R	H	E
Visitors															
Tri-City															

TRI-CITY LEAGUE ALL STARS

Pitchers—
Stan Slanina, City Bar
Nick Mariana, Helena
Joe Screnar, East Helena
Clarence Bartell, Helena
Ted Tabaracci, City Bar
Dan Merrick, Veterans

Catchers—
Pete Balzarini, City Bar
Joe Langenfus, East Helena

First Base—
Hal Scolpini, Selects

Second Base—
Burke Austin, City Bar

Shortstop—
Ellwood Kelley, Nicks Place
Ardo Nelson, City Bar

Third Base—
Ed Kovich, East Helena

Outfield—
Babe Young, Helena
Willie DeGratt, Helena
Cub Potter, Veterans

Manager—
Lee Mattingly, Selects

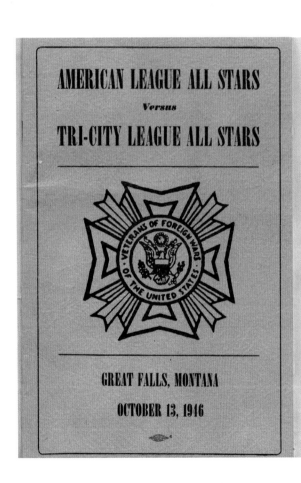

AMERICAN LEAGUE ALL STARS

Versus

TRI-CITY LEAGUE ALL STARS

GREAT FALLS, MONTANA

OCTOBER 13, 1946

James P. Outlaw

A third baseman and outfielder of no novice ability is James Outlaw. He comes from another successful season with the Detroit Tigers. A native of Tennessee, having been born in that state, at Orme, Jan. 20, 1913, he is five feet, eight inches tall, and tips the scales at 165 pounds. He attended Auburn College and knocked baseballs out of the park there. He started his baseball career in the M. A. League, went to the majors in 1937, playing for Cincinnati. He played for Syracuse and Buffalo in the International League and has been a Detroit Tiger since 1944, playing third base and outfield positions. His batting average is .271.

ROBERT SWIFT

From the Detroit Tigers comes Bob Swift, catcher, slated to appear in today's American League All-Star contest. He is a native Kansan, another right hander of the Tigers. He started his baseball career back in 1934, moved in to the American League in 1940, having been assigned to the St. Louis Browns from San Antonio. He went to Philadelphia in 1942 and was acquired by Detroit in 1944. He pounded out 65 hits in 1945 and his batting averaged .233.

Detroit

In a 1947 article in Alexander City, the announcement that I was leaving for Spring Training included the news that I had invested in the local ball club and had joined Poco Taitt in that enterprise. I'll have to admit that was a bad deal – it flopped.

Loyal and expectant fans crowded into Briggs for the first game of the 1947 year. They were ready for another world championship season.

At each season opener the Detroit Fire Department made a presentation of the Good Luck horseshoe of flowers to kick off the season.

The pregame ceremonies for the first game were emotional. The nation was still reeling from the impact of WWII and patriotism was at its height. The crowd stood at attention as the procession to the flagpole was led by the band and color guard.

"The traditional pregame ceremony for the first game of the season. Marine color guard stand at attention during the flag raising at Briggs stadium. The stands are packed with loyal baseball fans for the first game of 1947."

At one of the games the press wanted a photo of me giving an autograph to the Cotton Queen from Memphis, Hilda Seay.

I was the guest of honor at the GM Men's Club annual dinner, and C.S. Blocher, age 88, introduced me as his favorite ball player. Also there was Billy Evans, general manager of the Tigers.

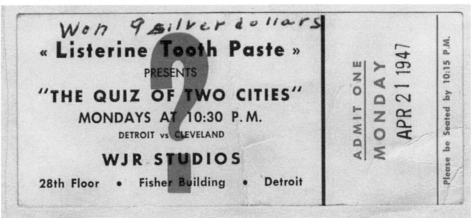

Jim Outlaw gives hunting advice to teammates during a rain break.

During a rain break, the guys in the dugout kept up their spirits by talking about all sorts of things. I am giving them hunting tips in this photo. Pictured are Bob Swift, Dizzy Trout, Fred Hutchinson, Johnny McHale, and Art Houtteman. We are waiting on the announcement for the second game of the double header with the Senators.

Eddie Lake and Jimmy Outlaw

Jimmy Outlaw slides hard, but Yogi Berra beat him to the punch.

Yogi Berra was a great player. I would have scored the tying run in the eleventh inning of this game, but Yogi caught a perfect throw from Billy Johnson.

Rudy York failed in an attempt to scoop up third baseman Glen McQuillen's bad throw in the first inning of a game between the Tigers and the Red Sox.

Tigers gladly signing autographs

We were always courteous to fans and I loved talking to them. After all, their support was really important to the club. Harvey Jebe and I are talking with Kenny Wohl, age nine, in Boston at the Prado Hotel before we leave for Comiskey Park for a game with the White Sox.

Steve O'Neill held training camps for high school and American Legion coaches. He used me to teach sliding techniques. Skeeter Webb (on the right) was also a part of the teaching staff. The clinic was the J.L. Hudson Baseball Clinic held in Briggs Stadium.

Jimmy demonstrates effectve sliding techniques.

In a series of columns, Detroit reporter Sam Greene interviewed a player from each position to solicit advice for players. His interview with Jimmy Outlaw was printed verbatim:

JIMMY OUTLAW: TIPS FROM TIGERS

Outfielders Warned of Shifting Wind

This is the third of a series of article in which the Tigers offer the benefit of their experience to scholastic and sandlot players. Other articles will follow daily until all positions have been covered.

When I was playing the outfield on sandlots down south, I learned to work with the wind. At the start of the game, I'd toss up a few blades of grass or a handful of sand to determine which way the wind was blowing and how hard.

Now that I'm in the big leagues, depend on the flags in centerfield or the pennants on top of the stands to give me the information. I check it every few innings. In this way, I gain an advantage that prevents many long balls from falling out of reach. The wind need not be of cyclonic proportions to make a difference of three or four strides in the instance you have to travel for a high fly.

It is my experience that the most important things in playing left field – or any other field for that matter – is the relay. The ball hit between the outfielders is often one that beats you.

After you have recovered the ball, be sure to give it to the relay man shoulder high so he has a chance for a quick and accurate throw. If your own throw is around his knees or over his head, he has to adjust himself so he can fire the ball back to the infield. Meanwhile, the chances are that the runner or runners are taking extra bases.

In handling more simple fly balls, I use varying methods. If there is a runner on third, tagged up for an attempted score, and the ball is in front of me, I try to catch it on the run. This provides momentum for the peg to the plate.

On the other hand, if the bases are empty or the ball is hit over my head, I hustle to reach the spot as quickly as possible. Suppose I've misjudged the ball, I still have time to reset myself for the catch.

The cardinal rule to follow, when possible, is to catch the ball shoulder high. It puts you in position for a normal throw and it gives you a second chance in case of a juggled ball. The outfielder who makes the catch waist-high, or lower, is pretty sure to lose the ball beyond recovery if it pops out of his glove.

When I am playing left field, I make it a practice to discuss the hitters of the opposing team with Hoot Evers or whoever is in center field. We decide whether to swing to the left or the right, according to our idea of the batter's habits and potential punch. We are guided, too, by the sort of stuff our pitcher is throwing and, as I said in the beginning, the way the wind is blowing.

> *Review of 1947 Season*
>
> *Quote from the 1948 Spring Training Press Release Booklet*
>
> *Detroit finished the 1947 season in identically the same spot that was occupied the previous year, in second place, twelve games behind the league leaders.*
>
> *From May 10 until June14, the Tigers had undisputed possession of the top rung and enjoyed at one time a four-game advantage, when Pat Mullin was hitting at better than a .400 clip. Injuries, failure of the highly regarded pitching staff to come up to expectations and weak hitting which resulted in the club's losing ten out of an eleven-game series on the road, sent it down in the percentage columns. Throughout the remainder of season, it failed to gain the league lead, although it finished strongly in the closing weeks of the campaign.*
>
> *In finishing second, the Tigers had no pitcher with 20 or more victories for the first time since 1942. Newhouser, who in the three preceding seasons had a record of 80 wins against 27 losses wound up with a .500 average with 17 wins and defeats. Trout, who had 17 and 13 in 1946, had 10 and 11 last year.*

1947 Detroit Tigers Salaries

Hal Newhouser $70,000.00

Dizzy Trout $25,000.00

George Kell $15,000.00

Eddie Lake $14,000.00

Al Benton $13,000.00

Doc Cramer $12,000.00

Bob Swift $9,000.00

Ben Steiner $6,000.00

> *Editor's Note: The 1947 Detroit Tigers played 154 games during the regular season, won 85 games, lost 69 games, and finished in second position. Jimmy played in 70 games and was at bat 127 times. His average for 1947 was .228.*

1948

Detroit

Jimmy and Hal Newhouser talk with fans and reporters at training camp in Lakeland, Florida. When Jimmy signed his contract, he was the 20th Tiger to come on board.

Jimmy Outlaw and mangaer Steve O'Neill in Tiger locker room, 1948

Briggs felt that the time for O'Neill was growing to a close. I saw the writing on the wall, or should I say the Press said that I was nearing the end with Detroit as well. I got really good press coverage, though. For the most part, I think the sportscasters liked me. Most of them wrote editorials saying I should be put on second base. Also, they gave me good reports while I was filling in for injured George Kell, Third Baseman. But I knew my age was becoming a factor and I was also having feelings about wanting to do something else.

Most of us ever paid much attention to what race a player was or where he came from. We were in it for the game, and that was all that mattered. Once Hank Greenberg told me that he felt it was harder for him to make it in the pros because he was Jewish. We had men from all over through the years. When this photo of Larry Doby was published, that was when it came to me that he was one of the first African American players to break the barrier in Major League. He was a regular good guy. Here Larry is sliding into third as I am reaching for the throw. He had come all the way from first on Ken Keltner's single in the fourth inning.

Doby slides into third

Jimmy Outlaw, Detroit Utility man, out at first by a step. Chuck Stephens, Brownie first baseman, beats Jimmy in race to bag.

Review of 1948 season as written in 1949 Spring Training Booklet press release

For the first time since 1943, Detroit finished out of the first division, 18 ½ games behind the Cleveland Indians. At home and abroad, the record was identical, 39 victories and 38 defeats.

In spite of this performance the club enjoyed the greatest attendance in its history with 1,743,035 cash customers passing through the Briggs Stadium turnstiles. Fourteen night games, played for the first time under the new $400,000 lighting systems, installed by Owner Walter O. Briggs accounted for 628,703 of the total.

After getting away to a good start in 1948 by copping their first three games, the Tigers commenced to skid, and it was not until May 1, that they were able to chalk up a victory at Briggs Stadium. As a result, the club was in, or hovered near, the second division throughout the greater part of the season.

Injuries and illness were large factors in the club's failure to land higher in the standings. Both Hutchison and Trout were idle for several weeks and Mullin and Newhouser for lesser periods. Perhaps the greatest loss was to the doughty George Kell, which permitted him to play but 92 games of the scheduled season. Houtteman, who had been counted on to be in 10 or 15 games, in view of his performance near the close of the 1947 season, disappointed the fans with his record of 2 victories and 16 defeats. Ineffective relief pitching and the scarcity of long ball hitters, also figured in the final result.

Over only three of its opponents, Philadelphia, Washington, and Chicago, the Tigers hold an advantage in games won. The Boston Red Sox proved to be the toughest opposition, taking 15 of the 22 contests waged.

June 30, the Tigers were the victims of the first no-hit, no-run game played at Michigan and Trumbell Avenues, since 1922, when Bob Lemon, of the Cleveland Indians, achieved the distinction, under the lights. The score: Cleveland, 2-5-0; Detroit 0-0-2.

Farm clubs were starting to emerge into what they are today. Before then they were very informal, and most trading and ownership was casual. Sometimes players were loaned to other clubs. In 1948 when the season began Detroit had 10 farm clubs associated. Four of them were owned outright by Detroit:

- Williamsport: A Rating. Eastern League, Manager Gene Desaltes
- Flint: A Rating, Central League, Manager Jack Teague
- Troy: D Rating, Alabama State League, Manager Robert Benish
- Thomasville: D Rating, Georgia-Florida League

The Detroit Club was also associated with Seattle (AAA), Buffalo (AAA), Little Rock (AA), Hagerstown (B), Rome (C), and Jamestown (D). By the end of the year, the number of players had almost doubled. There were then five teams owned outright by adding Toledo (AAA) to the list. There were also five clubs with working agreements with Detroit.

The Minor League Club Manager for Detroit was Robert Rolfe, who was selected as Tiger manager for the 1949 season. At that time, Ray Kennedy became Director of Minor League Clubs associated with Detroit. Rolfe had been very successful in the Minor League management role and Briggs wanted to see if he could do the big job.

I was at bat 74 times this year as outfielder and third base, finishing with a .283 average. I had twelve two-baggers. I was at third base mostly. I spent a lot of time the Winter of '49 in California working with baseball camps.

1949

Detroit/Sacramento

From 1949 Player Roster from Spring Training, 1949

Chosen from a field of 50, Rolfe takes over the job held for six years by Steve O'Neill, with no previous experience as a manager, but with a fine background as an intelligent and aggressive player, and the high regard of the fans of Detroit and Michigan.

The former star third baseman and coach of the Yankees did not seek the post. As head of the Tiger minor league chain, he had built up that organization in less than a year from 100 players to nearly double that number and was reluctant to make the switch. His knowledge of the farm set-up, it was felt by General Manager Evans, would be a great asset in the managerial position, however, and Red was finally persuaded into acceptance.

Trained under Joe McCarthy, after his graduation from Dartmouth and a period with the Yankee farm clubs, Rolfe was an outstanding member of the New York club for nine seasons, during which time it never finished out of the money. A participant in six World Series, Red was also chosen for All-Star honors on three occasions.

In his college days, the new Tiger pilot was a shortstop. He began his professional career with Albany in 1931, and it was not until he was switched to the "hot" corner as a Yankee that his ability as a fielder and hitter asserted itself. Previous to joining the Detroit organization, in August of 1947, Rolfe was coach of the Yankees and served in similar capacity with the Yale and Toronto basketball clubs.

His selection as Tiger leader, came in response to what was recognized as a definite demand for more aggressive play at Briggs Stadium. He is inclined to favor the younger players and it seems likely there will be little or no loafing on the field in this season.

Rolfe was born Oct. 17, 1908, at Peacock, New Hampshire. Previous to his entrance at Dartmouth, he attended Phillips Exeter. He was married Oct. 12, 1934, to Maud Isabel Africa. The Rolfes live in an attractive home in the outskirts of Detroit purchased a year ago.

1949 Detroit promo photo

The blurbs about the players in the 1949 Spring Training book said I was a utility player last year appearing in both infield and outfield and didn't even bother to comment on my performance in 1948. Of course, I had already made contacts with other teams.

I played in a few games, but sat out several, too. Obviously, Rolfe was vocal about preferring younger players. He went after them with an aggressive vengeance. One letter to the editor made me feel good, though:

Dear Lyall:

Perhaps you may be able to explain something that has been bothering quite a number of us for some time. Last season we were all scratching our heads and since the recent baseball meetings we have begun to scratch them again.

The question is: "What's the matter with playing Jimmy Outlaw at second?" Little Jimmy is one of the most aggressive ball players on the team, and if he could play regularly, he'd probably play rings around all these $180,000 prima donnas the management is trying to purchase.

Please pass this idea along to the front office as we are getting tired of seeing a good ballplayer ride the bench.

Truman did it. Why can't Outlaw!

Very Truly Yours,

Outlaw for Second Base Club

When I was placed on the inactive list, I called Grace in Alexander City to tell her I would be coming home.

"I hate to see Jimmy leave us," said Red Rolfe, "but, after all, he is 36 years old and we have to give the preference to younger players. I suppose you might say that Jimmy's number was up the day we got Kolloway. We had eight infielders and couldn't afford to carry that many."

In May when Kolloway was purchased, that put Detroit over the 25-player limit and Rolfe let three of us go. Besides myself, there were Don Lund and Saul Rogovin. Lund was sold to Toledo. Rogovin had been under an agreement with Buffalo, so he was returned there. I flew to Detroit to talk to General Manager Billy Evans to see what options were open to me. All major league clubs had waived on me, but Billy was helping me find a job in the minors.

Finally, at the request of General Manager Del Baker, I was sold to the Sacramento Solons. I had played under Baker when he was coach and manager for Detroit several years before that. Grace and Perry had been there some and she thought the move would be fine.

I had trouble getting to California and Baker showed how upset he was. He was

Outlaw at first practice with the Sacramento Solons

afraid it would take too long for me to get in shape. Another new player, Orv Grove, had been out of shape and said it took two weeks to be ready for the field. However, I had not been slack and hit the field for practice the night I got in. My signing made the Solons over limit; they optioned Merle Frick to Wenatchee in Western International League. I knew I was fast and had strong wrists.

George Klumpp hosted a party after the Solons worked up to second place in the league

We played a series in Seattle and worked up to second place in Coast League standings. George Klumpp threw a big party for us as soon as we got off the train. In this photo left to right; Dick Conger, Jimmy Outlaw, Bill Wilson (behind Jimmy), Walt Gropo, Vince Plumbo, Mann Salvo, Prexy Ed Sparks, and Tom Rose. I was busy looking at that cute little boy, missing mine.

That off-season, Eddie Lake and I again conducted baseball camps near San Francisco in the Sonoma Valley region. Grace and Perry had stayed in Alexander City during the season but moved to California in the fall. We got a house in Boyes Hot Springs, a wonderful little country town centered around the historic hot springs baths. Perry went to school there in a school so small they rang an old-fashioned school bell to start the day.

Editor's note: Mrs. Brown, the school bus driver, picked up lots of the children from the farms all around. I remember them dressed in overalls. After she took us to school, she went fishing all day, then returned to pick us up and take us home.

THE OLD FLOWERY SCHOOL beside Highway 12 at Agua Caliente is now utilized for the Agua Caliente High School for continuation students. For a time, the site was utilized as school district headquarters.

Front Row - *Manuel Salvo* *Jimmy Outlaw* *John Jorham* *Whitey Kitchmann* *Len Ratto* *Frank Kerr* *Fred Marsh* *Pete Coscarart*
Second Row - *Ralph Hodgin* *Frankie Dasso* *Vince Plumbo* *Bob Gillespie* *Tony Freitas* *Dolph Camilli* *Al White* *Dick Cox*
Third Row - *Bill Baker* *Carl Love* *Jim Tabor* *Walter Dropo* *Glenn Harmon* *Bill Wilson* *Don Jackson* *Joe Dee*

SACRAMENTO SOLONS 1949

1950

I did go to Spring Training with Sacramento but wasn't played much. They let me go after training. During that spring my back and legs were really bothering me, and I had a crazy skin rash. I was soon named manager of Miami Beach, of the Class D Florida State League. Jerry Crosby had just left the Flamingoes and I knew those guys from the All-Star games in Cuba I managed. I was always a free agent and made deals myself.

Draws Release

JIMMY OUTLAW

Third Sacker Is Dropped

I signed as a free agent May 17,1950, and went to Miami Beach to talk with Crosby, telling him I was not there after his job. I just wanted to get back in shape and try to help him. He resigned. He was worried about his own performance and had a leg injury as well. The team showings had not pleased him, and he felt he could still play ball if he stopped awhile and allowed his injury to mend. I met his wife and children who came for a vacation there, and then they all went back home to Houston.

Jim Outlaw (rear) and Tony Freitas (right) give Herm Reich of the Chisox the Sacramento news.

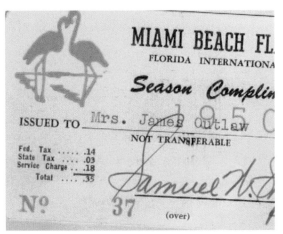

May 28: I had been in Miami ten days and played in seven games. I remember it was a Sunday morning when the president Sam Shapiro hauled me out of bed to see if I was willing to be manager and play third base for the final two-thirds of the season. I was honest and told them I just didn't know.

I think I helped a lot of those players. Art Bosch and Tommy Tabb made long strides. Bosch became a much better shortstop and batter. When we were playing in Havana, Deo Crose came down with the flu and Tommy asked to fill in first base, one of the few positions he had never played. It was funny, he didn't even want to use the first baseman's mitt for six games. The first ball thrown to him hit him between the eyes and his nose bled for five minutes. He got so much better, I kept him there most games.

We were in the game to determine the teams for the Shaughnessy Playoffs, and lost. In the locker room I announced that it was time for me to retire. There was an unsettled climate with the Flamingoes, and I doubted if they would want me back anyway. I did go to the Minor League Convention in St. Petersburg, but nothing felt as right as going home with my family in Alexander City. It was time to start a new stage of my life. At the time, I was interested in becoming a partner in an oil distributorship.

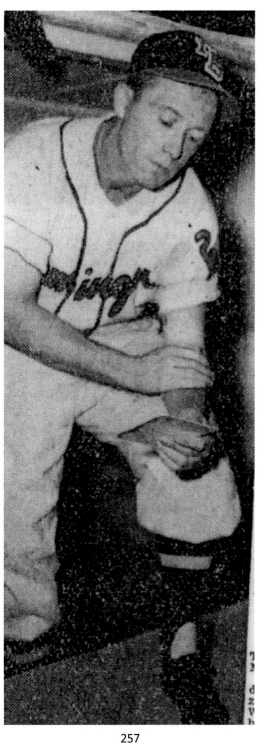

Extra Inning Ten
Life After Pro Ball
1950-2006

My wife's family was still living in Alexander City, so we went to stay with her mother awhile until we rented an apartment. Perry had made friends there from the past off-seasons and fit right back into the old group at the school and in the neighborhood. I took my old job at Russell Mills and was told they would like for me to be a spokesperson and use my name in promotions, but that never did pan out.

Careers

MACK OUTLAW, BROTHER OF JIMMY

We were back and forth to Jackson a good bit, and I decided to go into partnership with my brother Mack. Mack had a filling station in downtown Jackson and in a part of the building ran a little loan company. Across the street was A1 Cleaners. The owners and I worked out an agreement for me to open a cleaning business in Mt. Vernon, which is about 30 miles south of Jackson on Highway 43. Mack and I also put a loan company office in the tiny building next to it. I would work in the cleaners during the day and take the dirty clothes to Jackson each night. We delivered the cleaned clothes to customers back then.

I had a really bad wreck one day coming back from Mt. Vernon in the dry-cleaning truck. I still have a scar to prove how bad it was. It didn't make me afraid of driving though. I soon saw that the loan business and dry cleaners were not going to ensure enough income to support my family.

I got a job as a distributor with Dairy Fresh Milk company, whose headquarters were in Prichard, Alabama. I will have to say they were a good company to work for and I stayed there until I retired. I loved seeing the people in the little stores all across my area and loved taking the milk into the school cafeterias. When I made deliveries during the school hours, those fabulous cooks always had something good for me to eat.

I I

all

Family and Friends

Perry was in the sixth grade when we made the move and we lived in apartment near the school until our house was built.

We bought a piece of land from the Bollers.

259

It was actually part of their lot. We built behind them and the street running in front of our house we named James Street. Our house was the only one facing that street.

Grace and I had a wonderful group of close friends. She was a perfect bridge player and met with those ladies each week. I think she always won. We had a western party one time with our friends. I was game to dress up for that. I was a good sport. We were in a supper club; Grace was a wonderful cook and had the best meals of all.

Our son Perry went college in Auburn and then married in 1966. He was working in Mobile and Grace and I adored our grandchildren when they came along. They would spend a week or more with us in the summers and we enjoyed taking them to the huge pool that Vanity Fair had built in the town. The developers used the cold spring water to feed it and then built concrete walls and bottom for part of it. They also built a golf course, club house and community center. Later on, they sold it to the city of Jackson.

The hardest thing I have ever had to do was face the death of my wife. She died in 1974, and we buried her in the cemetery on the road to Walker Springs, north of downtown Jackson. Every month I take a fresh bouquet of red roses for her grave. She loved red roses. I retired in 1978 from Dairy Fresh and soon bought a long Chevy custom van so my friends and family could enjoy some trips and we sure did.

Joe Brown, local pharmacist, was one of my best friends and we went all over the United States. It seems he knew someone in every city we went to, and we always went to visit them. We went to quite a few bowl games and Auburn games as well. There were lots of family trips, too. We went all the way across country once and to Washington DC once. I went to Mexico and Hawaii with my son's family, and I could keep up with everyone. Back then I was just in my seventies and eighties.

Joe Brown's Drugstore Coffee Club

I was active in First United Methodist Church in Jackson and served on several committees. I was very involved in our Sunday School class taught by Dr. Lamar McLeod.

I was also in the Civitan Club. The Civitan Club kept me going all the time. We sold fruitcakes, put the flags out for holidays, and sponsored a festival each fall. I went to some of the conventions with those guys.

I kept up my health by walking and riding my bike. I had to have a pacemaker when I was 80, but that did not slow me down. I still rode my bicycle to town every day and had coffee with the coffee club at Joe Brown's Pharmacy. We ran the city and the world from that back table over strong, black coffee. One evening I was riding my bike and two thugs ran out from behind a building and tried to jump me. They didn't expect this old man to fight back, but I showed them what I was made of and they ran off. My bike did get damaged, though, darn it.

Citizen of the Year

The nicest thing that happened in my hometown was that I was named Citizen of the Year for 1983.

Jimmy Outlaw is presented the award of Citizen of the Year from Mrs. Lamar "Coo" McLeod who introduced Jimmy as the recipient for 1983

Sense of Humor

Editor's Note: Dad was an unbelievably funny guy. He had the quickest sense of humor I have ever seen. He was a master of comeback one-liners that would make us all burst into laughter. Here are some examples of our memories of his quips and actions:

David Outlaw:

"Once, Dad was driving and Papa was riding shotgun. Dad probably cut somebody off and when the driver passed us on the right, the driver stuck his hand out the window and gave an emphatic middle finger. Papa was right there at him and gave him one right back, "Yeh, yeh, we're number one. You think you are number one, but we are number one. Number one all the way. You're number one, we're number one, we are all number one."

Perry Outlaw:

"We were at the Cotton Bowl up in the stands. About three rows below us two men were obviously upset with each other. The shouting escalated until they were standing up and taking punches at each other. Dad jumped up where we were and started pumping his fists back and forth punching the air. He was yelling, 'Give him a good one. There you go – upper cut. Get him. Get him. Go, go, go at it.'"

"He was at the Christmas Eve candlelight service at Jackson United Methodist Church. Near the end of the service, the ushers walked down the center aisle with a candle. They were lighting the candle of the first person in each pew, who then passed the light down that row. When the usher got to Dad sitting on the seat next to the aisle, Dad said, 'But I ordered a Bud Lite.'"

"Dad went to his sisters' house, the old family home, every day for lunch. His sister Edith had been the dietician at Jackson Hospital for most of her life. Gladys taught school for about 40 years. The Good Sisters had a relationship built on spatting with each other. Dad would usually try to get them going. After they were all getting up in years, and Gladys had already passed away, he and Edith were together most of the time. She traveled with us on several trips and Dad

OUTLAW FAMILY HOME ON COLLEGE AVENUE, JACKSON, ALABAMA

still went to her house every day, sometimes bringing a hamburger to help out with the meals. One day after lunch, Dad was sitting in the rocking chair and Edith walked across the room, tripped and fell right in front of him. He immediately said, 'Now, Edith, you know I can't pick you up.' That has become a family quote!"

"When he finally traded in the van for a car, he got a big four door sedan. He still visited the nursing homes, and he also transported friends back and forth to doctors in town. Each week he would go to Leroy to visit with his sister, Mildred Farish. One day on the way back to Jackson on the Coffeeville Road, he was in the right lane, a turning lane, and when he realized he was in the wrong lane, he swerved to the left lane. There was a concrete median that was not well marked at all. Anyone could have missed seeing it. Anyway, as the car hit the median, it was thrown into the guard rail. There were three passengers in the car, and thank goodness, there were no serious injuries. When I asked him why in the world he was driving there at his age, he answered, 'Well, someone has to drive the old folks around.' He was ninety and the oldest one in the car."

"He was determined to buy a new car, so I obliged him and took him to the car dealership. The salesman pulled me aside and asked, 'You're not going to let him buy one, are you?'"

ONE OF THE ANNUAL BIRTHDAY DINNERS FOR JIMMY OUTLAW. THIS ONE IS AT HIS HOME IN JACKSON

"We always made a big deal of his birthday each year. On his eighty-fifth, we held a large reception for him at the Kimbell House in Jackson. He enjoyed that a lot. Some years we had parties at his house and sometimes we had his friends come to our home in Fairhope. As they were all getting older, once we hired a limousine to go to Jackson and pick them all up, bring them to Fairhope, and return them each home. He made all his friends meet at the school to get in the limo, and then he told them it belonged to the funeral home. Actually, we lived next door to a funeral home owner, so I guess he just assumed that was where it came from."

HANK GREENBERG "HALL OF FRAME" PLAQUE

"He was invited to Texas for Hank Greenburg's induction into the Texas Sports Hall of Fame. He and Joe Brown went to the airport in Dallas to meet him. When Hank got off the plane, he was carrying his tennis racket. As soon as Dad saw him, he pointed to the racket and said, 'I see you finally found a sport you could play.' At the ceremony, the plaque presented had a typo on it. It said, 'Hall of **Frame**.' Hank accused Dad of doing that and he gave him the plaque. 'This sounds like something you would do. You deserve this more than I do!'"

"At the ceremony for naming Dad Citizen of the Year for Jackson, Alabama, one of the speeches was given by his good friend Joe Brown. Joe told a story that showed Dad's sense of humor. During the 1945 series, Lamar McLeod happened to be in the hospital and was enthusiastically following the series on the radio. He bragged to the hospital staff that he knew two of the players in the series, Ray Prim and Dad. The news stories accurately named Prim from Salitpa, and it named Dad as being from Tennessee, where he was born. None of the staff believed that Lamar knew them. To prove it, Lamar sent a telegram to each of them asking them if they knew him. Prim immediately replied in the affirmative and thanked him for his good wishes. But then the telegram from Dad arrived, it said simply, 'Never heard of you.'"

Harriet Outlaw

"In 2000, the Jewish Film Festival in Mobile, Alabama, featured a documentary about Hank Greenburg. Jimmy was asked to be there for the opening remarks. The master of ceremonies, a well-known radio announcer, asked Jim to come to the front of the theater. The announcer introduced him, and then began a speech about Hank and his career. After quite a lengthy talk, he turned to Jim and asked, 'Jimmy, do you have anything to say?' Without missing a beat, he replied,' I have a lot to say if you will ever quit talking.' The crowd burst into laughter. Dad's remarks about his memories were touching and emotional. It was a perfect introduction to the film."

"On one of our trips, we crossed the Canadian border to visit Niagara Falls. At the crossing, the usual questions were asked. When the officer asked, 'Do you have any guns?' Dad threw his hands up in the air and turned around to the passengers, 'Guns, guns, who's got a gun? Who's got a gun?'

"Needless to say, the guard did not appreciate his style of humor and the van was totally emptied and searched. There were no guns."

School Visits

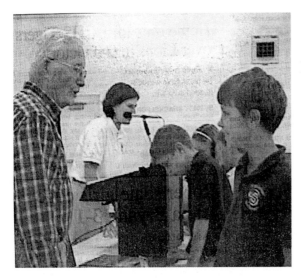

I was asked to come talk to lots of classes and schools. They looked at me as some kind of hero. I told them I was just lucky enough to get to play pro ball and to live long enough to enjoy talking about it. I always had signed photos to give them and was happy to give them autographs. You know, I never would sign autographs for people I thought would sell them. That is just not who I am.

I visited Daphne Middle School to talk to the kids about old times in baseball. It was the 50th anniversary of the World Series I was in. The year before, the baseball season suffered because of fans being frustrated about money disputes. I can't understand why grown men like the players and the owners couldn't get together and work it out. The fans got the bad end of the deal, but I am glad to see the excitement again. A lot of things have changed since I played ball.

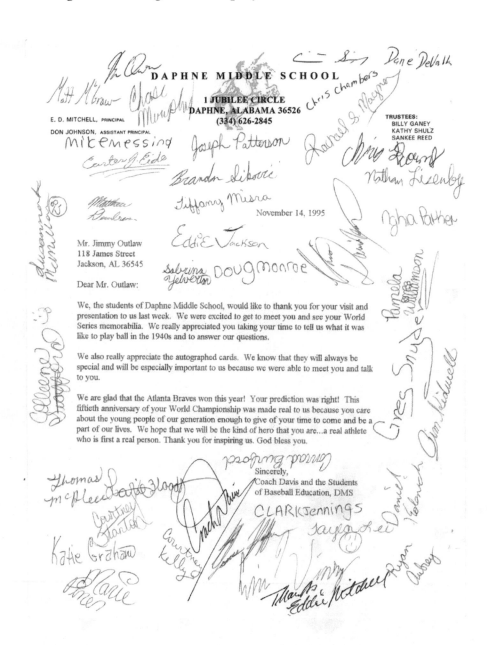

DAPHNE MIDDLE SCHOOL

1 JUBILEE CIRCLE
DAPHNE, ALABAMA 36526
(334) 626-2845

E. D. MITCHELL, PRINCIPAL
DON JOHNSON, ASSISTANT PRINCIPAL

TRUSTEES:
BILLY GANEY
KATHY SHULZ
SANKEE REED

November 14, 1995

Mr. Jimmy Outlaw
118 James Street
Jackson, AL 36545

Dear Mr. Outlaw:

We, the students of Daphne Middle School, would like to thank you for your visit and presentation to us last week. We were excited to get to meet you and see your World Series memorabilia. We really appreciated you taking your time to tell us what it was like to play ball in the 1940s and to answer our questions.

We also really appreciate the autographed cards. We know that they will always be special and will be especially important to us because we were able to meet you and talk to you.

We are glad that the Atlanta Braves won this year! Your prediction was right! This fiftieth anniversary of your World Championship was made real to us because you care about the young people of our generation enough to give of your time to come and be a part of our lives. We hope that we will be the kind of hero that you are...a real athlete who is first a real person. Thank you for inspiring us. God bless you.

Sincerely,
Coach Davis and the Students
of Baseball Education, DMS

When I visited Spanish Fort School, George Fuller, editor of the *Spanish Fort Bulletin*, ran a column (*The Return of the Runt* October 28, 1987) about me. He quoted me:

"Today's baseball bat is much thinner at the handle than the Louisville Sluggers of yesterday. But the biggest difference is in the uniforms. The uniforms of 1945 were made of flannel. When the season started the suits were so big and bulky that the sweat from your body would soak into the flannel and make it difficult to run the bases. The pants hung around your legs like wet croaker sacks. It was not until toward the end of the season when the flannel shrank that you could run with comfort. Today's uniforms are form-fitted and are cut from synthetic fabric."

When he asked me if I would like to go back to the "good old days," I quickly answered, "NEVER!" The pay was very low, and a player was obliged to negotiate his own salary. There were no agents, no players' union, and precious few perks such as insurance or pensions. Baseball teams rode trains to the site of their next game, and most of those rides were at night. The only good thing about the old days are the memories."

Fan Mail

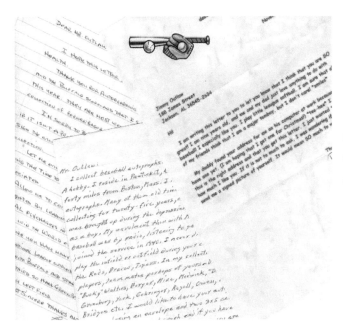

Samples of fan letters

It seemed like I got a letter about once a week with a photo or card enclosed, asking for my autograph. I always felt honored to be asked.

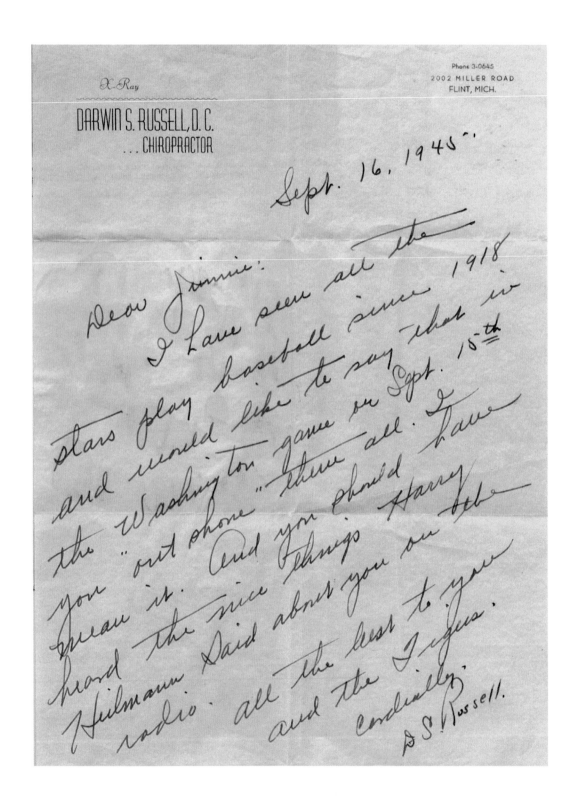

X-Ray

Phone 3-0645
2002 MILLER ROAD
FLINT, MICH.

DARWIN S. RUSSELL, D. C.
... CHIROPRACTOR

Sept. 16, 1945

Dear Jimmie:

I have seen all the
stars play baseball since 1918
and would like to say that in
the "Washington game on Sept. 15th
you "out shone" them all. I
mean it. And you should have
heard the nice things Harry
Heilmann said about you on the
radio. All the best to you
and the Tigers.

Cordially,

D S Russell.

SEPTEMBER 18, 1945

DEAR JIMMY,--I HOPE YOU DONT MIND.

I AM GOING TO MAKE AN ATTEMPT TO MAKE A VERY FEEBLE
ATTEMPT AT WRITING YOU A FAN LETTER. I AM NOT VERY GOOD
AT THIS SORT OF THING BUT I JUST WANTED TO SAY THAT I
THINK YOUR A VERY WONDERFUL BALL PLAYER AND I DONT SEE
HOW THE, DETROIT TIGER TEAM EVER GOT ALONG WITHOUT YOU.
YOU MOST CERTAINLY HAVE ADDED GREATLY TO THE MORALE OF
THE TEAM IN THIS VERY IMPORTANT TIME.

THERE IS NO DOUBT IN MY MIND THAT THE TIGER TEAM WILL
TAKE THE PENANT WITHOUT THE LEAST BIT OF EFFORT. BELIEVE
ME WHEN I SAY THAT THE WHOLE TOWN IS BEHIND YOU AND WE
DARE ANYONE TO SAY A WORD AGAINST THE TEAM.

I HEARD THAT GAME ON S ATURDAY - EXCUSE THE ERRORS-
WHEN YOU MADE THAT TERRIFIC DOUBLE PLAY FROM LEFT FIELD,
YOU SURE ARE WONDERFUL AND EVEN IF THE WASHINGTON FANS
DIDNT CHEER YOU CAN BET YOUR LIFE EVERYBODY AT MY HOUSE
CHEERED, IN FACT THAT IS THE FIRST TIME I HAVE EVER SEEN
MY DAD SWING O N THE CHANDALIER.

WELL I HAVE TO STOP AND GO TO WORK NOW. BUT GOOD LUCK
AND I WILL BE CHEERING FOR YOU AT BRIGGS STADIUM AND SO
WILL ABOUT 50,000 OTHER PEOPLE. YOU ARE ONE SWELL GUY
AND HAVE A GRAND BUNCH OF TEAM MATES. GOOD LUCK.

A FAN

When I was 85, the Little League and Dixie League in Jackson invited me to throw out the first ball. If I remember correctly, it was a strike!

Play ball!

Extra Inning Eleven
Honors and Awards

- 1959: 100th Baseball Anniversary, Washington
- 1963: Syracuse All Timers vs Old Timers' Games.
- 1980: Cubs Old Timers' Game
- 1990: Alabama Sports Hall of Fame
- 1991: Syracuse Wall of Fame
- 1992: Detroit Tenth Inning Alumni Party and Softball games
- 1999: Tiger Stadium Final Game Sept. 27

1959: 100th ANNIVERSARY BIRTHDAY OF BASEBALL IN WASHINGTON, DC

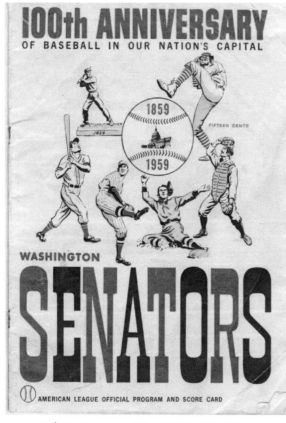

100th Anniversary of Baseball in Washington

The Washington Senators sent former American League players a couple of tickets to the 100th Anniversary game in Washington. The first one played there was in 1859. Griffith Stadium is the place where the President of the United States pitches out the first ball to start the Major League season. It has held dignitaries and famous people from all over the world. Even before the stadium as it is today, it housed Washington's National League team, and was known as Boundary Field because it was at the end of the horse-drawn trolley line. In 1912, fire burned down the old wooden stands and a concrete and steel stadium was built in the same place. It claims that from its mound Walter Johnson pitched his first major league victory and Babe Ruth hit his last American League homerun.

1963: Syracuse Old Timers and All Timers Game August 26

One of the first honors I got after I retired from pros was from the Syracuse Chiefs. In 1963 the club hosted a lot of old-timers for a weekend of festivities and to play a two-inning game before one of their regular games. They played it up big and there were more than 6,000 fans there to see us. We had fun joking and kidding around, and the spirits of the guys were way up high. They put us in our old numbers as much as possible. It fit just like it did way back in '39. Most of the guys had kept up their fitness and looked very much like they had 20 years ago. They had a host assigned to each of us who met us at the airport and drove us around wherever we needed to go. Our hotel was the Hotel Syracuse where they had a press room set up for interviews and laughs before we went to the field for the pre-game activities.

Ten of the eleven players elected to the All-Timers team were there.
The only one missing was Ens, the only one voted in posthumously,
having died in 1950 after seven years of managing the team in some of
its most successful years.

273

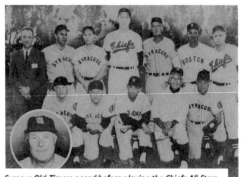

Syracus Old-Timers posed before playing the Chiefs All-Stars at MacArthur Stadium.

We were to play a two-inning game at 7:30 before their regular International League game against the Richmond Virginians. We played against a group they called their Old-Timers team, some were former Chiefs players too. Frankie Drews, Dutch Dotterer Jr., Tommy Henrich, Johnny Gee, Hal Erickson, Al Lakeman, and Frank Carsell, preset pilot of the Syracuse club. The inset is Manager Benny Borgmann, former Chiefs manager. Front row: Bill Stinton, Dutch Dotterer Sr., Preston Gomez, Bob Shawkey, and Hal Schumacher. Borgmann is in this photo but he took leave from the regular Old-Timers team to manage our team of All-Timers in the place of deceased Jewel Ens. Bob Shawky managed the Old-Timers that night.

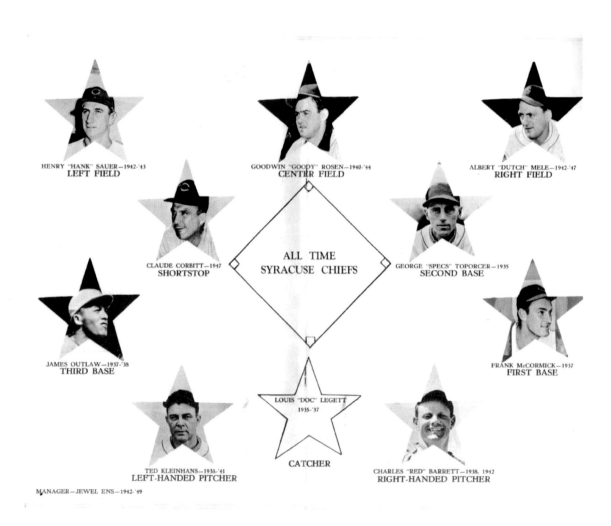

HENRY "HANK" SAUER — 1942-'43
LEFT FIELD

GOODWIN "GOODY" ROSEN — 1940-'44
CENTER FIELD

ALBERT "DUTCH" MELE — 1942-'47
RIGHT FIELD

CLAUDE CORBITT — 1947
SHORTSTOP

ALL TIME
SYRACUSE CHIEFS

GEORGE "SPECS" TOPORCER — 1935
SECOND BASE

JAMES OUTLAW — 1937-'38
THIRD BASE

FRANK McCORMICK — 1937
FIRST BASE

LOUIS "DOC" LEGETT
1935-'37
CATCHER

TED KLEINHANS — 1938-'41
LEFT-HANDED PITCHER

CHARLES "RED" BARRETT — 1938, 1942
RIGHT-HANDED PITCHER

MANAGER — JEWEL ENS — 1942-'49

Jimmy shown being presented his award as All-Time Third Baseman by Bill O'Donnell, sports director of WYSE Radio and TV

All-Timers for each position were selected by vote of fans and press: Holding Plaques: Frank McCormick, Specs Torporcer, Jimmy Outlaw, Claude Corbitt, Hank Sauer, Goody Rosen, Dutch Mele, Doc Leggett, Ted Kleinhaus, and Charles (Red) Barrett

Bennie Borgmann in the Cardinal Uniform managed the All-Timers team: Red Barrett, Ted Keinhans, Doc Leggett, Dutch Mele, Gordy Roser, Hank Sauer, Claude Corbitt, Jimmy Outlaw, Specs Toporcer, and Frank McCormick.

Most people don't understand the relationship between the clubs and the press, at least the way it was back in my days. The sports reporters were as much of the club as anyone. We read their remarks with all seriousness, and their opinions mattered a lot to the owners. In his column in the Syracuse Herald Journal on the Tuesday, August 27, 1963, after the Monday night game, the article summed up the inspiration we all got from George 'Specs" Toporcer:

The reunion served as a tonic to all of the men selected as the top Chief at his position, but, perhaps, the one who got the biggest kick out of "seeing" the old gang again was George "Specs" Toporcer.

Totally blind for the past decade, the cheerful and alert Toporcer who served as a vacuum cleaner around second base for the championship Chiefs of 1935, still has the clear-thinking mind of a quiz-kid.

"Actually, I think I keep up better on baseball today," beamed George, "than I did years ago. I listen to every game over the radio and receive all kinds of press releases...press books...The Sporting News. Everything to keep abreast of the game. Not just because I do some writing and speech-making, but because I thoroughly enjoy it."

Then, just as though the '35 season were yesterday, Toporcer ticked off some of the great plays that led to Syracuse's first Governor's Cup Championship.

"I'll always remember that series with Montreal," detailed Toporcer. "Montreal had beaten us out of the pennant. We beat Newark four straight, then took on Montreal. The series went seven games, and it was a strange one, for neither team won a game at home. We took two up there, then dropped three at home, before going back up to with the sixth and seventh games, both by 2-1 scores."

It   seems   like our horseplay and joking around was what made everyone feel so good. And we were still the same guys we were 25 years ago in our minds. Sauer was quoted saying what we all felt: "You know, we had fun in the Minors. More than in the Majors where we had to watch our P's and Q's. But that's what is wrong with baseball today. Everyone is so serious. No one is having any fun. "

When we took the field, they put Specs on his regular second base position but was replaced by Hall White. Specs looked upset, then walked right behind the catcher to take his place as umpire. The ump said, "That's my place." Specs answered, "I can see better than you can." The crowd roared with laughter. Then the umpire Augie Guglielmo ordered him off the field. He wasn't silent, though. He said to the ump, "You've got the fastest thumb in the league." Then from the dugout he yelled out to pitcher Red Barrett, "Red, you're faster now than when I had you in Buffalo." Specs managed Buffalo until his failing eyesight forced his retirement.

When catcher Louis (Doc) Legett, then a dentist in New Orleans, yelled at pitcher Lefty Ted Kleinhaus, "I am going to have to retire. My hand is swollen up twice its size. I hope you are my patient while it is no good."

In the second inning with Barrett on the mound, batter Prince Hal Schumacher halted the game and claimed that Barrett was throwing spitballs. The ump refused to take him out, but told him to wipe his hands before he pitched the next one. He did, but then promptly wet his fingers again before the throw.

After the game, each player was presented a plaque and members of both All-Timers and Old-Timers were presented engraved lighters.

1980: CUBS OLD TIMERS GAME, JUNE 14, WRIGLEY FIELD

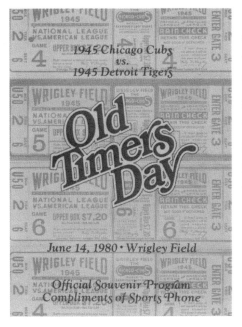

It was a lot of fun to go to the Old Timers game at Wrigley Field. The Cubs gave us a fantastic weekend to get together as many of the 1945 series players as they could to replay a couple of innings. They flew me, my son, and my grandson, David, to Chicago and treated us like royalty. The invitation letter had a funny part. It said that Chicago was bringing in some ringers to be sure the final score would be different than in 1945. They were wrong – Detroit still won, 1-4!

Skeeter Webb signs autgraph for David Outlaw, grandson of his teammate Jimmy Outlaw. Cubs Old-tImers Game, june 14,1980.

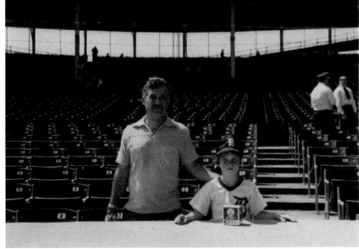

Perry and James David Outlaw, son and grandson of Jimmy Outlaw, Wrigley Field, 1980

279

The first night we were there Radio station WGN, Continental Broadcasting Company, and WGN Television 9 hosted a party at the Chicago Marriott where we were staying. It was lots of fun to see so many of the old guys.

CLAUDE PASSEAU, CUBS PITCHER

Claude Passeau has always been one of my best friends. Actually, he had stopped by Joe Brown's Drug Store in Jackson earlier that spring (April 17, 1980) looking for me to find out if I was going up to Chicago for the game. He knew where I would be, but unfortunately that was one of the few days I was not there. Probably had a doctor's appointment or was off visiting grandchildren in Baldwin County. Anyway, the Jackson newspaper interviewed him and ran a long column.

Passeau Signs Autograph: former Chicago Cubs pitching ace Claude Passeau autographs a photo of himself in a book owned by Mrs. Pam brown. She once lived in Chicago and is an avid fan. (courtesy of Mike Breedlove)

The article which was written by Mike Breedlove for the South Alabamian ran on April 17, 1980. Claude said he wasn't too crazy about old timer appearances, and had turned down several invitations, but thought he would go to Chicago if I was going. When asked about his pitching career, he remembered pitching against Dizzy Dean before they played together for the Cubs. "The last time I pitched against him we hit four homeruns and I wouldn't be telling about this game if we hadn't won."

As far as the World Series goes, he said, "They ought to put Jimmy up in bronze. He won the series for the Tigers. In the sixth game, I held the Tigers 5-1 through the fifth inning with Virgil Trucks on the mound for them, but a ball Jimmy hit back to the mound injured my pitching hand and I had to be taken out of the game the next inning. It wasn't a line drive like you reporters printed, but it was a knuckle-like ball he hit off the end of his bat. I took my eye off it looking at the runner on first that I hoped to double off. I believe they put in Red Primm and Hank hit a homerun off him to tie the game up in the ninth."

For the Chicago weekend, it was an added attraction for the Cubs to have Ernie Banks and former Milwaukee Braves star Eddie Mathews have a homerun contest. Banks hit good, but on the last ball (12th) pitched to Matthews he connected and hit the only homer in the contest. Another cool thing was that Paul Richards, who was the oldest in his seventies, suited up and was catcher in two innings of the Old Timers game. I remember hoping I could do that when I got as old as he was. I was a young sixty-seven at that time!

At the dinner afterwards, they presented each of us a framed drawing which they had commissioned. They had used these drawings in the special program printed for the event. The blurbs say something unusual about each participant.

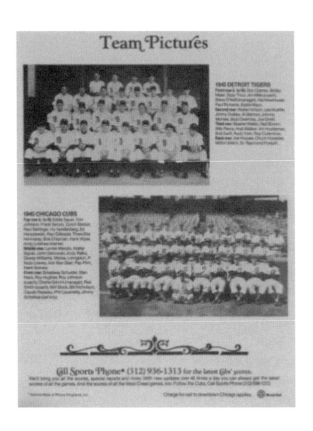

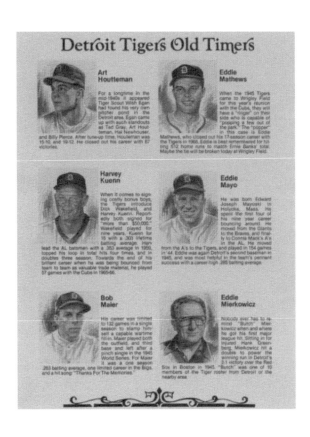

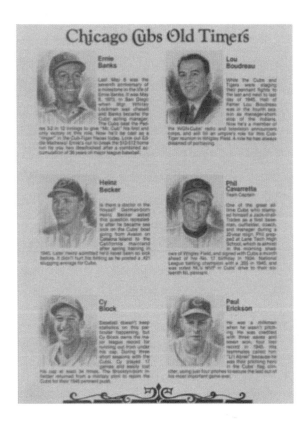

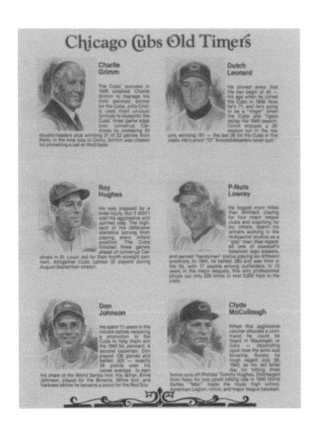

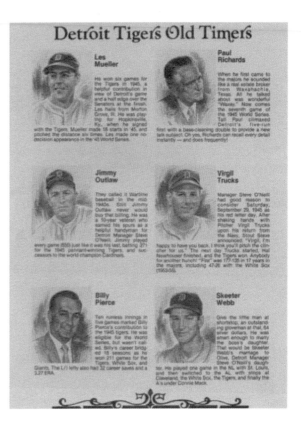

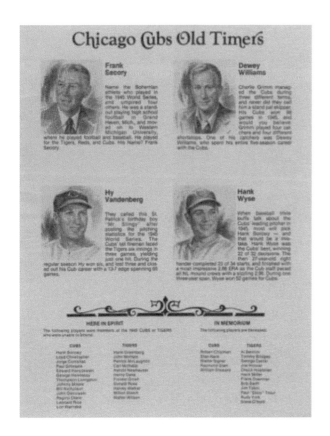

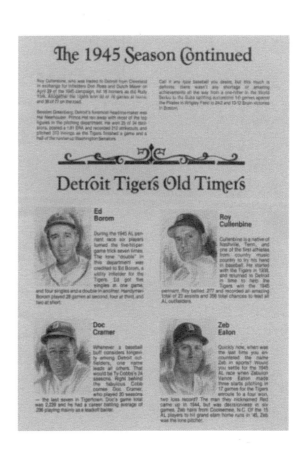

1990: ALABAMA SPORTS HALL OF FAME

FEBRUARY 24, 1990

I guess, besides family events, the second most memorable thing that happened to me (First was winning the World Series in 1945) was my induction into the Alabama Sports Hall of Fame, Class of 1990, in Birmingham. Alabama.

I was nominated the previous year but failed to be elected. The Board of Directors actually changed the voting committee for the Old-Timers' category and chose some people who were more in tune with the old days of sports. This was way back in 1988, actually. There were 10 nominated and they could only elect two. In the modern category, there were 20 nominated and they could elect four.

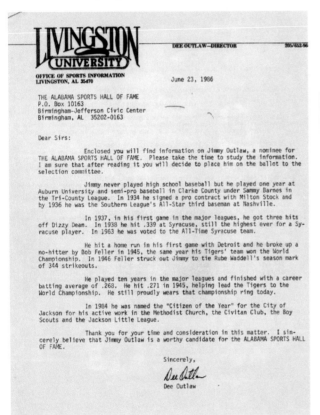

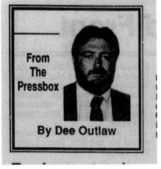

Keep your fingers crossed for the upcoming vote on the Alabama Sports Hall of Fame. Uncle Jimmy Outlaw is on the final ballot again for the Oldtimers section. Jimmy Outlaw, relation or not, deserves to be in the Alabama Sports Hall of Fame.

I won't go into details on his career in this column but you readers in Jackson know all about Jimmy, or "Runt" as he is affectionately known in the Clarke County city.

How many people do you know that got three hits off of Dizzy Dean in their first big league game or broke up a Bob Feller no-hitter with the only hit given up by the hard-throwing Hall-of-Famer?

Jimmy Outlaw is in the Outlaw Hall of Fame right now. All members of the Outlaw family are proud of him and all the people in Jackson are proud of him, also. The state of Alabama should be, too.

My nephew Dee Outlaw, Athletic Director at Livingston University (now University of West Alabama) completed tons of paperwork to have me nominated, and he got lots of people to write letters in support of me. I was notified in August 1988, (age 75) that I would be on the ballot for the 1990 awards. I think that was one of the nicest things anyone has done for me. I know it took Dee hours and hours of work. The Jackson newspaper, *The South Alabamian,* even ran an editorial giving the names and addresses of all the judges, encouraging people to join the newspaper in a campaign. Dee Outlaw was a columnist for the *South Alabamian* as well. His column, *From the Pressbox,* also encouraged letter writing

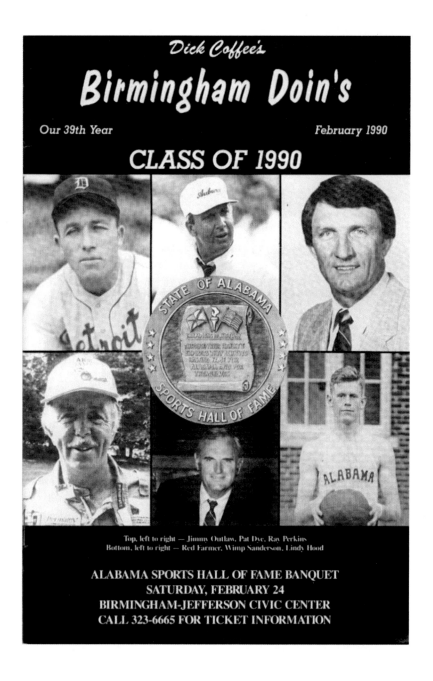

PRESENTING THE
STATE OF ALABAMA
SPORTS
HALL OF FAME
22nd ANNUAL
INDUCTION CEREMONY

PAT DYE
RED FARMER
LINDY HOOD
WIMP SANDERSON
RAY PERKINS
JIMMY OUTLAW

RAY SCOTT
DISTINGUISHED ALABAMA SPORTSMAN

BIRMINGHAM-JEFFERSON CIVIC CENTER
EXHIBITION HALL—SOUTH ADDITION
FEBRUARY 24, 1990

JIMMY OUTLAW

By DENNIS SMITHERMAN

Everyone who knows him calls him "Runt."

"I wouldn't think they were talking to me if I were called anything else," says James Paulus "Jimmy" Outlaw, of Jackson, Ala.

But Outlaw is another of those perfect examples of not having to be a giant in physical proportions to be a big man in the world of athletics.

Or specifically, in his case, in the realm of major league baseball.

Jimmy—or "Runt"—earned his way into this 1990 class of inductees into the Alabama Sports Hall of Fame the usual way: by his outstanding accomplishments in the higher echelons of professional sports.

He spent most of his ten seasons in the majors with Cincinnati, Boston, and Detroit, accumulating a lifetime batting average of .268.

A speedy, slick-fielding third baseman who oftentimes was called upon to play other positions, Outlaw also realized that dream of all major leaguers by playing in—and starring in—a World Series.

Jimmy was flawless afield, drove in three runs and was an inspirational leader to his teammates as his Detroit Tigers outlasted the Chicago Cubs four games to three in the 1945 fall classic.

Seven of his 10 seasons in the majors—his career in organized baseball totalled 16 years—were spent with Detroit.

There were also other notable highlights in his illustrious diamond career, such as:

He got three basehits off Baseball Hall of Famer Dizzy Dean in his very first game in the majors as a Cincy Red in 1937;

He hit a homer in his first game with Detroit in '43;

He once outran the great Pepper Martin of the St. Louis Cardinals in a prearranged and much ballyhooed pregame footrace;

He once got the only hit off Bob Feller in one of the latter's many one-hit masterpieces;

And he led the Three-I League in hitting in only his second year in organized baseball with a nifty .361 average; and he was voted to the All-Time team at Syracuse in the Tripple-A International League after leading that club with an all-time team high of .339. He was also an All-Star third baseman at Nashville in the Southern League.

All this by a fellow who never played high school baseball because he "only weighed 125 pounds, and in my senior year (1931) I broke my arm before the season started."

Although his only experience up to that time was on sandlot and semipro diamonds, young Outlaw nevertheless was awarded a scholarship to Auburn, and played a freshman season with the Tigers in '32.

It was shortly after that spring season that he was signed to a baseball contract by Milton Stock, a famed minor league manager of yesteryear and the father-in-law of another Alabama Sports Hall of Fame member, Eddie Stanky, also of major league renown.

Now 76 and fully retired in his native Jackson, Outlaw recalls playing in the World Series as the "most interesting time" and "the highlight" of his life in baseball. "It has to be the climax of any major leaguers' career," he states.

Still an avid fan of all sports, Jimmy says he often travels to Mobile to see high school football games, and is "an Auburn fan" who travels to the Plains to see the gridiron Tigers, also.

He has a son, Perry Outlaw, Jr., who is the principal of B. C. Rain High School in Mobile, and has six grandchildren and one great grandchild, all of whom reside in the Daphne and Spanish Fort areas of Baldwin county.

Continued on page 109

Jimmy Outlaw Continued from page 63

"It's a real thrill to be picked for the Hall of Fame," modestly admits Jimmy, "it's real nice company to be in. I thought they were just kiddin' me when I got the telephone call telling me I'd been selected .

"I guess it's pretty good for a little guy who, as a kid, just got a bunch of guys together to play baseball on the sandlots around Jackson."

"Pretty good" is more than right for this latest representative from southwest Alabama in his state's Sports Hall of Fame.

And what is he doing mostly these days? "I just go down to the drug store every morning and drink coffee and shoot the bull with the boys."

Pat Dye was born November 6, 1939, in Blythe, Georgia. He became an All-American guard at the University of Georgia and was also named an Academic All-American. Following an Army tour of duty he played two years in the Canadian Football League. In 1965 he joined the coaching staff of Paul Bryant at the University of Alabama where, during the next 9 years, he was part of two national championships. After head coaching stops at East Carolina and Wyoming, he was named the head coach at Auburn University in 1981. During the decade of the eighties, he established one of the premier programs in the country, winning or sharing four SEC titles with an 81-25 won-loss record. He retired from coaching at the end of the 1992 season. He resides in Reeltown, Alabama.

Charles "Red" Farmer was born October 15, 1932, in Nashville, Tennessee. He began his racing career in 1949 in Florida and moved to Birmingham in 1960. He has won more than 790 feature races and has won NASCAR National Championships in three decades, the 50's, 60's and 70's. He won the nation's premier sportsman race at Daytona International Speedway in 1971 and ARCA races at Talladega Super Speedway in 1984 and 1988. He finished fourth in the 1972 Talladega 500 and has been rated most popular driver by his NASCAR peers several times. He, along with Bobby Allison, became known as the "Alabama Gang", a name that has stuck. Red presently lives in Hueytown, Alabama.

Lindy Hood was born July 30, 1907, Leesburg, Alabama. He was the University of Alabama's first All American basketball player, and he gained that status without ever having played the game until he was a college freshman in 1927. He came to Alabama to play football and was on the Rose Bowl team in 1931, but basketball turned out to be his game. Urged by Coach Hank Crisp, he went out for the team and became its starting center as a sophomore. One season later as a junior, Lindy led Alabama to the conference championship and the only undefeated season ever. For almost half a century he remained the only University basketball player to be named All-American. He passed away October 17, 1972.

Jimmy Outlaw was born January 20, 1913, Orme, Tennessee. Played shortstop one year for Auburn in 1932. In 1934 he signed a professional contract with the Cincinnati Reds. After 4 years in the minor leagues with batting averages of .250, .340, .351, and .330, and being named the All Star 3rd baseman for Nashville and Syracuse, he made his major league debut by getting 3 hits off the great Dizzy Dean. He played 10 years in the major leagues, 2 at Cincinnati, one at Boston, and seven at Detroit. In 1945 while hitting .271, he helped lead the Detroit Tigers to the World Championship over the Chicago Cubs four games to three. When he finished in the major leagues he had a career .268 batting average. He died April 9, 2006.

Ray Perkins was born November 6, 1941, Mount Olive, Mississippi. For three years (1964, 1965, 1966) he was outstanding as a wide receiver for the Crimson Tide. During this time the Alabama teams compiled a 30-2-1 record including 2 national championships (1964-65) and 3 SEC titles. As a senior he was team captain, SEC player of the year and All American. He played in 2 Orange Bowls and 1 Sugar Bowl, and set records in both. He was drafted by the Baltimore Colts and played five years there. He played in Super Bowl III in 1969 and Super Bowl V in 1971 when the Colts were World Champions. In 1979 he was named head coach of the New York Giants. In 1983 he returned to the University of Alabama as head coach. In 1987 he became the head coach of the Tampa Bay Buccaneers. In 1992 he was named the head football coach at Arkansas State University. From 1993-96 he was with the staff of the New England Patriots. In 1997 he was the offensive coordinator for the Oakland Raiders.

Wimp Sanderson was born August 8, 1937, Florence, Alabama. He attended Coffee High School and the University of North Alabama. In 1960 he became the graduate assistant at the University of Alabama, and in 1961 he was made a full time assistant. He served in this capacity for 20 years until 1981 when he was named Alabama's head basketball coach. In ten years as head coach his teams averaged 21.8 wins a year, with a 218-100 record, and they won 4 SEC tournaments. They played in one NIT and eight NCAA tournaments making the "Sweet 16" five times. The only coach in Alabama history to win 200 or more games in his first 10 years. He was the SEC Coach of the Year in 1987, 1989 and 1990, and was the National Coach of the Year in 1987. He resides in Birmingham, Alabama.

ASHOF

CLASS OF 1990 HALL OF FAME HONOREES

93

PAGE FROM LATER HALL OF FAME GIVING HIGHLIGHTS OF THE 1990 INDUCTION CLASS

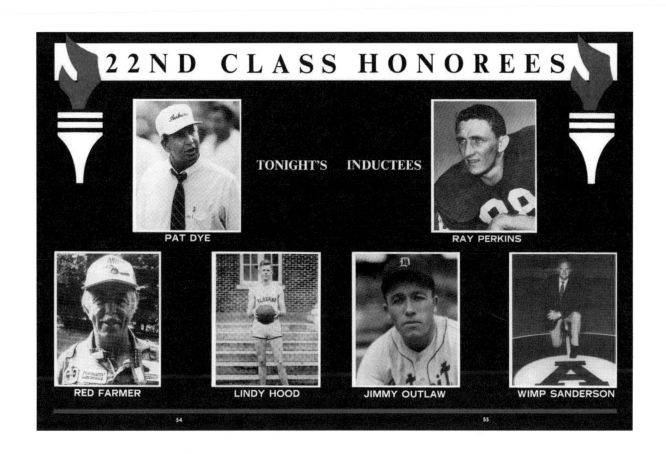

In the official program book the Hall of Fame presented to Jimmy, the inside cover had a typed list of all the family and guests who were there for the induction ceremony:

Harriet and Perry Outlaw and children, David, Mandy, Paul, Linor, and Joe.
Mike and Liz Outlaw- Mobile
Drew and Connie Outlaw – Jackson
Maurie Outlaw – Jackson
Anja and David Pace – Jackson
Cornell Outlaw – Jackson
Bert Outlaw and son, Ken- Pace, Florida
Mike and Beth Blount – Jackson
Mildred Farish – Leroy
Bobby and Viki Farish and daughter Summer – Leroy
Edith Outlaw – Jackson
Gladys Outlaw – Jackson
Dottie and Dan Outlaw – Jackson
Dee Outlaw – Livingston
Darryl Outlaw – Birmingham
Mary and Max Johnston - Nashville, TN
Sam and Nina Whiteside - Hampshire, TN
Walker and Peggy Grimes – Nashville, TN
Dot Mayfield - Columbia, TN

Friends:
Joe Brown – Jackson
John Winters – Jackson
Helen and Billy Guy – Jackson
Cecil McMullin – Jackson
Mike and Linda Breedlove – Jackson
Theodore Pearson – Leroy
Gary Green – Coffeeville
Red Borom and friend - Dallas, TX (former Detroit teammate)
Ricky Elmore - Jackson

Dee Outlaw's column eloquently expresses the emotions of each family member:

> *Saturday night February 24 proved to be a whirlwind of excitement for the Outlaw family of Jackson. Jimmy Outlaw, my uncle, was inducted into the Alabama Sports Hall of Fame and his induction has been well documented in all the daily papers in Alabama as well as the weekly newspapers.*
>
> *The pride, the emotions, the love and the family bond was not documented. Many well-known people were present at the Birmingham-Jefferson Civic Center that cold night. Also present were many, many Outlaws.*
>
> *My father, Dan, talked me into leaving early for downtown Birmingham to make a visit to the Alabama Sports Hall of Fame Museum. It was much, much better than I expected and I had tears in my eyes looking at Bear Bryant's houndstooth hat and Shug Jordan's Auburn staff jacket.*
>
> *Well over 1,000 people attended the pre-banquet reception and there were autograph seekers everywhere. I chuckled as I watched cousins Beth Blount and Liz Outlaw gather enough courage to ask former Alabama football great Johhny Musso for an autograph.*
>
> *Musso's handsome features and winning smile had all the ladies present in awe.*
>
> *Livingston's Jeff Coleman, a member of the Hall, had three or four people looking for me at the reception so we could exchange Livingston notes. We found each other and had a nice chat. Coleman Coliseum at the University of Alabama, by the way, was named after him.*
>
> *Other HOF members I met were Fred Sington, Harry Walker, Frank Howard, Virgil Trucks, Billy Hitchcock, Frank Lary and new inductee Pat Dye.*
>
> *The two people I enjoyed the most were Howard and Hayden Riley. Howard, a native of Barlow Bend, is the retired head football coach at Clemson University and a spinner of many, many tall tales. He said, "Hi" to his old home of Clarke County.*
>
> *Coach Riley the former Commissioner of the Gulf South Conference, is still recovering from a stroke, but is doing fine. He asked about so many people in Livingston and is still a man I admire tremendously.*

The banquet finally started and Uncle "Runt" was third on the list. The late Lindy Hood was up first and his nephew accepted for him. Aunt Mildred Farish, an Outlaw by birth, leaned over to me with tears in her eyes and said, "I'm so glad Jimmy got to see this day."

I am too, Aunt Mildred, I am too

When it came time for Uncle Runt to accept his award, he told of how my grandmother took a rock and wrapped string around it to make a baseball for him. He told of how he used to bounce a rubber ball off the house to play catch, much to the chagrin of my grandfather.

He also talked about his late wife, Aunt Grace, who was with him all through the good days, and the bad." Believe me, there are a lot of bad days in baseball," he noted.

Uncle Runt then asked his family and friends to stand. We all took a deep breath, poked chests out and with pride and restrained ourselves from breaking down in a chorus of "We Are Family" by the Pointer Sisters.

I didn't get much of a chance to talk to Uncle Runt when the banquet was over. He was too busy signing autographs.

I chuckled again when I looked at the autograph line. Beth and Liz were getting Uncle Runt's autograph, too.

That's it this week...From The Pressbox. 'Till next week....see ya in the finals.

DEE OUTLAW

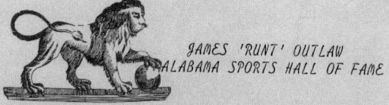

JAMES 'RUNT' OUTLAW
ALABAMA SPORTS HALL OF FAME

The Detroit Tigers, very quiet in the 'pen'
Steve O'Neil with fists clenched tight, looks at
the batter on deck-
as he swings a bat on two;
    He hopes to get a hit to check-
the no-hit game that is due.
    Two walks on base and one man out,
the batter then fans-
    The Tigers hear the shouts
that ring throughout the stands.

    Runt picks his bat and takes his place,
the 'ump' dusts off the plate;
    The pitch, a hit! Ball over the wall, three men
race-
Oh boy! Runt feels great!
    Quickly he eyes the bleachers everywhere,
as pride swells in his heart;
    The elatation! The crowd goes wild out there,
proudly, Runt feels he did his part.

    With pride Runt will show you his bat and uni-
form from 'pro days-'
    He will tell you some of the 'stories' from the
past, but still in his memory lays.
    Now the final glory has come to Runt in this
small town-
    His name in the 'HALL OF FAME' beside the other
greats, give Runt his final encore, the 'HALL OF
FAME CROWN.'

                CONGRATULATION!!
Marguerite G. Jones
9/89

299

1992: DETROIT ALUMNI ASSOCIATION 10TH INNING

JULY 25, 1992 TIGER STADIUM

"10th Inning"

July 25, 1992 Tiger Stadium

Alumni Participants

Hank Aguirre
Pitcher
Michigan

Reno Bertoia
2b, 3b
1953-58, 1961-62
Ontario

Gates Brown
Michigan

Jim Delsing
Outfield
1952-56
Missouri

Walter Dropo
1b
1952-55
Massachusetts

Paul Foytack
Pitcher
1955-63
Michigan

Doug Gallagher
Pitcher
1962
Ohio

Bill Hoeft
Pitcher
1952-59
Michigan

Ned Garver
Pitcher
1952-56
Ohio

Steve Gromek
Pitcher
1953-57
Michigan

Ray Herbert
Pitcher
1950
Michigan

Fred Holdsworth
1972-74
Michigan

Don Kolloway
1b
1949-53
Illinois

Dick Littlefield
Pitcher
1952
Michigan

Cliff Mapes
Oklahoma

Leo Marentette
Pitcher
1965
Ohio

Mickey McDermott
Pitcher
1958
Arizona

Jimmy Outlaw
3b
1943-49
Alabama

Larry Pashnick
Michigan

Dan Petry
Pitcher
Michigan

Jack Phillips
1b
1955-56
New York

Dave Rozema
Pitcher
Michigan

Walter Streuli
North Carolina

Jon Warden
Pitcher
1968
Ohio

Milt Wilcox
Pitcher
Michigan

Jake Wood
1961-67
New Jersey

Kip Young
Pitcher
1978-79
Ohio

Bill Zepp
Pitcher
1971
Michigan

Detroit Tigers Alumni Association
Tiger Annex
1401 Michigan Ave.
Detroit, MI 48216
313-340-9611
616-668-3233

July 15, 1992

Mr. Jimmy Outlaw
118 James Street
Jackson, AL 36545

Dear Jimmy:

It's nearly time to take the field for the "10TH INNING"! We are pleased that you will be participating. Hopefully, this note will answer any questions that you may have. If not, please don't hesitate to call (313-930-3885).

The alumni that are staying overnight will have accommodations at the Best Western Domino's Farms Hotel, 3600 Plymouth Road, Ann Arbor. Tiger Stadium is 35 minutes from the hotel. On Friday evening, July 24, you are encouraged to attend the Alumni meeting at the hotel beginning at 7:00 p.m. Following the meeting there will be a get-re-acquainted party for you, other celebrities that will be participating, the planning committee and perhaps some media. You'll want to be there for sure---we'll plan on you unless I hear otherwise.

The games will begin on Saturday at 4:00 p.m. All players will use the visitor's clubhouse. The stadium will open at 2:00 p.m. Alumni players are invited to park in the player's lot. I will need the names of all drivers by Saturday morning for stadium security. We anticipate at least two slow-pitch softball games of approximately one-hour duration. Stadium management has advised that **NO CLEATS MAY BE WORN**. Thanks for your cooperation on this.

Cocktails and dinner will be served in CENTER FIELD after the games. Alumin participants and their spouses are invited as guests of the event. The fans are looking forward to meeting you in an informal setting. Dress is casual. We'll have plenty of professional photographers on hand, great food, beverages, music, good company---all the makings of an enjoyable evening.

The non-professional players are really excited about this event---meeting you, playing on Tiger field (we're using the electronic scoreboard, authentic programs, p.a. system, Fat Bob's doing the National Anthem, etc.), and supporting a worthy cause. We've distributed over 13,000 complimentary admission tickets so we expect to hear some cheering from the stands. Thanks for a super weekend. I look forward to seeing you on the 24th.

Sincerely,

Judith A. Tice

In Association With
Domino's Pizza, Inc.

1999: SYRACUSE WALL OF FAME INDUCTION

The same year of the final game in Tiger Stadium, I got news from Syracuse that I had been selected for the Sky Chiefs' Wall of Fame for 1999.

Right now, I still hold the teams' record batting average, set in 1939 at .339.

The 1999 induction class included Frank Verdi, Rob Gardner, Jim Bottomly, Dutch Mele, Bill Kelly, and Lawrence Skiddy. Bottomly, Mele and Skiddy were all inducted posthumously. The induction ceremony was held before the 7:00 game between the Syracuse Sky-Chiefs and the Ottawa Lynx at the P&C Stadium. I was 86 at the time and had not been back to Syracuse since the 1963 game that named me All-Time Chiefs Third Baseman.

It was a nice ballpark back then, too: McArthur Stadium, then known as Municipal Stadium. It was built in 1934 and was there until it was torn down in 1996 to build the new McArthur Stadium. When I played for the Chiefs, they were affiliated with the Cincinnati Reds, who I had signed with in 1934 when I was only 21.

This was the second year of the Chiefs' Wall of Fame. The year before in the first class, they had inducted Hank Sauer, Mack Jones, Dave Giusti, Grover Alexander, Red Barrett, and Bill Dinneen.

Syracuse Baseball Wall of Fame:

Class of 1999 featuring Frank Verdi and Rob Gardner

By Bob Snyder

Was 1970 the greatest year in Syracuse baseball history? Arguably it was. That season, the Chiefs won everything attainable ... The International League pennant, Governor's Cup Playoffs, and the Junior World Series.

It was a year that forever linked Frank Verdi and Rob Gardner in the annuals of Syracuse baseball. That year, they were named International League Manager of the Year and Most Valuable Pitcher, respectively.

Now, the skipper and his All-Star lefthander are, fittingly, being inducted into the ballclub's Wall of Fame together.

Verdi would win other pennants elsewhere, but this was his first. And it is the only championship ring he wears. He had played and managed here before, with far lesser clubs. And he'd return, as well, with the Chiefs and against them. But the Verdi who took over a 1968 Syracuse team seemingly dead in the water - Gary Blaylock having resigned after a 10-20 start - and coming within a whisker of the playoffs, then capturing Syracuse's first Governor's Cup in seven decades in '69 and winning it all in '70, was as good a manager as this franchise has ever had.

And that championship season, Gardner was among the most reliable pitchers ever to wear a Syracuse uniform. Gardner posted a 16-5 record, a 2.53 ERA, and overall won 20 games that season.

In light of his post-baseball career as a Southern Tier fireman, perhaps Gardner should have been a reliever. Instead, it wasn't that often hat he needed help in putting out fires; Gardner had 13 complete games in '70. Gardner's curve ball was almost unhittable that season. He was the ace of the staff, particularily in postseason play, in which, for the second consecutive season, the Chiefs captured the Gov's Cup by beating Columbus both times in five games. And in the '70 JWS, Gardner fashioned a one-hitter against Omaha. His career winning percentage (.673, 37-18) is the best in franchise history.

Frank Verdi

Verdi believed in developing a strong bench and bullpen. He irritated some parent New York Yankee brass from time to time, not necessarily filling his lineup card the way NY always wanted. Quite simply, he played to win. And Verdi won.

The '70 Chiefs did not have a single player who'd go on to major league stardom during his playing days. But the team had an All-Star double play combination of Frank "HomeRun" Baker and Len Boehmer, and a creaky-kneed third baseman named Bobby Cox, who is still making his managerial mark in the big leagues.

That ballclub played .600 ball. No other Syracuse team since 1927 had done that. During his '60-'70 tenure, Verdi-managed teams played 45 games over .500. He was as volatile as Gardner appeared calm, cool, and collected. But they fit together perfectly, skipper and stopper.

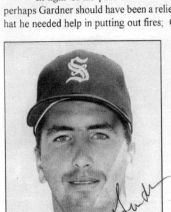

Rob Gardner

Gardner was Verdi's kind of pitcher. Pencil him in, he'd be ready to pitch. And if the Yankees never appreciated him, thinking his fastball lacked pizzazz, that was their misguided opinion. He even proved them wrong one year in New York. He'd proved it earlier to Verdi.

Now, the Syracuse Baseball Wall of Fame includes the best of the best, two guys most instrumental in a Syracuse season that has remained unequalled.

Along with these two distinquished inductees, the Wall of Fame also welcomes these four other athletes into as the class of 1999.

Jim Bottomley
April 23, 1900-Dec. 11, 1959
Syracuse Stars - 1922, hit .349 in 119 games
Syracuse Chiefs player-manager - 1938
National Baseball Hall of Fame Inductee - 1974

Bill Kelly
Dec. 28, 1889-April 8, 1990
North High School
Dean Academy - All-New England honors
I.L Baseball Hall of Fame Inductee - 1954
Buffalo Baseball Hall of Fame Inductee - 1985
Greater Syracuse Hall of Fame Inductee - 1994

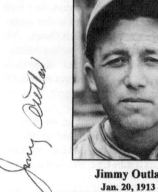

Jimmy Outlaw
Jan. 20, 1913 -
Chiefs Third Base - 1937-1938
All-Time Chiefs Team Selection - 1964

Albert "Dutch" Mele
Jan. 11, 1915-Feb. 12, 1975
Most Games played as a Chief - 1087
(1942-1947, 1949-1950)
All-Time Chiefs Team Selection - 1964
L.L. All-Star Team - 1947

I was reading the newspaper about Joe DiMaggio dying on March 8, when Mike Breedlove, reporter for *The South Alabamian* came to do an interview about the Syracuse Wall of Fame coming up that summer. He asked me about my memories of playing against him. "He was never one to brag. He wasn't very talkative, but he wasn't stuck-up. Everybody really liked Joe, but he was modest and really just wanted to be by himself.

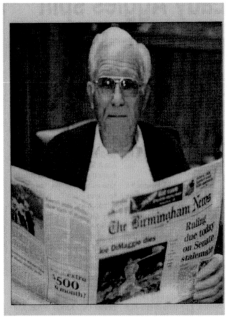

Interview and photo with permission from
Mike Breedlove

"One day I was sitting on the bench and DiMaggio came up and lined a one-hopper to third. George Kell was playing third and the ball took a bad hop and caught George under the chin. It was hit so hard it broke his jaw, and he had to be wired up.

"They sent me in, but I didn't know if I wanted to be against DiMaggio or not. He was as good an outfielder as he was a batter; had a sense of where the ball was going as soon as it was hit. Along with Boston Red Sox outfielder Ted Williams, and Cleveland Indians pitcher Bob Feller, he was one of the three best ballplayers I played against."

1999: LAST GAME AT TIGER STADIUM

SEPTEMBER 27, 1999

- Sunday event at Fox Theatre
- Beach Balls and waves were all through the stands.
- All-Time Team voted by fans
  - Sparky Anderson
  - Right-handed pitcher: Jack Morris
  - Left-handed pitcher: Mickey Lolicch and Hal Newhouser
  - Relief Pitcher: Jon Hiller
  - Catcher: Bill Freehan
  - First Base: Hank Greenburg
  - Second Base: Charlie Gehringer
  - Third Base: George Kell
  - Short Stop: Alan Trammell
  - Outfield: Ty Cobb, Al Kaline, and Kirk Gibson
- As a tribute to the players, Detroit provided uniforms with their original numbers to wear
- Tigers vs Royals 4:15; Hour long ceremony followed
- Tigers first played at Bennett Park, predecessor to Tiger Stadium at corner of Michigan and Trumbull Avenues, April 28, 1896
  - April 20, 1912 first pitch thrown at Navin Field
  - Renamed Briggs in 1938
  - Renamed Tiger Stadium in 1961
  - July 13, 1934, Babe Ruth hits his 700th career homer, a 480 footer to right field
  - May 1, 1939, Lou Gehrig plays his 2,130th consecutive game – the last of his then record streak
  - October 14, 1984, Tigers win World Series with an 8-4 win over San Diego
- Last game, Robert Fick hit a grand-slam in the eighth inning to beat Kansas City 8-2; fans shouted "Fick, Fick" after the game when he doffed his hat to the crowd.
- Ceremony led by Ernie Harwell, announcer – age 65
- 65 former Tigers names called and they lined up chronologically from home plate to the flagpole in center field.
  - Eldon Auker played in 1933
  - Brad Ausmus 1999

- When the Tiger Stadium logo flag was lowered, it was passed from player to player all the way to home plate.
  - When Auker then said, "Behind me stands over 70 years of baseball history. Each of us has touched this flag today as this stadium has touched millions of fans who have attended games here. Never forget us, for we live on by those who carry on the Tiger tradition and who so proudly wear the Olde English D."
  - Home plate was ceremoniously dug up and carried to Comerica Park about a block away.
- Harwell closed with, "Tonight we say goodbye, but we will not forget. Open your eyes, take a look around, and take a mental picture. Moments like this will live on." His voice was choked with emotion, "Farewell, old friend, Tiger Stadium. We will remember."
- A few fans reached down over the fence to grab a handful of dirt.

FORMER TIGER PLAYERS AT FINAL GAME AT TIGER STADIUM

Homerun
By Harriet Outlaw

How amazing to have this collection of memories from Jimmy Outlaw. His final years were full of laughter with friends and family, but also tears as other family members were laid to rest. He was active until the last year of his life and his memory was clear until his last few months. His attitude continued to be inspirational and uplifting for all his many daily visitors.

He passed over to the Home Field on April 9, 2006 from his hometown of Jackson, Alabama knowing he was surrounded by a loving family and feeling grateful that he had lived a blessed life.

The visitation was filled with laughter just as he would have wished, and the funeral was a truly religious ceremony. After the final prayer in the church, the pall bearers, his grandsons, each donned a Detroit Tigers Baseball Cap and marched out of the church to the organ bellowing "Take Me Out to the Ballpark."

As the coffin was guided down the aisle, there was not a dry eye in the assembly. Those were not tears of sadness, but of rejoicing in a life well-lived and cherished. His humble nature, Christian faith, self-discipline, devotion to family and friends, and his loving actions combine to make a veritable lasting legacy.

James Paulus Outlaw was laid to his final rest next to his wife Eleanor Grace Windham Outlaw in Pine Rest Cemetery in Jackson. However, he is not there, for as his tombstone reads. "He rounded third and the Master waved him home."

Perry James Outlaw with his father, Jimmy Outlaw
at Jimmy's 85th birthday party.

ABOUT THE AUTHOR

Perry Outlaw is a retired education administrator, teacher, and coach. He grew up in Jackson, Alabama, with his father being a major influence in his life. Perry is a historian with a passion for reading and verifying written history with primary source information. His library of a vast number of books includes many on the history of baseball as well as American and European history. He listened intently to his father's recollections of his years as a ballplayer and was able to give inside stories that add keen human interest to the recorded baseball facts. He is an avid collector of information about Jimmy Outlaw, as well as many other players and coaches. He welcomes any additional information which fans might have.